MW00804574

LUFTWAFFE

ADVANCED AIRCRAFT PROJECTS to 1945

Volume 2: Fighters & Ground-Attack Aircraft
Lippisch to Zeppelin

Luftwaffe Advanced Aircraft Projects to 1945
Volume 2: Fighters and Ground-Attack Aircraft – Lippisch to Zeppelin

ISBN (10) 1 85780 242 X
ISBN (13) 978 1 85780 242 9

Translation from original German text
by Ted Oliver

English language edition published 2006 by
Midland Publishing
4 Watling Drive, Hinckley, LE10 3EY, England
Tel: 01455 254 490   Fax: 01455 254 495
E-mail: midlandbooks@compuserve.com

Midland Publishing is an imprint of
Ian Allan Publishing Ltd

Worldwide distribution (except North America):
Midland Counties Publications
4 Watling Drive, Hinckley, LE10 3EY, England
Telephone: 01455 254 450   Fax: 01455 233 737
E-mail: midlandbooks@compuserve.com
www.midlandcountiessuperstore.com

North American trade distribution:
Specialty Press Publishers & Wholesalers Inc.
39966 Grand Avenue, North Branch, MN 55056
Tel: 651 277 1400   Fax: 651 277 1203
Toll free telephone: 800 895 4585
www.specialtypress.com

Design concept and layout
© Ingolf Meyer, Dr. W Bergt
and Midland Publishing

Colour illustrations, drawings
and text by Ingolf Meyer
Technical supervision by Dr. W Bergt

Printed in England by Ian Allan Printing Ltd
Riverdene Business Park, Molesey Road,
Hersham, Surrey, KT12 4RG

Visit the Ian Allan Publishing website at:
www.ianallanpublishing.com

LUFTWAFFE
ADVANCED AIRCRAFT PROJECTS to 1945

Volume 2: Fighters & Ground-Attack Aircraft
Lippisch to Zeppelin

Ingolf Meyer

MIDLAND
An imprint of
Ian Allan Publishing

Contents

Skoda-Kauba

Sombold

Stöckel

Von Braun

Zeppelin

Camouflage

Camouflage *always* makes sense – something that is proven by history. Camouflage initially served to disguise aircraft on the ground from optical reconnaissance by enemy aircraft, or as optical protection for higher-flying aircraft which made the camouflaged machine very difficult to recognise from the ground.

The higher and faster the aircraft flew, the more superfluous became the question of disguise. At high altitudes, camouflage was seldom of use since aircraft were easily visible from above against low-lying clouds.

During the Second World War, camouflage initially consisted of earth hues and green and brown tones. In the inter-war years, camouflage was not a subject of discussion and especially with the British there were no end of silver-finished machines, undoped or unpainted and in natural metal finish. Other than national insignia, wing and/or squadron emblems as well as decorative additions, there were no colour coatings on aircraft like the Fury or Gladiator.

During the long period of the Cold War, it was a very similar case on both sides. The Republic Thunderstreaks, North American Sabres and Super Sabres and McDonnell Voodoos were equally silver-metallic like the MiGs, Sukhois and Tupolevs on the Russian side. It was only in the Vietnam War that camouflage was again used, and even then only sparingly were the old camouflage patterns applied which, still exclusively according protection against being visible from the ground, were displaced by such colour tones that made the aircraft optically very difficult to recognise against the sky. Today, grey and blue tones predominate and the old schemes – green and blue or diverse desert tones only make more sense when the operational profile is suitable, as for example, with the Fairchild A-10 Warthog tank-buster or other low-flying aircraft.

Machine-gun or cannon armament was considered obsolete for a time, largely superseded by ever more effective rockets, but was re-adopted after Vietnam, as a result of the Americans finding their lack of such weapons in aircraft an extremely painful experience.

The dogfight and the machine-gun were regarded as dead but, even so, continued to live on. With optical aiming of the machine-gun and cannon, camouflage in the air (against a sky background) again became a topic.

Yet again! For the story was by no means something new. In the Second World War, lone-flying aircraft especially, had the problem of not wanting to be recognised. There was no formation in which one could seek shelter and in which one could hide as one of several. As a result German aircraft appeared that were completely in light blue. For their fast reconnaissance aircraft such as the Spitfire, the British preferred pink or rose-coloured tones. The aircraft flown by the Royal Navy, which operated over the Atlantic against U-boats, were completely in white. That made sense. The unavoidable shadows on the underside of the aircraft caused by the sun above, falsified the white into a bright grey which dissolved into the colour of the sky.

The Germans also adopted the same practice. Grey and light blue on the night fighters had the effect of becoming diffuse in darkness, whereas an aircraft that was completely black threw conspicuous shadows at dusk or on moonlit nights.

These light grey and light blue tones were also applied to the sides of the aircraft (fuselage and fin and rudder) so that with machines flying at the same high altitude as the enemy machine, the German aircraft blended in with the horizon. Hence, the current blue and grey tones of modern aircraft are really a rebirth as are the machine-gun weapons and the dogfight.

Camouflage, however, has some disadvantages, one of which is the effort needed to alter the colour tones after each operational theatre (tundra, desert, forested areas) or time of year (winter camouflage).

Colour happens to account for weight and with a large aircraft, this amounts to some hundreds of pounds – and this results in reducing the payload, the speed, and the range.

A Ju 88 night fighter pilot once related to me that when he took over his machine, it was the 'slowest duck'. He therefore issued the instruction to have his aircraft, which had been overburdened with several layers of dope, to be completely stripped of colour and redoped. As a result, and without any further measures being necessary, he had the fastest aircraft in his unit.

To put it bluntly: when one has air superiority, one can dispense with camouflage. Performance is better than camouflage. Towards the end of the war the Americans increasingly flew with 'silverbirds'. For them, camouflage was no longer necessary.

What would have paid off for the Luftwaffe in 1945/46? To begin with, camouflage! The enemy would have had the ascendancy, but air superiority – at least over the Reich – would doubtless have been the Luftwaffe's had they followed the American example. The numbers of 'silverbirds' would have increased.

It is thus fully legitimate to portray the aircraft that would have flown, without camouflage. Everything is possible to imagine, even to a degree of gaiety of colouring on the German machines that, in reality, remained only projects. The one thing that is certain is that had Germany survived the war, the conflict in the East would have continued and the 'cold war' would have been played out between Germany and the USA.

Flying-Wing Aircraft

Flying-wing or all-wing aircraft are not a German invention, although in Germany, just at the end of the war a number of such designs were favoured, among them the sole Horten 8-229 tailless fighter that was intended to be used operationally. This aircraft only progressed to the status of test flights; it did not attain series production due to the war. The aircraft was, however, so far developed that, following on after the He 280, Me 262 and He 162, it would have been, to all intents and purposes, Germany's fourth turbojet-powered fighter.

In 1942, the He 280 was tested in mock combat against the then new Fw 190 (in service since 1941) and clearly came out as the victor, but did not enter series production. This, however, by no means represented blindness on the part of the Luftwaffe leadership. It was no different from the introduction of the Me 262, which had not been hindered through alterations of plans (such as Hitler's wish to see it as a Schnell-bomber), but rather, due to a fear of the unreliability of the turbojets, and it was precisely for this reason that series production of the He 280 was abandoned. It could at an early date have been *the* air superiority fighter and was a first-class fighter. But even the jet engines developed in Great Britain did not function as they should have done; in the USA their engines were not only so weak that the performance of their first jet aircraft lay below that of their piston-engined fighters, but they also technologically lagged behind the far advanced German designs.

After the 'number one' – the He 280 – had dropped out, and despite the Me 262 with its grouped-component construction method which helped to save on highly-skilled workers, but was only able to be introduced gradually into service use, the He 162 appeared to be a good solution. The use of much wood in its construction hence saved on strategic raw materials. Its single powerplant was mounted above the fuselage so that it did not become damaged in belly landings. Although a portion of JG 1 in Leck was equipped with the aircraft, only a sole encounter is known in which a Hawker Tempest was shot down.

Number Four was to have been the Gotha-built 8-229, but it did not progress beyond the phase of a few flight tests. If one takes into account the innumerable projects of the German air equipment programme, it would appear that much faith was expressed in the all-wing concept, not only for fighters but also for bombers.

The Horten Brothers were the primary address for this type of construction, since they had many years of experience in their design and manufacture as well as with the tricky behaviour of such aircraft. These suffered, above all, from their poor stability and very often led to improvised solutions.

The true all-wing aircraft, as the term suggests, consists *solely* of a flying wing. This purity is often obliterated by the presence of small tail and stabilising surfaces. With large bombers whose poor stability could not be compensated for even by an experienced pilot because of the aircraft's bulk, the undercarriage was often enclosed in massive contusions which in reality served as stabilising surfaces.

What advantages does an all-wing aircraft offer? Here, the wing is the lifting surface; the remainder of a conventional aircraft has of necessity to be 'tagged along'. There were also attempts to conceive a lifting fuselage in which the underside of the fuselage was given a similar profile to the wing, but that was not a good solution. The ultimate appeared to be to design the entire aircraft as a single lifting surface or wing.

The problem with that, however, is that the wing cross-section has to be such that an excess pressure is developed on the underside which lifts the aircraft and on the upper side, a sub-pressure which lifts the wing. These effects result from the different airflow speeds on the under and upper sides of the wings, and the drag must be kept as low as possible. Assistance is provided by the wing geometry, which on modern aircraft is often made variable (Grumman Tomcat, General Dynamics F-111 and Panavia Tornado). With an all-wing aircraft, what counts is the optimum of combining a lifting surface with the least possible air resistance. In an orthodox aircraft, the total drag consists of the sum of the drag of all the components lying in the airstream: the fuselage, wing, empennage, undercarriage and so on.

The overall drag is, however, greater than the sum of the component drags (aerodynamic interference). These vary considerably but in their significance, one factor remains paramount: the drag of all those parts which do not generate lift is denoted as interference drag. On the wing itself there are two kinds of resistance, surface and parasitic drag, but in the latter case the entire lift is produced by the wing, so that these drags are acceptable. Some can be reduced by means of high aspect ratios and by other design measures.

If one seeks to create the optimum flying wing, however, one problem still remains: assuming the correct geometry has been selected to meet the desired speed and the correct profile to provide maximum lift for the lowest drag, the shape, which also has to ensure structural stability, limits the space available for payload. If however, the carriage of a suitable payload has been taken into account, the wing would then be of necessity too thick, resulting in aircraft that only have a small speed advantage.

In such cases the advantage of new types of powerplants ought to bring the aircraft into ever higher speed ranges, something that cannot be accomplished with a thick wing profile. A part of the problem can be solved by employing a swept or delta wing, but this in turn causes problems to the disadvantage of flight stability and controllability.

The high-speed all-wing aircraft finally became realised in the shape of the Northrop B-2 bomber. But this in turn consists of components made of light but strong synthetic materials, has powerplants that produce many times the power of early engines, stabilises itself with the aid of high-performance computers and is unbelievably expensive. Even so, it is not a truly all-wing aircraft, since on the upper surface it has a fuselage segment that houses the crew and thus incorporates something of a fuselage, whereas on other designs, there is usually always the presence of a tail.

It is thus even more astounding that the Horten 8-229, with its similar configuration, displayed an enormous performance for the year 1945. Here also, there was a fuselage centre section that was nevertheless of low profile plus a cockpit and engine cowlings that projected from what was an otherwise all-wing configuration. With a quoted maximum weight of 9,000kg (19,840 lb), maximum speed was 977km/h (607mph), the ceiling an astonishing 16,000m (52,500ft) and range 3,170km (1,970mls), the latter figure with auxiliary fuel tanks and cruising speed 635km/h (395mph). The performance actually attained was certainly rather less, but nevertheless ...

Several flying-wing as well as all-wing projects existed, except that a whole series of them (Arado Ar I, Gotha Go P.60) were in fact tailless aircraft of large thickness at the wing root. The Go P.60A only was a pure all-wing aircraft, but nevertheless featured miniature vertical stabilising surfaces at the wingtips that could not be dispensed with. The externally-mounted turbojets, however, destroyed the picture of an all-wing aircraft. Would it be possible for me to discover another one?

Yes! It was the Horten H XVIII B-1 bomber project. All in all, one can certainly view it more generously and speak of an all-wing aircraft, when the wing forms some 85 to 90% of the aircraft.

One of the most prominent of the aircraft firms that favoured the all-wing concept was the Northrop Corporation in the USA – and that even before the year 1945.

The Germans had conceived and developed much in advance of others, but even so, certainly not everything. And it was precisely the Americans who have been so successful in this sphere.

Notes on Aircraft Configurations

In a novel, it was very lucidly described what problems the flak had at the end of the war in connection with some German aircraft. They shot at a small aircraft until someone shouted: 'Captain, that aircraft has German markings!' 'Cease fire!' 'What type is it?' 'No idea! Type unknown, Captain!' 'Er ...' came the rough reply: 'Monoplane – no tailplane – no undercarriage – no engine!' The Captain, half furious, half bewildered: 'Is everyone drunk around here ...?' What the flak had in front of their muzzles was a Messerschmitt Me 163.

Secret designs suddenly appeared, of which nobody had any knowledge. For quite some time already there existed a 'definition' for aircraft so as to identify the various types that clearly fitted into a particular configuration. It described design details that distinguished the configuration of one type from another. Despite this, at the present time confusion still reigns and has not been eliminated even among the knowledgeable. In the flying world, clarity of description exists, but even among pilots today, has become increasingly indistinct – and especially among journalists.

The 'Flieger' (flyers) are not the aircraft but the men in the machines, and even a service grade in the Luftwaffe is called a Flieger, as is likewise the small sail in the rigging of a ship. An aircraft does not have 'wings' like a duck or an albatross, but instead 'lifting surfaces', at best 'lifting wings'. And the 'wheels' that are external when it lands, are in fact the undercarriage. The wheels form only a part of what is today an exceedingly complex mechanism. Such amateur appellations have entered more and more into everyday usage, even though such descriptions are false or misleading.

In this respect, no-one would think of describing the front windscreen of a car as a 'front window' or the rear one as a 'rear window'. Specific terms exist that provide a correct description, and everything else is nonsense. Hence, one should correctly apply the terms in a competent manner.

One finds, for instance, that a number of specialists describe the American Lockheed Lightning as a 'twin-fuselage aircraft'. However, it has only *a single* fuselage between its wings. The components that support the tail surfaces are therefore 'twin booms' and the aircraft should thus be correctly described as such.

A true 'twin-fuselage aircraft' was the planned Me 609 (the Me 109 with two fuselages and a connecting structure between them), or else the He 111Z (for Zwilling, meaning 'twin'). In order to eliminate such misconceptions, it pays to explain such terms by means of graphical illustrations. In this way, there exists a good deal of difference between a 'shoulder wing', whereby the lifting surfaces are attached to the upper fuselage, and a 'parasol wing' whose wings are supported by struts or stays. Various terms for such types of construction were used in the early days of flight. And not every design (often with delta wings) without a tailplane but with a few *fixed* stabilising surfaces at the forward end of the fuselage qualifies as a 'canard' aircraft. A true 'canard' has *movable* elevators ahead of the wings; its design thus provides a completely different form of manoeuvrability than is inherent with 'normal' designs and hence has completely different loading moments in its overall design.

When therefore an aircraft is correctly 'described', it often provides a clue as to its performance and its limitations. A braced or strutted parasol aircraft with rectangular wings, conventional tailplane and fixed undercarriage – independent of its powerplant – because of its design configuration, cannot fly at supersonic speed. High-performance piston-engined aircraft with a high HP rating would for example, hardly perform with a 2-bladed propeller. The term 'propeller' really belongs in the realm of ships, but has embedded itself in describing 'propeller-driven aircraft', as opposed to jet engines. To describe an aircraft as a 'jet aircraft' is likewise rather vague, since rocket motors also have exhaust 'jets'.

In the former DDR (East Germany) there once existed a book that – without being something special – was concerned exclusively with such (correct) basic terminology. Since the 1960s, I have unfortunately not come across such a publication.

Worst of all is when authors of aviation literature describe a tailless aircraft as a 'flying wing'. This often happens with the Me 163 and with similar designs. The Me 163 has a very short fuselage, the fin and rudder being close to the wings at the fuselage rear. The function of the elevators is performed by wing trailing-edge flaps. Since a long extension of the fuselage is missing and a tailplane is superfluous, it is thus a 'tailless' monoplane with a slightly swept wing and fixed fin and rudder and retractable undercarriage. As the powerplant inside the fuselage is not easily recognisable to determine, this term for the aircraft is therefore appropriate.

Never, however – *never* – is an aircraft having a fuselage and a tailplane in the fashion of the Me 163 a 'flying wing'. All such tailless aircraft (and particularly among the projects there are several) in being described as a flying wing, only displays lack of basic knowledge on the subject of aeronautics. And those who are of the opinion that the 'area rule' has especially something to do with the wings, would do well to consult an aviation dictionary to familiarise themselves with basic terminology.

Acknowledgements

It is not an easy task to produce a technical and historical work which simultaneously attempts to satisfy the need for a graphical and creative presentation of this nature. Not only is an in-depth knowledge required, but a considerable amount of enthusiasm as well.

Especial words of thanks are due here to Dr. Wolfgang Bergt, who as an engineer for aircraft and rocket production, has supervised the technical aspects involved and advanced them to a respectable degree and who, beyond this, played an important role in the overall presentation.

I should like to express my thanks also to those who, by means of the computer, were involved in wading through a mass of material, illustrations and categorising the projects.

Last but not least, the same holds true for all those authors, technicians, illustrators and historians whose own published works have contributed to the compilation of this chapter of aviation history which should not be consigned to oblivion.

Ingolf Meyer

Bibliography

Die Deutsche Luftrüstung [German Air Armament] *1939-1945*: Heinz J Nowarra; Bernard & Graefe Verlag, Koblenz, 1993 (4 Volumes)

Geheimprojekte der Luftwaffe – Jagdflugzeuge 1939-1945, Band 1: Walter Schick & Ingolf Meyer; Motorbuch Verlag, Stuttgart, 1994 *

Geheimprojekte der Luftwaffe – Schlachtflugzeuge und Kampfzerstörer 1939-1945, Band 3: Dieter Herwig & Heinz Rode; Motorbuch Verlag, Stuttgart, 2002 †

Reichdreams and Unknowns – Series: Justo Miranda; Miranda Mercado C / Tutor 53 Bj-C, Madrid, Spain

Jet Planes of the Third Reich – The Secret Projects, Vol.1: Manfred Griehl; Monogram Aviation Publications, Sturbridge, Massachusetts, 1998

* English language edition:
Luftwaffe Secret Projects – Volume 1: Fighters 1939-1945: Walter Schick & Ingolf Meyer; Midland Publishing, 1997

† English language edition:
Luftwaffe Secret Projects – Volume 3: Ground-Attack & Special-Purpose Aircraft 1939-1945: Dieter Herwig & Heinz Rode; Midland Publishing, 2003

Glossary & Notes

Firms and Institutes

AG	Aktiengesellschaft – Joint-Stock Company (suffix); for instance, Daimler-Benz AG
eV	eingetragener Verein – Registered Association (suffix); for instance, DFS eV
GmbH	Gesellschaft mit beschränkter Haftung – Limited Liability Company (suffix); for instance, Focke-Wulf GmbH
KG	Kommanditgesellschaft – Limited Partnership Company (suffix); for instance, H Walter KG

AVA	Aerodynamische Versuchsanstalt (Aerodynamics Experimental Institute), Göttingen
BMW	Bayerische Motorenwerke (Bavarian Engine Works), Munich, Berlin-Spandau
DFS	Deutsche Forschungsinstitut für Segelflug (German Research Institute for Sailplane Flight), Darmstadt, Ainring
DVL	Deutsche Versuchsanstalt für Luftfahrt (German Aviation Experimental Institute), Berlin-Adlershof
HeS	Heinkel-Strahltriebwerk (Heinkel jet engine), Rostock, Stuttgart-Zuffenhausen
HWA	Heereswaffenamt (Army Ordnance Office), Kummersdorf, Peenemünde-East, Berlin
HWK	Hellmuth Walterwerke KG, Kiel, Beerberg, Hirschberg, Bosau
Jumo	Junkers Motorenwerke (Junkers Engine Works), Dessau
OKL	Oberkommando der Luftwaffe (Luftwaffe High Command), Berlin
RLM	Reichsluftfahrtministerium (German Air Ministry), Berlin

Aircraft Types and Projects

Entwurf	design, project, plan, scheme, model, sketch, outline, draft
Vorschlag	proposal, suggestion, offer

Bordjäger	air-launched fighter
Flitzer	single-seater jet fighter – literally 'dasher' or 'whizzer'
Höhenjäger	high-altitude fighter
Jabo	Jagdbomber – fighter-bomber
Rammjäger	Ram-fighter
Stuka	Sturzkampfflugzeug – dive-bomber
Volksflugzeug	People's Aircraft
Volksjäger	People's Fighter
Zerstörer	heavy fighter (literally 'destroyer')

Armament and Bombs

BK	Bordkanone – aircraft cannon
BT	Bombentorpedo – bomb-torpedo
FHL	Ferngerichtete Hecklafette – remotely controlled tail barbette
LT	Lufttorpedo – air-launched torpedo
MG	Maschinengewehr – machine-gun, up to 20mm
MK	Maschinenkanone – machine canon, over 20mm
Rüstsatz	field conversion pack
SC	Splitterbombe, cylindrisch – standard high explosive fragmentation bomb
SD	Splitterbombe, dickwändig – thick-walled high explosive fragmentation bomb
SG	Sondergerät – special device
A-Stand	forward-firing weapon position
B-Stand	fuselage dorsal weapon position
C-Stand	fuselage ventral weapon position

Armament Designations

Armament manufacturers were also identified by the first numeral of a three-digit designation, namely: 1 Rheinmetall-Borsig; 2 Mauser; 3 & 4 Krieghoff, beginning in the 100-series.

Where not stated in the text, airborne weapons developed had the following calibres:

7.9mm MG15	20mm MG FF	30mm MG 213/C	45mm SG113
7.9mm MG17	30mm MK101	37mm BK 3.7	30mm SG116
7.9mm MG 81	30mm MK103	50mm BK 5	30mm SG117
13mm MG131	30mm MK108	75mm BK7.5	30mm SG118
15mm MG151/15	55mm MK112	50mm MK 214	30mm SG119
20mm MG151/20	55mm MK114	30mm MK 303	50mm SG 500
20mm MG 204	55mm MK115	55mm MK 412	88mm Düka 88

Radio, Radar and Cameras

APZ	Automatische Peilzusatz – automatic supplementary D/F equipment
EiV	Eigenverständigungsanlage – crew intercom in aircraft
FuBl	Funk-Blindlandeanlage – radio blind-landing equipment
FuG	Funkgerät or Funkmeßgerät – radio or radar equipment
PeilG	Peilgerät – homing or direction-finding (D/F) equipment
Rb	Reihenbildgerät – camera

Aero-Engine Designations

Aero-engines bore the fixed prefix 9, followed by three digits, except that each manufacturer was accorded a first digit identifier. The series ran as follows:

9-090 series: (small firms, eg Breuer Werke GmbH 9-091)
9-100 series: BMW (later 800-series)
9-200 series: Junkers-Jumo
9-300 series: Bramo (absorbed by BMW June 1939)
9-400 series: Argus
9-500 series: Hirth
9-600 series: Daimler-Benz
9-700 series: Deutz (KHD)
9-800 series: BMW

To distinguish jet-propulsion engines from orthodox piston-engined types, the RLM introduced the prefix 109, followed by 3 digits that began from 001 onwards. These were initially allocated in numerical sequence regardless of manufacturer, up to 109-011. Thereafter, each manufacturer was allocated a fixed end digit as identifier, corresponding to the reciprocating engine series. These end digits were allocated as follows:

1 Heinkel-Hirth Examples: 109-011, 109-021,109-051
2 Junkers-Jumo Examples: 109-012, 109-022
4 Argus Examples: 109-014, 109-024, 109-044
5 Porsche (reserved)
6 Daimler-Benz Examples: 109-016
8 BMW Examples: 109-018, 109-028

Code letters were also introduced for the different types of reaction-propulsion -Antriebe (drives) or -Triebwerke (engines), the following list does not claim to be complete:

L Luftstrahl (jet) or Lorin (ramjet – invented by Réné Lorin).
R Rakete (rocket).
PR Pulver-Rakete (solid-fuel);
FR Flüssig-Rakete (liquid-fuel).
LR Lorin-Rakete (ramjet-rocket).
RL Rakete-Lorin (rocket-ramjet).
ERL Einstoff RL (single-fuel RL).
I L Intermittierendes Luftstrahl (intermittent combustion unit pulsejet)
ML Motor-Luftstrahl (engine-driven jet unit without airscrew).
PML Propeller-ML (ML unit with airscrew drive)
TL Turbinen-Luftstrahl (turbojet)
PTL Propeller-TL (turboprop)
ZTL Zweikreis-TL (two-circuit turbojet)
TLR TL + Rakete (turbojet-rocket combination).
GTW Gas-Turbine mit Wärmetäuscher (turboprop with heat-exchanger). AEG & BBC-type

When R-Geräte (Rauch = smoke-trail devices, a codename for the still secret Raketen = rocket motors) began to be developed by the HWA Kummersdorf and the HWK Kiel for aircraft use in 1935, these were divided into two categories, prefixed by the identifiers RI for short-duration rocket motors, and RII for longer-duration sustainer motors. Individual units were assigned a three-digit number, beginning in the 100-series. Initially, each manufacturer was assigned a leading digit as identifier:

RI-100 series: HWA. Examples: RI-101; RII-101a
RI-200 series: HWK. Eg: RI-201, 203, 260; RII-203, 211, 213
RI-300 series: BMW. Eg: RI-301, 302, 305; RII-301, 302, 303
RI-500 series: Rh.-B. Examples: RI-501, 502, 505

This designation system was still in use in December 1942, after which time it was replaced by numbers in the 109-500 to 109-999 series. Like the turbojet designations, these were initially applied sequentially as follows:
109-500 to -503 HWK; 109-505 Rheinmetall-Borsig; 109-506 WASAG; 109-507 HWK; 109-509 HWK; 109-510 and -511 BMW. Thereafter, a fixed end digit was assigned to each manufacturer:

2. WASAG. Examples: 109-512, 522, 532
3. Schmidding. Examples: 109-513, 533, 603
5. Rh.-Borsig. Examples: 109-515, 525
8. BMW. Examples: 109-548, 558, 708, 718
9. HWK. Examples: 109-559, 709, 729

Characteristics of the engines mentioned in the this volume are as follows:

Piston Engines

Manufacturer	*Model*	*Take-off power*
Argus (As)	9-413	4,000hp
BMW	9-801 D	1,600hp
	9-801 D-2	1,730hp
	9-801 E	2,000hp
	9-801 J	2,000hp
	9-802	2,600hp
	9-803	4,000hp
Daimler-Benz	9-600 A	1,000hp
(DB)	9-601 A/B	1,100hp
	9-601 C/D	1,300hp
	9-601 N	1,175hp
	9-603 E	1,800hp
	9-603 EB	2,250hp with MW-50
	9-603 EC	2,400hp with MW-50
	9-603 G	1,900hp
	9-603 L	2,000hp
	9-603 LA	2,100hp with MW-50
	9-603 LM	1,825hp; 2,100hp with MW-50
	9-603 N	2,750hp
	9-605 A	1,450hp
	9-605 B	1,475hp
	9-605 D	1,550hp
	9-606 A/B	2,700hp
	9-606 C/D	2,600hp
	9-609	2,660hp
	9-605 E	1,550hp
	9-610 A/B	2,950hp
	9-610 C/D	2,870hp
	9-613 A/B	3,500hp
	9-613 C/D	4,000hp
	9-614	2,000hp
	9-619	4,540hp
	9-623	2,000hp
	9-627	2,000hp
Junkers-Jumo	9-213 A-1	1,750hp
	9-213 A-2	1,750hp
	9-213 S	2,400hp
	9-213 E	1,750hp; 2,100hp with MW-50
	9-213 J	2,240hp with MW-50
	9-222 A/B	2,500hp
	9-222 C/D	3,000hp
	9-222 E/F	2,500hp; 2,900hp with MW-50

Jet Engines

Manufacturer	*Model*	*Take-off power*
Argus (As)	109-014	335kP, IL-unit
	109-044	500kP design, IL-unit
BMW	P 3302	600kP design; up to 550kg prototypes
	P 3303	2,000kg project, precursor of 109-018
	P 3304	600kg design, RLM 109-002
	109-003 A	800kP – for A-0, A-1, A-2
	109-003 C	900kP
	109-003 E	800kP – for E-1, E-2 (in Hs 132, He 162)
	109-003 R	2,050kP = 003 A + 109-718 rocket motor
	109-018	3,500kP design; 3,400kP initially expected
	109-028	6,570eshp design, PTL unit
Daimler-Benz	109-007	1,400kP design, ZTL unit
	109-021	2,400shp + 770kP jet thrust, PTL unit
Heinkel (HeS 8)	109-001	720kg design; 600kP prototypes
Heinkel-Hirth	109-011 A	1,300kP initially; 1,500kP design
	109-011 B	1,500kP
	109-011 R	1,300kP 011 A + HWK 509 A-2 rocket motor
Junkers-Jumo (T1)	109-004	635kP – early units 1941/42
	109-004 A	840kP initial production
	109-004 B	900kP for B-1, B-2; 930kP B-4
	109-004 C	1,015kP dry; 1,200kP with reheat
	109-012	3,000kP design, 2,800kP initially expected
	109-022	4,600eshp design, PTL unit
Porsche	109-005	500kP
Schmidt	SR 500	500kP, IL-unit
	SR 1000	1,000kP, IL-unit

Rocket Motors

Manufacturer	*Model*	*Take-off power*
BMW	P 3390A 109-510	1,500-300kP regulable
	P 3390 C 109-708	2,500-600kP + 500-100kP cruising chamber
	P 3395 109-718	1,250kP design, 1,000kP initial prototypes
HWK	RI-203	400kP – in DFS 194
	RII-203	750-150kP regulable
	109-509 A-0	1,500-200kP regulable
	109-509 A-1	1,600-200kP regulable
	109-509 A-2	1,700-200kP regulable
	109-509 B/C	2,000-100kP with 300kP cruising chamber
	109-509 S	2,000kP
Rheinmetall-Borsig	RI-502	1,500kP x 6 secs, RATO unit
Schmidding	SG 9 109-513	1,000kP x 10 secs
	109-533	1,000kP x 12 secs, RATO unit

Rocket Motors and Fuels

A-Stoff	liquid oxygen
C-Stoff	30% hydrazine hydrate +57% methanol + 13% water
GM-1	nitrous oxide boost
M-Stoff	methanol
MW-50	methanol-water 50/50 mixture
R-Stoff (Tonka 250)	organic amine mixture of 50% xylidine F + 50% triethylamine
S-Stoff (Salbeik)	96% potassium nitrate + 4% iron chloride
SV-Stoff (Salbei)	98-90% nitric acid + 2-10% sulphuric acid
T-Stoff	80% hydrogen peroxide
Z-Stoff C	calcium permanganate
Z-Stoff N	sodium permanganate solution as catalyst

Dates

Sometimes dimensions could vary significantly during the life of a project. Where this occurred, the reader is given a date on which the figures shown were valid.

Measurements

All German aircraft measurements etc are given in decimal (or SI – Système International d'Unités, established in 1960) units. The following may help:

aspect ratio wingspan and chord – expressed as a ratio. Low aspect ratio, short, stubby wing; high aspect ratio, long, narrow wing.

ft feet – length, multiply by 0.305 to get metres (m).

ft² square feet – area, multiply by 0.093 to get square metres.

fuel measured in both litres/gallons and kilograms/pounds. The specific gravity (sg) of German fuel varied considerably during the war and conversions from volume to weight and vice versa are impossible without knowing the specific gravity of the fuel at the time.

gallon Imperial (or UK) gallon, multiply by 4.546 to get litres. (500 Imperial gallons equal 600 US gallons.)

hp horse power – power, measurement of power for piston and turboprop engines. Multiply by 0.746 to get kilowatts.

kg kilogram – weight, multiply by 2.205 to get pounds (lb).

kg/m² kilograms per square metre – force, measurement of wing loading, multiply by 0.204 to get pounds per square foot (lb/ft²).

km/h kilometres per hour – velocity, multiply by 0.621 to get miles per hour (mph).

kP kilopascal – force, for measuring thrust, effectively a kilogram of static thrust. Present day preferences are for the kilo-newton (kN), one kN = 224.8lb or 101.96kg.

kW kilowatt – power, measurement of power for piston and turboprop engines. Multiply by 1.341 to get horse power.

lb pound – weight, multiply by 0.454 to get kilograms (kg). Also used for the force measurement of turbojet engines, with the same conversion factor, as pounds of static thrust.

lb/ft² pounds per square foot – force, measurement of wing loading, multiply by 4.882 to get kg per square metre.

litre volume, multiply by 0.219 to get Imperial (or UK) gallons.

m metre – length, multiply by 3.28 to get feet (ft).

m² square metre – area, multiply by 10.764 to get square feet.

mm millimetre – length, the bore of guns is traditionally a decimal measure; no Imperial conversion is given.

mph miles per hour – velocity, multiply by 1.609 to get kilometres per hour (km/h).

Horten Flugzeugbau

To bring the design offices of Horten and Lippisch, which were not aircraft firms in the sense of Heinkel or Messerschmitt, into one book, was by no means simple. The 'fulfilment' firm for Horten was the Gothaer Waggonfabrik, and that for Lippisch was the Messerschmitt AG. I have therefore combined the designs of the Horten Brothers and Alexander Lippisch under the rubric K for Komplex (Family) and have placed them at the beginning. Strictly speaking, the Gotha proposals belong to the Horten Brothers, but were executed under the Gotha name. On the other hand, there exists a visual connection in the configuration of their designs and verbally eases the transition to the other Lippisch proposals and to those of the Messerschmitt firm.

H IX B

H IX B / H IX C

Regardless of what one does to secure confirmatory documents on the known Horten projects, in contemporary literature much is manipulated. Profuse descriptions of the aircraft add nothing, as this is best accomplished by the illustrations. Occasional sketches are of doubtful origin, the dimensions vary, and performance data are nebulously transformed. Added to that are the differing nomenclatures – at times with Roman (Ho IX) and at times with Arabic (Ho 9) numerals. I would be grateful for any documents.

The H IX B and the H IX C possess similar contours. The first is portrayed with a delta wing with unswept trailing edges and a superimposed surface which functions as a sort of fuselage (cockpit) plus fin and rudder, and powered by a single turbojet. The H IX C has a swept wing with swept trailing edges, powered by two turbojets, and with a forward-set cockpit blended into the lengthened fin. According to post-war models and drawings, the H IX C was dimensionally larger and in terms of speed, both were aimed at close to the sonic region.

In the event that the Ho 9 and planned H IX are identical, these (B or C?) were expected to be ready for series production in 1946. Powerplants have been quoted as two Jumo 004s with a crew of two, and armament and bombload was to have corresponded to the Go 229 V5. In the planning stage, these details were given for the B, whilst that powered by two turbojets is quoted in literature as the C variant.

H IX C

The colour illustration and 3-view drawing show differences.

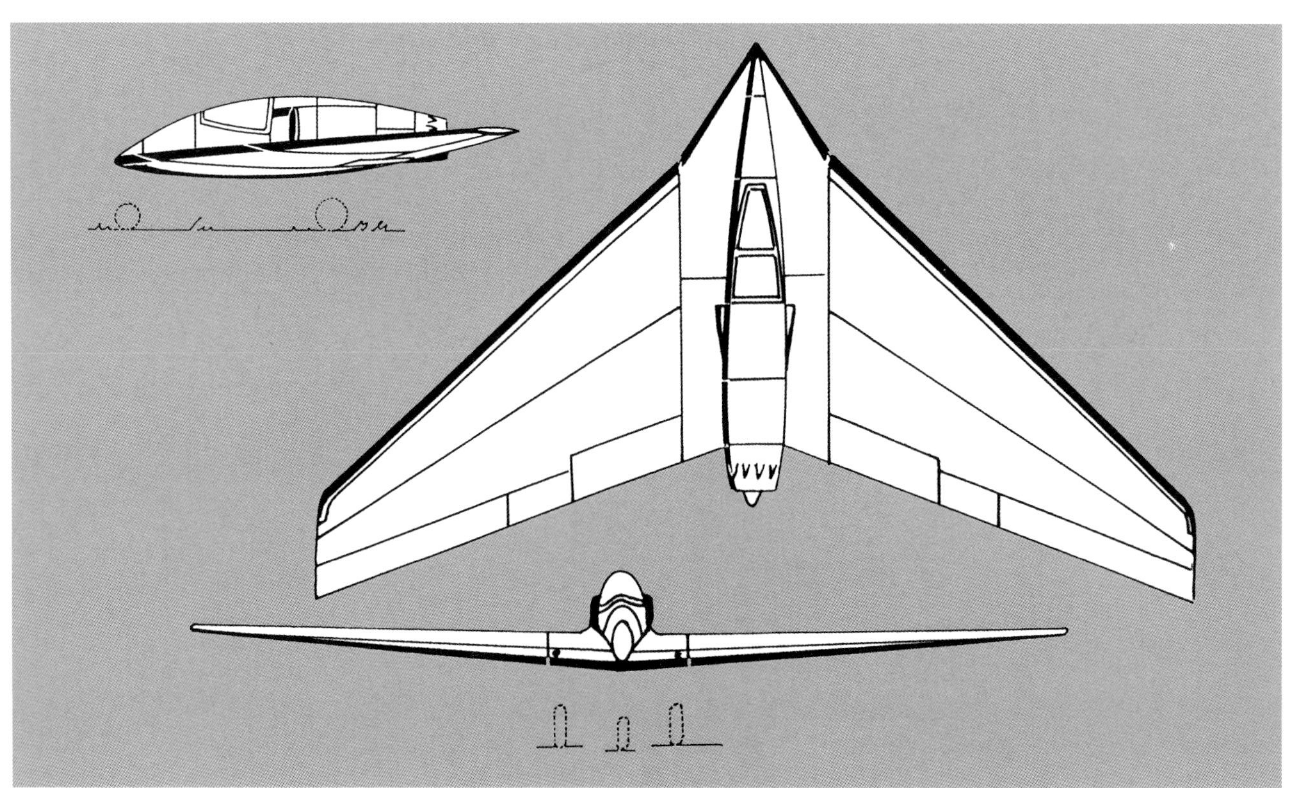

H X A

Details are also lacking here. The relatively small delta aircraft with semi-prone pilot, turbojet installed far aft on the centre fuselage and fin and rudder superimposed on it, appears to have served a similar function as did the DM-1 for the Lippisch projects, and hence was more of a test aircraft for the planned operational machines.

H X (1)

This project was apparently evolved as an intermediate step from the basic layout; an aircraft developed into a flying wing and featuring a raised fuselage. The colour illustrations depict both this intermediate and the final stages of the design.

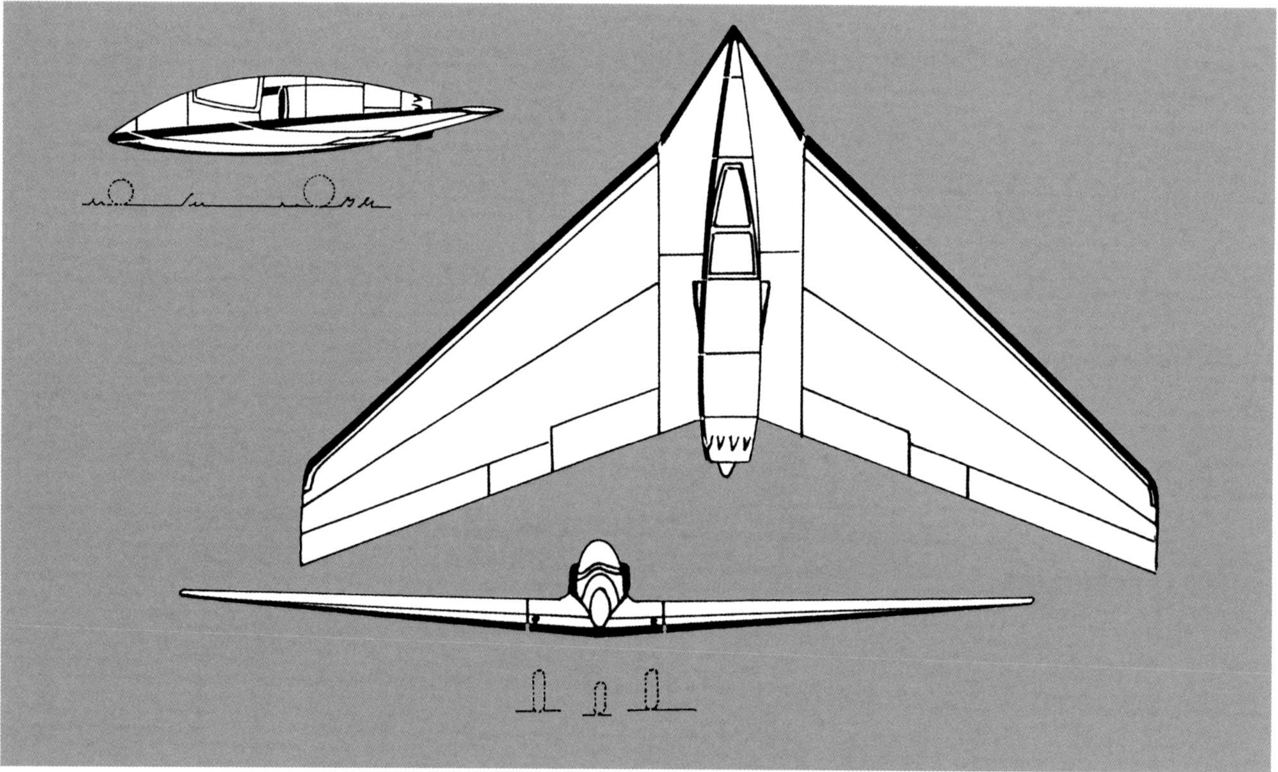

H X (1) and H X (2)

A lightweight single-seat fighter within the scope of the Jägernotprogram (Fighter Emergency Programme). For initial trials up to 500km/h, it was planned to power it with a 240hp As 10C and in its final form, with a 1,300kp thrust HeS 011 turbojet (1946).

The 'almost' flying wing features swept wings with compound sweep on the leading edge, a flat wedge-shaped fuselage with nose pressurised cockpit and rear dorsal turbojet, one variant having lateral air intakes behind the cockpit. Armament was 3 x MGs or MKs.

Horten H X (2)

H XIII B (1)

In terms of calculation and design, this aircraft was evolved based on studies conducted in 1944, aimed at an aircraft capable of attaining 1,800km/h at 12,000m. The problems occurring at high supersonic speeds were expected to be overcome by use of a sharply swept wing of low aspect ratio. Having taken care of the theoretical side, practical tests began with the H XIII A glider in Göttingen and Göppingen to investigate the control and slow-flight behaviour of such wings. From the structural aspect, a new centre section was attached to the outboard wings of the H III. The pilot was housed in a ventral gondola and on landing, in addition to the central wheel, a fixed skid absorbed the landing shocks.

Like the H XIII A, the H XIII B had a wing leading edge sweep of 60° but of greater chord, and as with earlier projects featured a vertical fin which enclosed the cockpit, the tricycle undercarriage retracting inwards into the centre section. The planned powerplant, a BMW 003R, consisted of an 800kp thrust 003A turbojet and a 1,000kp thrust BMW 718 liquid-propellant rocket motor. As a result of a special method of fuel feed (from various tanks), a stable centre of gravity position was to have been assured in flight. Under construction at the end of the war, it was expected to be ready to fly in 1946 and is one of the relatively well documented aircraft. In view of the speed strived for, a pressure cabin and ejection seat were obligatory.

In other literature, the powerplant has been quoted as a 1,300kp thrust HeS 011A turbojet and an HWK 509 S2 rocket motor, with expected maximum speed of Mach 1.40.

Dimensions

Span	11.90m
Length	11.70m
Height	3.80m
Wing area	37.80m^2

Weight

Flying weight	7,000kg

Performance

Max speed	1,800km/h
Range	2,000km
Ceiling	18,000m

Armament

3 x MGs or MKs

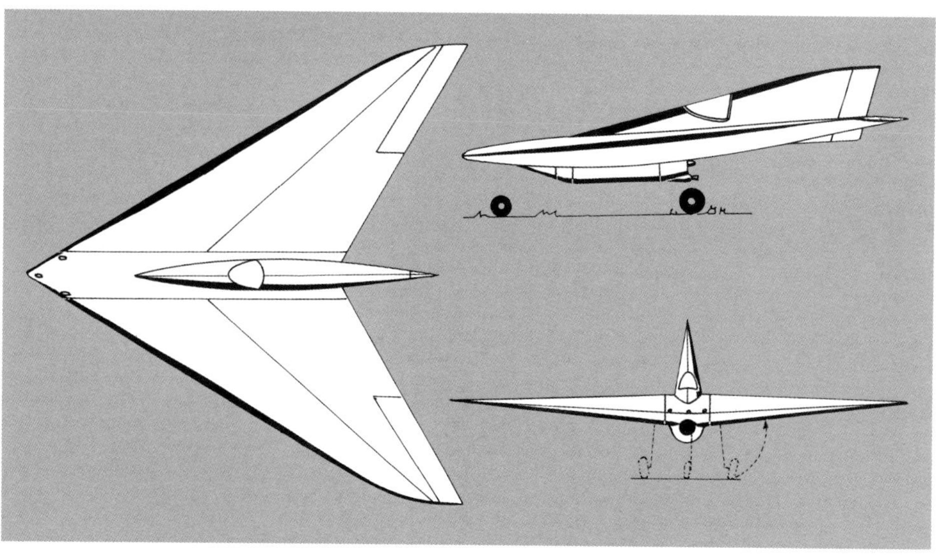

Since several different drawings exist under the designation H XIII B, it is possible that two differently-powered variants were proposed. A third scheme shows air intakes on either side of the fuselage nose, so that it is not clear whether these represent intakes for one or for two turbojets.

H XIII B (2)

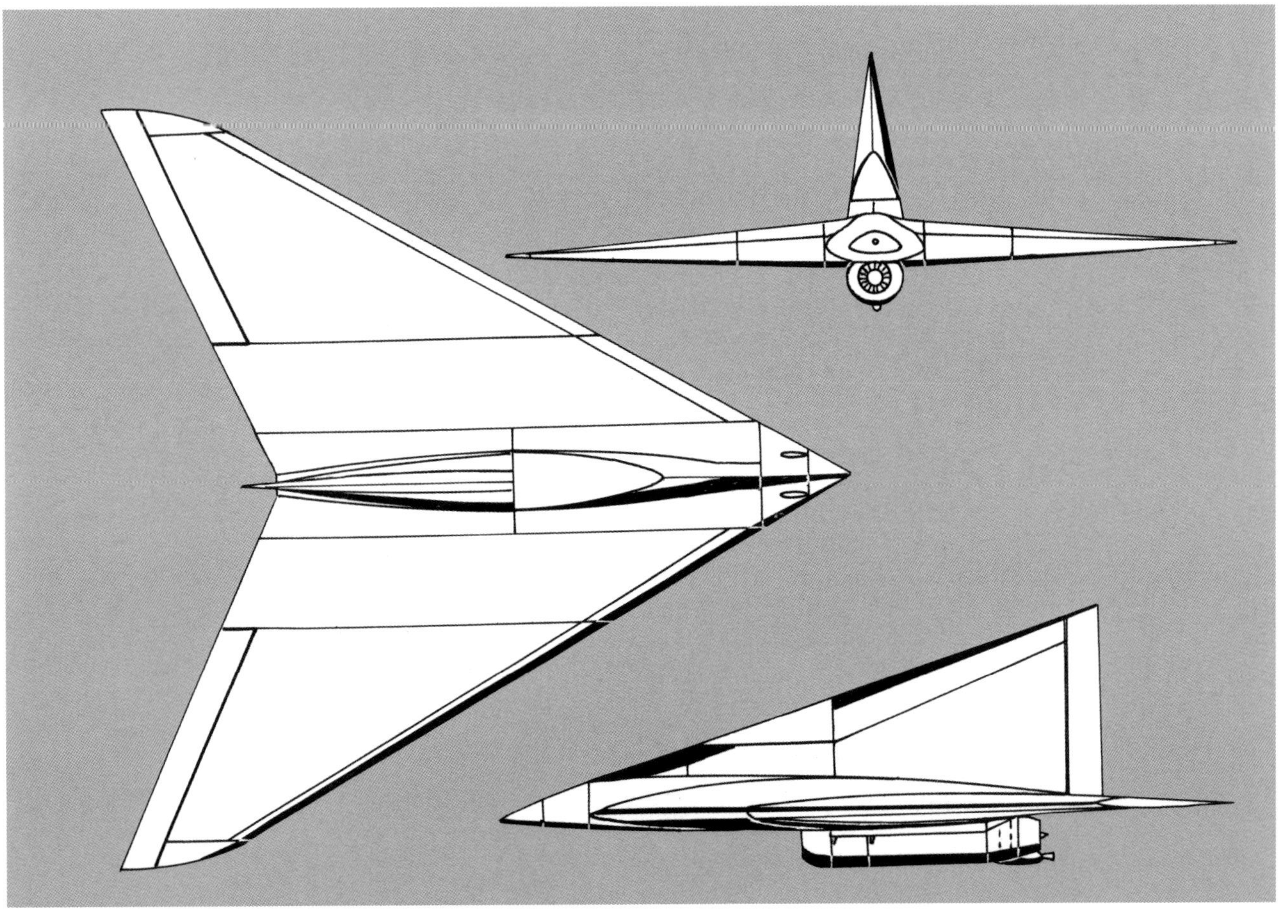

H XIII B (3) / H XIII C

H XIII B (3) with lateral wing leading-edge air intakes

Only a wind tunnel model of the H XIII C is known whereas dimensions, weights, powerplant and performance are not.

Lippisch Flugzeugbau

Li P 09 (05.05.1942)

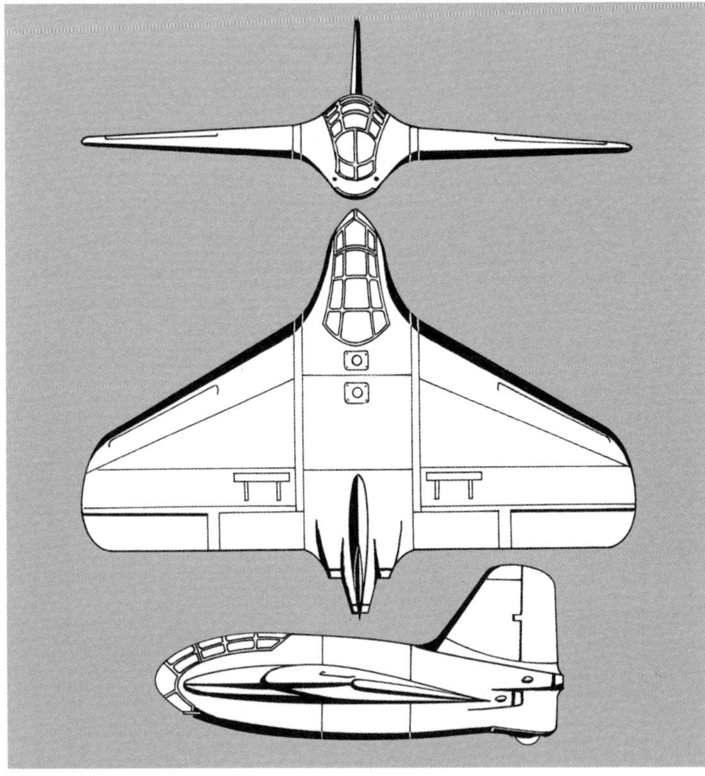

There were two very different aircraft designs designated Li P 09, one of which was a turbojet-powered fighter of 1941, the other having been a Schnellbomber and ground-attack aircraft of 1942. As seen in the illustrations, as a fast bomber it had a generously-glazed cockpit canopy and a main undercarriage consisting of two skids retracting into the fuselage, and a tailwheel. Wingspan was a mere 10.00m, length 7.40m and height 3.10m. The wings had fixed leading edge slots outboard and brake flaps, the fuselage accommodating an internal bomb-bay and two large fuel tanks. Possible weapons were an LT 350 or a BSB 1000/XIII and 2 x MG 151/20s. Powerplants were 3 x 1,500kp thrust HWK 509 rocket motors, maximum speed c.1,000km/h, range 300km and ceiling 12,500m.

Li P 11 (Delta VI)

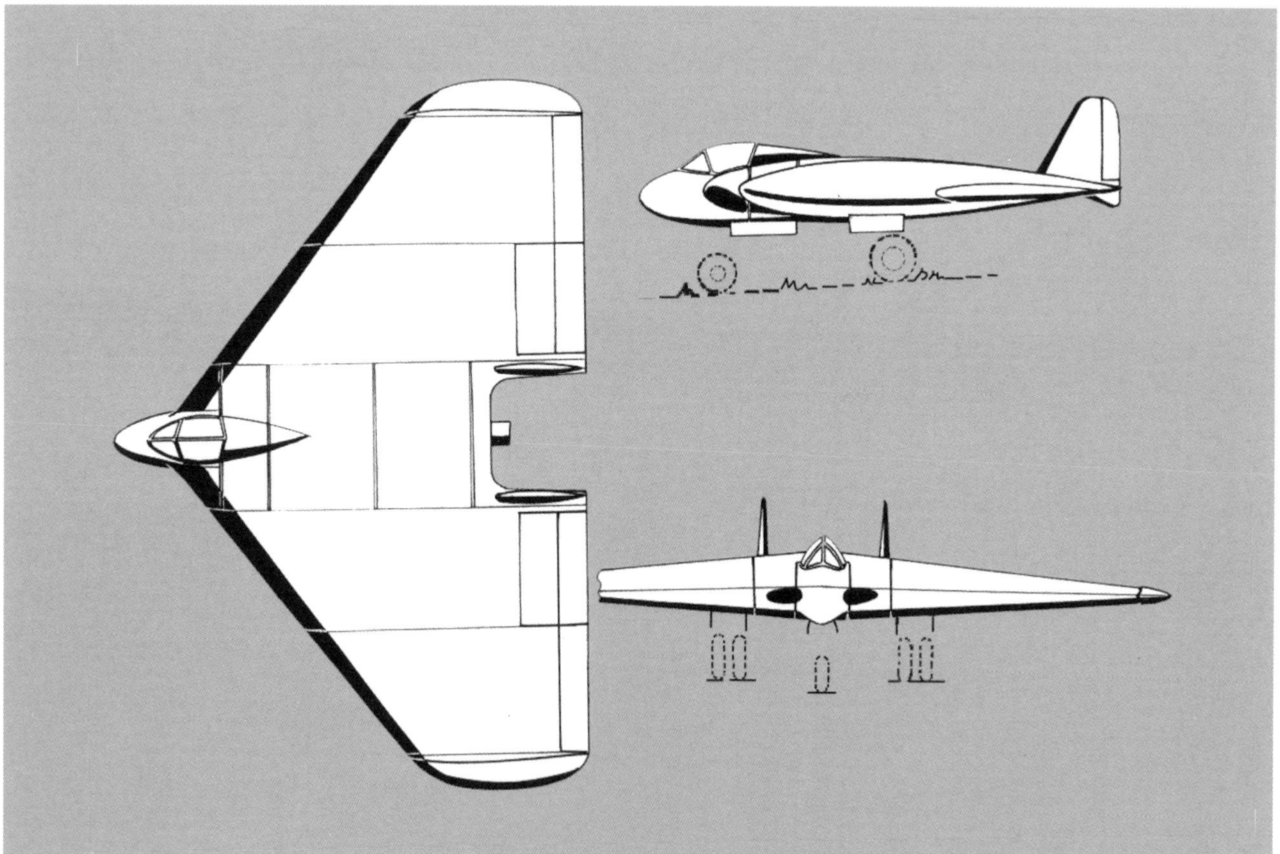

Li P 11 (Delta VI)

The Lippisch P 11 prepared from post-war literature.

Li P 11 (Delta VI) and P 11-121

Among the several proposals under the P 11 designation, the broad-chord delta-winged turbojet-powered model shown opposite dated from May 1943. Work on it was initially interrupted until the RLM officially placed an order for a fast bomber in August 1943. The LFW Vienna built models and conducted wind tunnel tests and preparations were also made for manufacture. Up until February 1944, design of the Delta VI V2 prototype was almost completed, the P 11-121 being envisaged for the fighter, fighter-bomber and Zerstörer roles. The external structure was to have consisted of a thick-walled shell contoured over a core without a load-bearing framework formed of two layers made of Dynal and Tronal, between which was a filling material. With an airframe consisting of 50-60% of synthetic materials, it would have been the first such aircraft – decades before similar synthetics were used abroad in such proportions in aircraft construction. The use of synthetics and their shaping, moreover, was a forerunner in the realm of Stealth aircraft, added to which a low wing loading promised a good climb rate and high manoeuvrability.

For the P 11 V1 twin-finned prototype (2 x Schmidding RI-503 RATO units), span was 10.80m, length 7.485m and height 2.76m. The data given below is for the P 11-121 single-fin variant which is illustrated on the following page.

Dimensions and Weights

Span	10.60m
Length	6.80m
Height	2.70m
Wing area	50.00m²
Flying weight	7,260kg
(as fighter-bomber)	8,000kg

Performance

(with 2 x Jumo 004C)

Maximum speed	
at 6,000-8,000m	1.040km/h
Range	
at 8,000-10,000m	c.3,000km

Powerplants

2 x Jumo 004C initially
2 x HeS 011A (later)

Armament

1 x 1,000kg bomb
2 x MK 103

Li P 11-121 (17.05.1943)

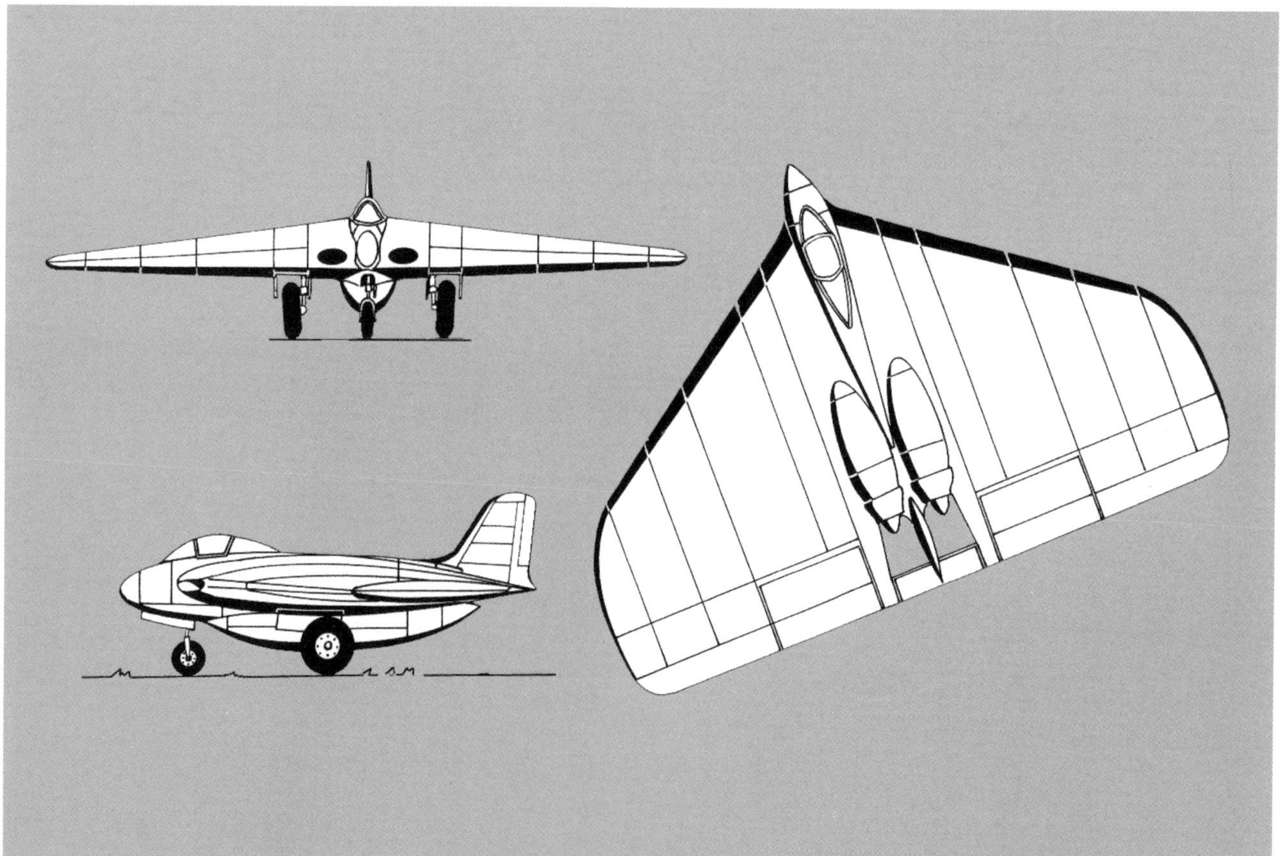

Li P 12 (March 1944)

The illustration is prepared from post-war literature.

The P 12 was one of those proposals which sought to solve problems simultaneously: to establish a new form of motive power which with relatively little fuel would provide high performance, and an increase in speed in the Mach 1 to Mach 3 region. In effect, it would have served to pave the way in this direction.

With the exception of the cockpit, the entire aircraft centre section formed the powerplant. The air intake ducts for the liquid-fuel ramjet led past the cockpit enclosure, fuel ignition for the ramjet taking place in this region. For landing, a single central wheel was extended, and each wingtip featured a down-turned 'winglet'. Exactly how the necessary ram pressure was to be achieved in order to start the ramjet is not known, as the presence of a rocket motor is not visible in the drawings. Even so, an armament of two MG 151/20 has been mentioned in literature, so that it can be assumed that the P 12 would have served as a powerplant testbed.

In the P 12 Entwurf IV ('Supersonic'), the aircraft has a prone pilot above the ramjet and an extensible skid beneath the fuselage. The exhaust gas efflux is in the form of a wide orifice of narrow depth containing adjustable horizontal and lateral flaps to deflect the exhaust to assist during climbing and diving, a rudder having been dispensed with in favour of a small fixed stabilising fin. This variant could also be viewed as a step towards the goal of a supersonic fighter.

The P 12 designation was used earlier in September 1942 – described later on, for a fighter proposal that resembles more a turbojet-powered Me 163 in its overall configuration.

Li P 12 Entwurf III

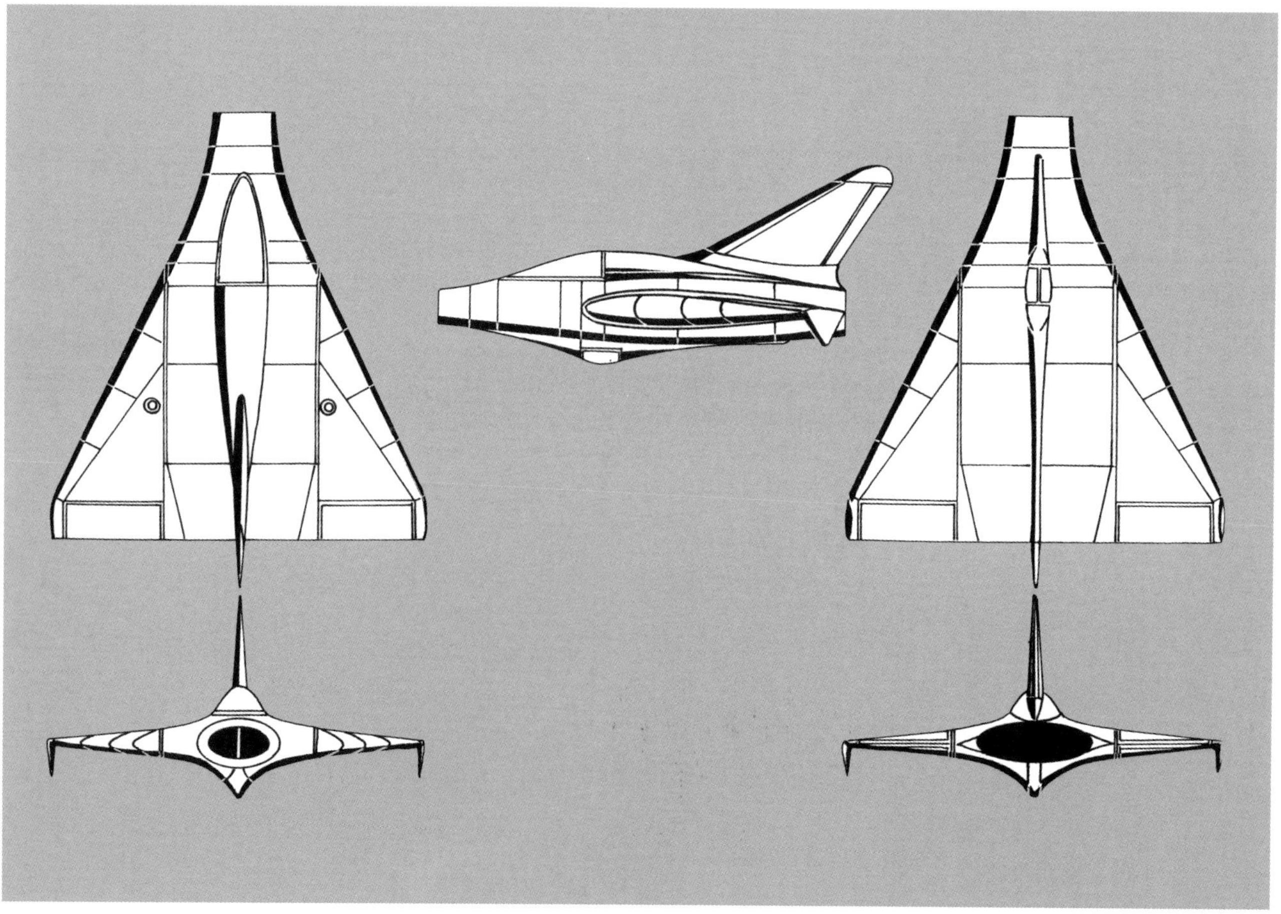

Li P 12 Entwurf IV

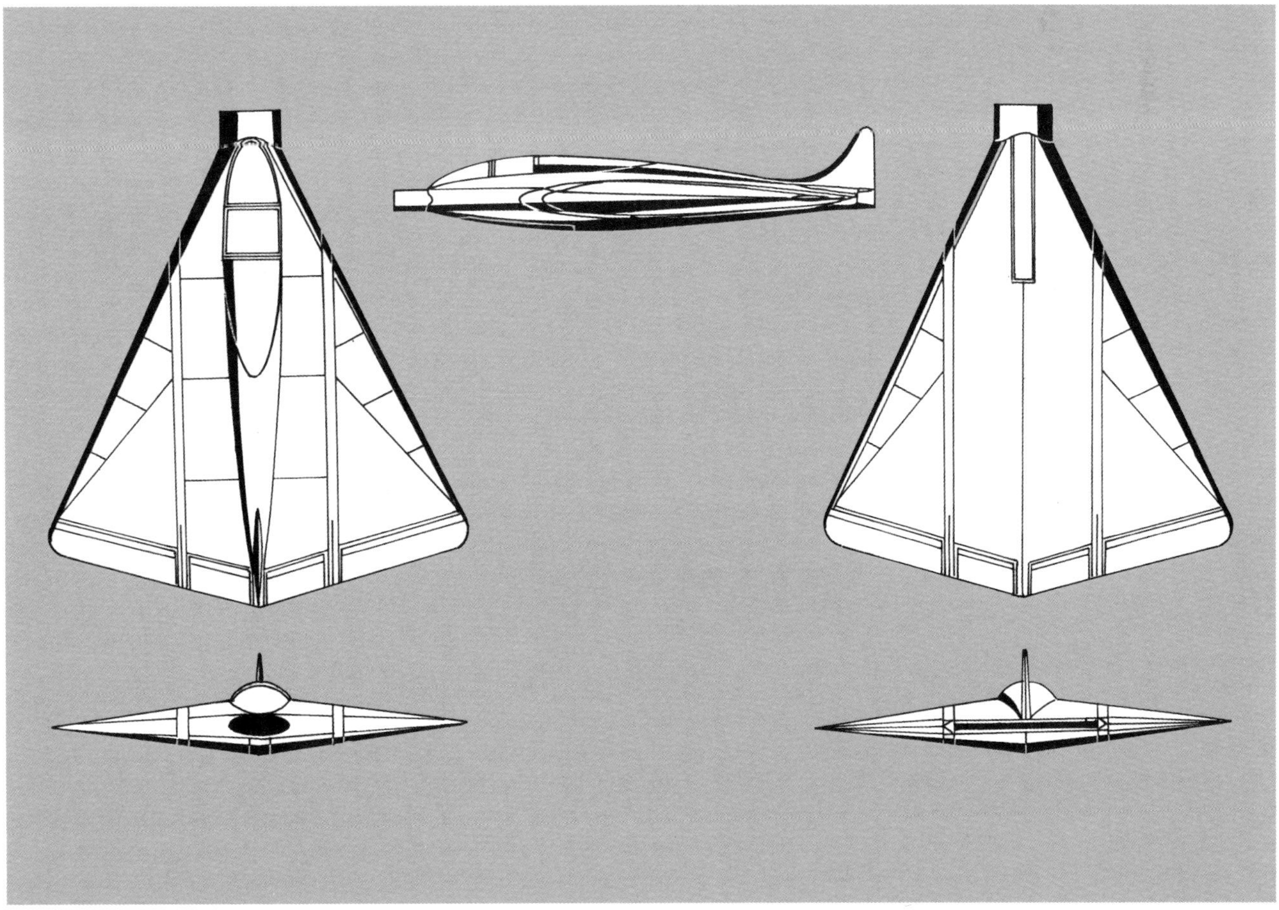

Li P 13a Entwurf I

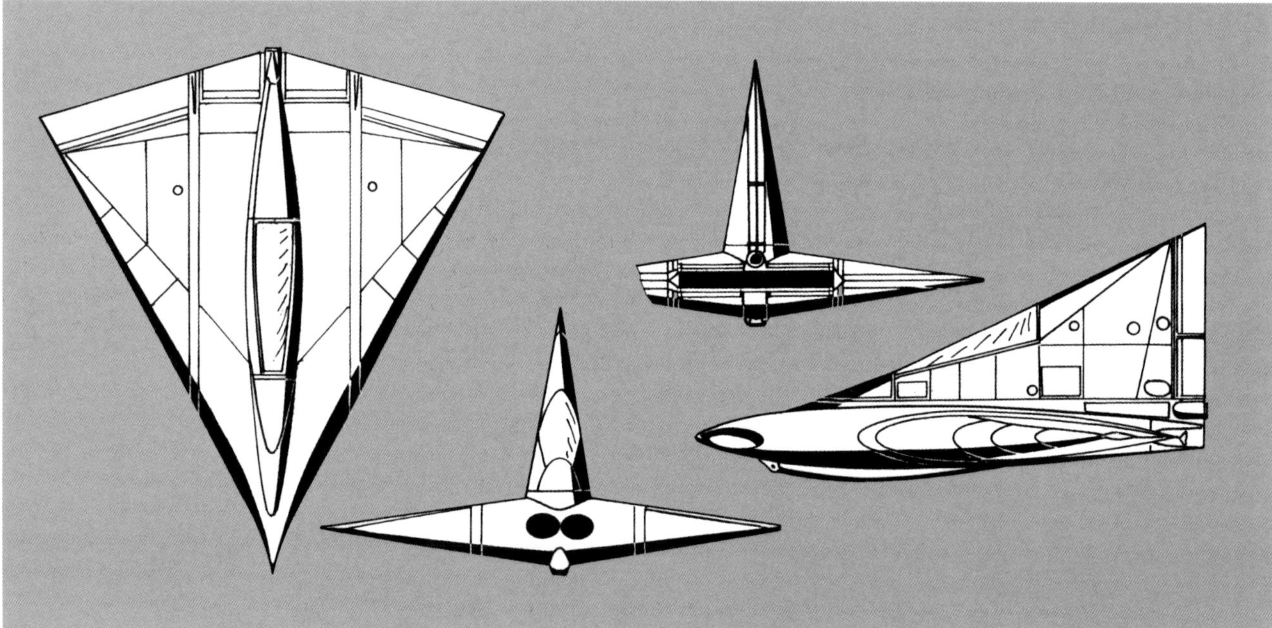

With the P 13a, Lippisch approaches the Horten designs in overall configuration. From the powerplant aspect, he introduces the idea of using coal dust as the fuel. The DM 1 glider, which paved the path towards a fast fighter, was intended to have been flown by the Americans after the war (but was not) and ultimately led to the delta layout being used by Convair for its supersonic fighters.

The three variants of the P 13a show slight differences from one another, all three having the slot-shaped ramjet exhaust orifice equipped with adjustable flaps. In the P 13a/I, the air intakes were on either side of the pointed nose whereas in the II and III, they were in the shape of a circular opening in the fuselage nose. Significant internal differences existed in the I and II, the former containing the pulverised ramjet fuel in the shape of a mattress whilst in the III, which is also very well documented, it was in the shape of a flattened rotating basket.

Take-off was to have been from a wheeled trolley equipped with a 2,000kp thrust HWK 509 S2 liquid-propellant rocket motor that would have provided the initial speed and ram pressure necessary for the ramjet, the aircraft landing on a central skid. Constructionwise, it was to have been an all-metal aircraft, the ramjet estimated to provide 60,000hp that would enable it to be brought to Mach 2.

Li P 13a Entwurf III

Li P 13a Entwurf III

In the P 13a Entwurf III, the C-Stoff tanks in each outer wing section were protected from the hot combustion gases by longitudinal cooling channels on either side of the wing centre section. The T-Stoff, housed in the thickened vertical fin aft of the cockpit, was likewise protected by a cool-air shaft. In addition to the pressurised cabin and ejection seat, the armament was also impressive.

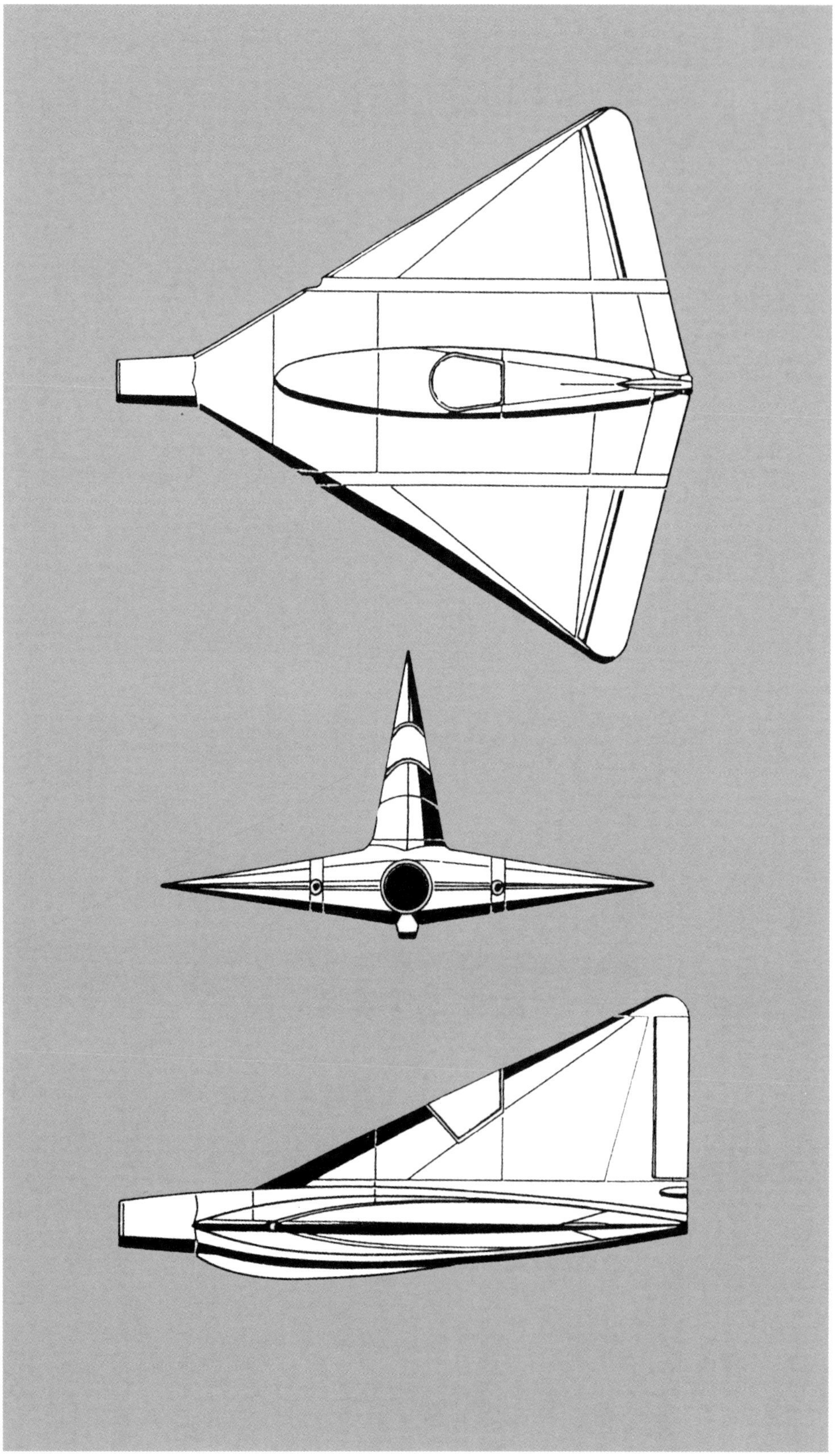

Dimensions

Span	6.70m
Length	6.00m
Height	3.25m
Wing area	20.00m^2

Weights

Empty weight	1,800kg
Take-off weight	3,000kg

Performance

Maximum speed	Mach 2
Ceiling	30,000m
Endurance	45min

Armament

2 x MG 213/20 or
2 x MG 213/30 in wings
24 R4M or
2 x SG 500 *Jägerfaust* projectiles

Li P 13b (December 1944)

There is currently little to relate on the Li P 13b due to lack of documentation. In its construction it has the appearance of a test aircraft for the ramjet, the coal fuel being in the form of a flattened circular basket. Span was 6.90m, length 7.20m and height 3.47m.

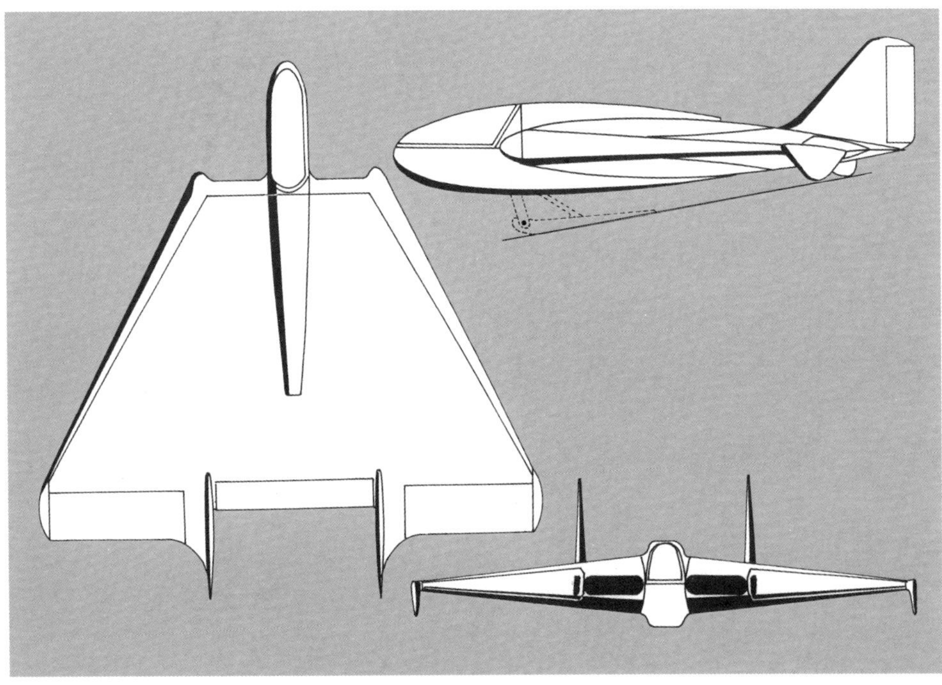

Li P 14 (Spring 1945)

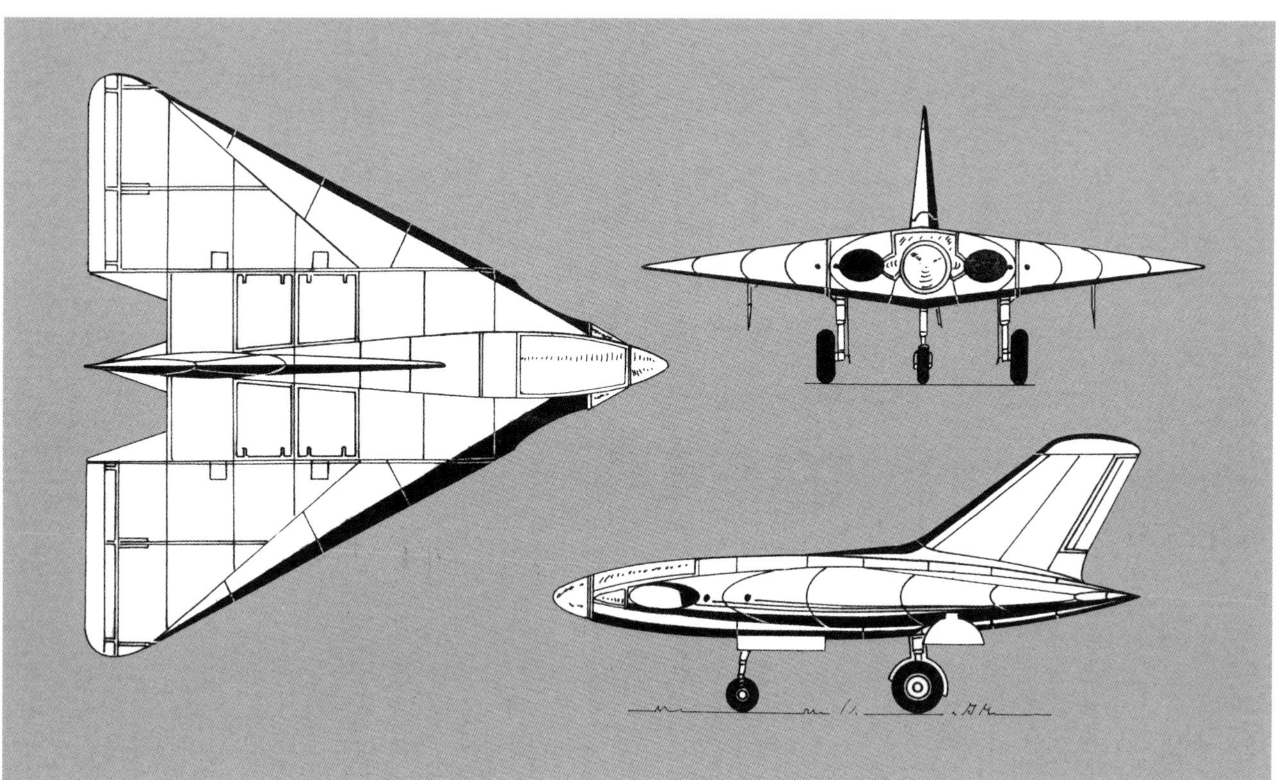

A wind tunnel model of the Li P 14 is known to have been completed, together with the statement that it consisted of a delta-wing fighter powered by two HeS 011 turbojets. The wing, of only 6% thickness/chord ratio, was to have brought it close to Mach 1. In the absence of documentation of my own, the above illustration and 3-view have been prepared (in conformity with the model photo) from research undertaken by my Spanish colleague J Miranda. Design data are not known.

Li P 15 Entwurf I

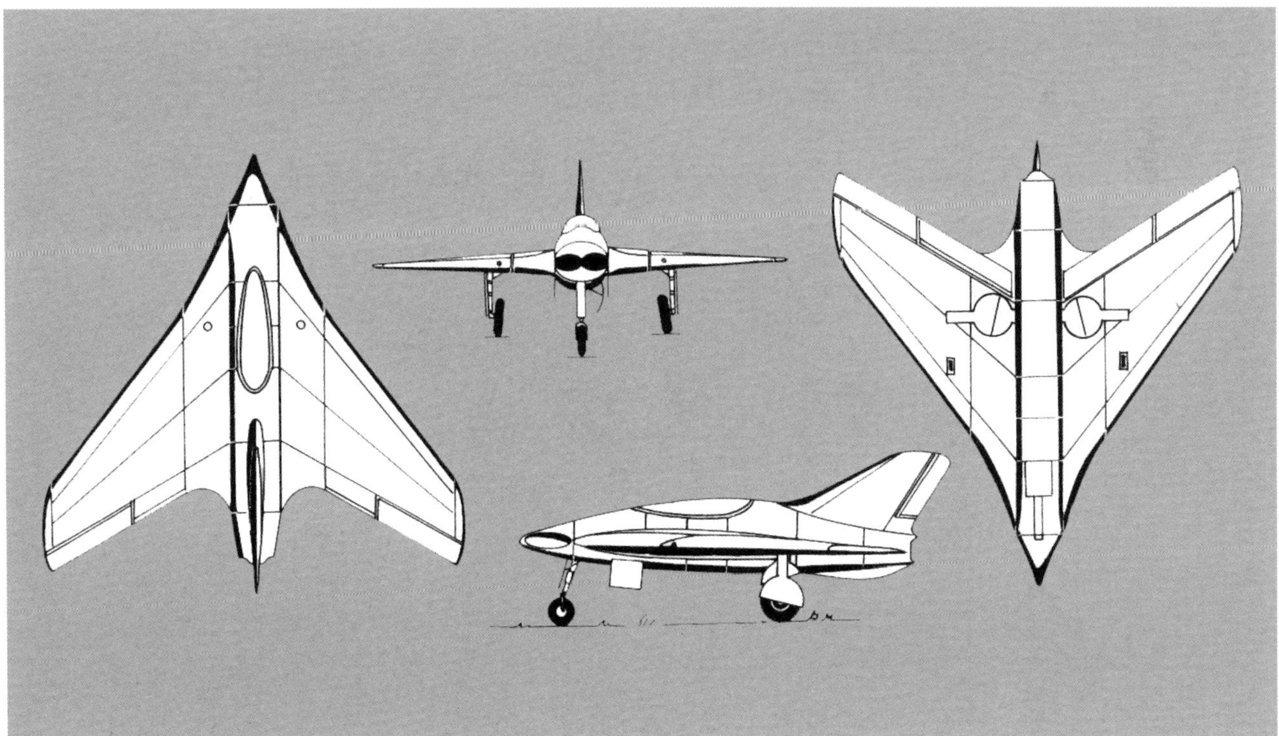

What was valid for the P 14 applies here to the P 15 also, the latter a project for a single-jet fighter which at the time, was dimensionally relatively small, having an extremely sharply-swept wing and a large swept fin and rudder. Without the cut-outs along the wing trailing edges it could be described as a delta – but in this case the limit to the 'flying triangle' is reached, thus ending this particular episode.

It should be noted that the designations P 11, P 12, P 13 and P 15 'Diana' were also used for a completely different series of projects described later on.

Li P 01-106 (13.04.1939)

The Lippisch P 01-106 of 13.04.1939. Span was 6.00m, length 5.48m, height 2.72m and powerplant an unknown (but presumably Junkers) early jet engine.

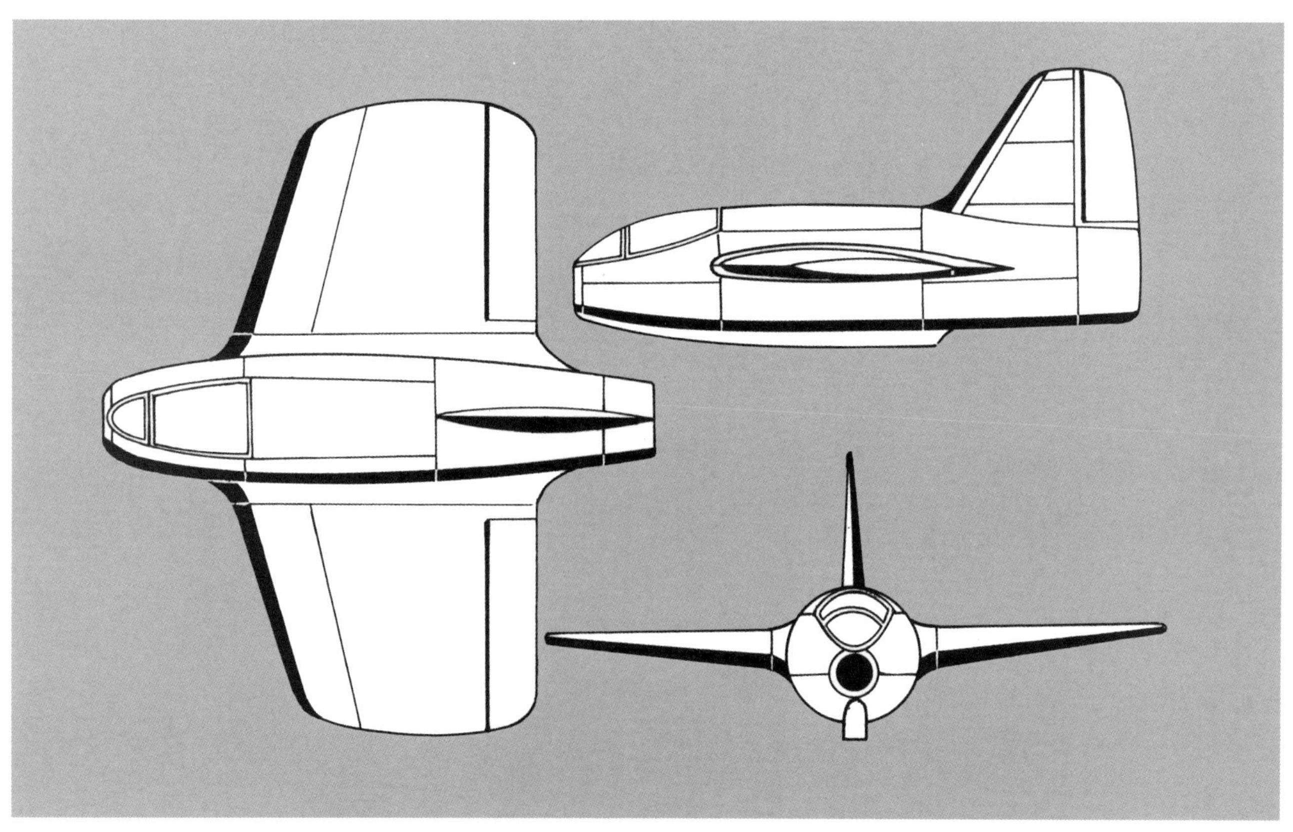

Li P 01-111 (20.10.1939)

Further Lippisch Projects

With the P 01-series Lippisch turned towards the configuration adopted for the Me 163 with which all these aircraft have a common layout, namely, that of a tailless swept wing. The propulsion, however, varied from rocket motors to turbojets and hybrid powerplants, but also included piston engines, not to mention ramjets that were indicated in one or other variants of a basic design. All the projects of this series were equipped with skid landing gear.

Dimensions
Span 7.50m
Length 6.60m
Height 3.20m
Wing area 19.00m²

Weights
Empty weight 2,200kg
Loaded weight 4,270kg

Powerplant
1 (unidentified) turbojet

Armament
2 x MG 151/15 in wing roots

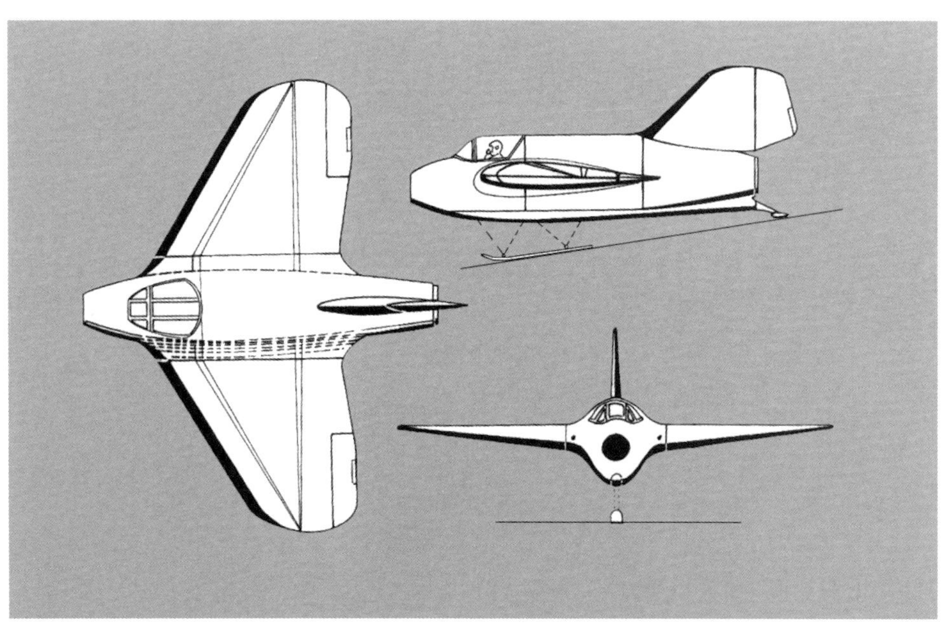

Li P 01-112 (12.02.1940)

With a comparably large fuselage and without armament, an experimental aircraft was to have been created to investigate the influence of the boundary layer, whereby a part of the incoming air in the turbojet intake would be diverted and, with increased energy, blown out over the upper side of the aircraft's outboard wing surfaces. From this concept, an armed fighter was derived in February 1940, its two 600kp thrust early BMW turbojets lying side by side in the fuselage.

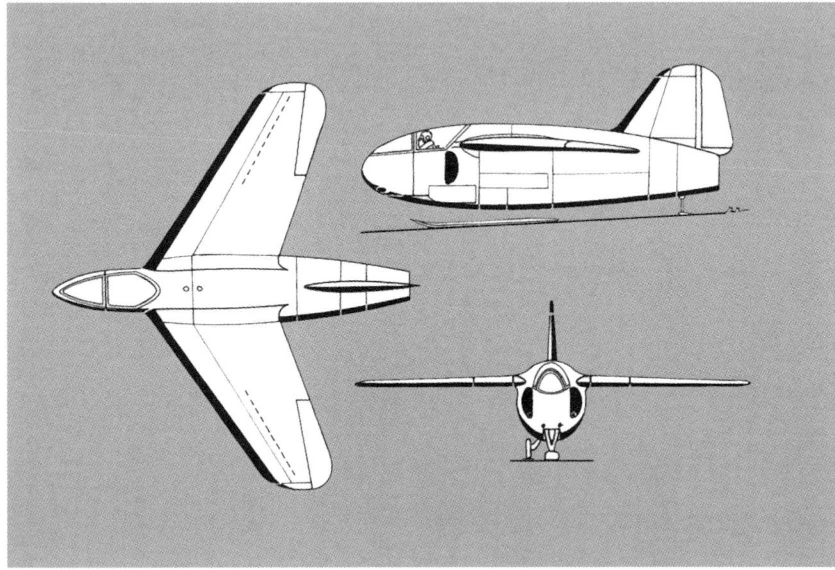

Dimensions and Weight

Span	8.00m
Length	7.50m
Height	3.20m
Wing area	16.00m^2
Flying weight	4,000-4,500kg

Performance

No data available, estimated at	c.1,000km/h

Armament

2 x MG 17 in intake ducts
2 MG 151/15 in fuselage nose

Li P 01-113 (17.07.1940)

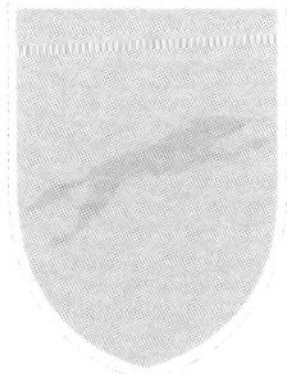

Dimensions

Span	9.00m
Length	6.75m
Height	3.00m
Wing area	18.00m²

Powerplants
2 x 600kp thrust BMW P 3302 or P 3304 turbojets + 1 x HWK RII-203 rocket regulable from 150-750kp thrust.

Armament
2 x MG 151/20

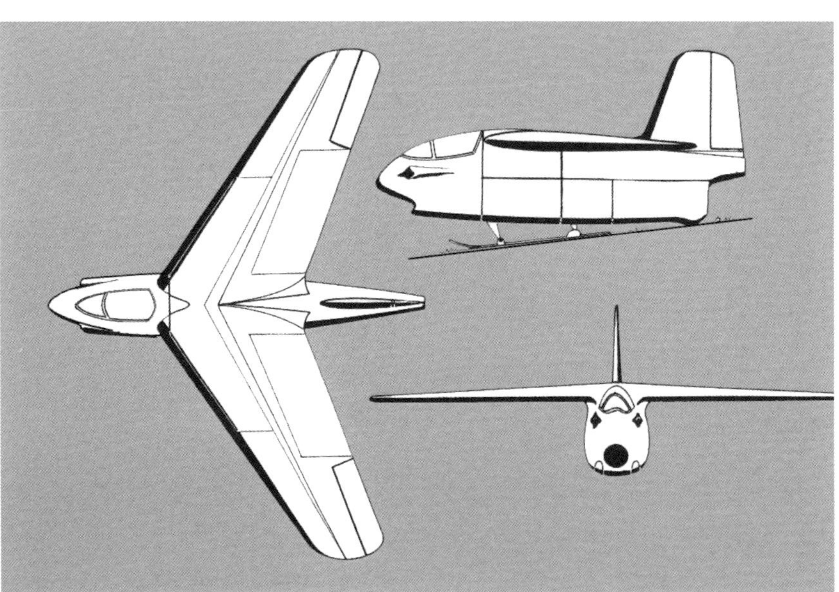

Li P 01-114 (19.07.1940)

A shoulder-wing aircraft which was to be powered by 1 x HWK rocket motor as employed in the previous project.

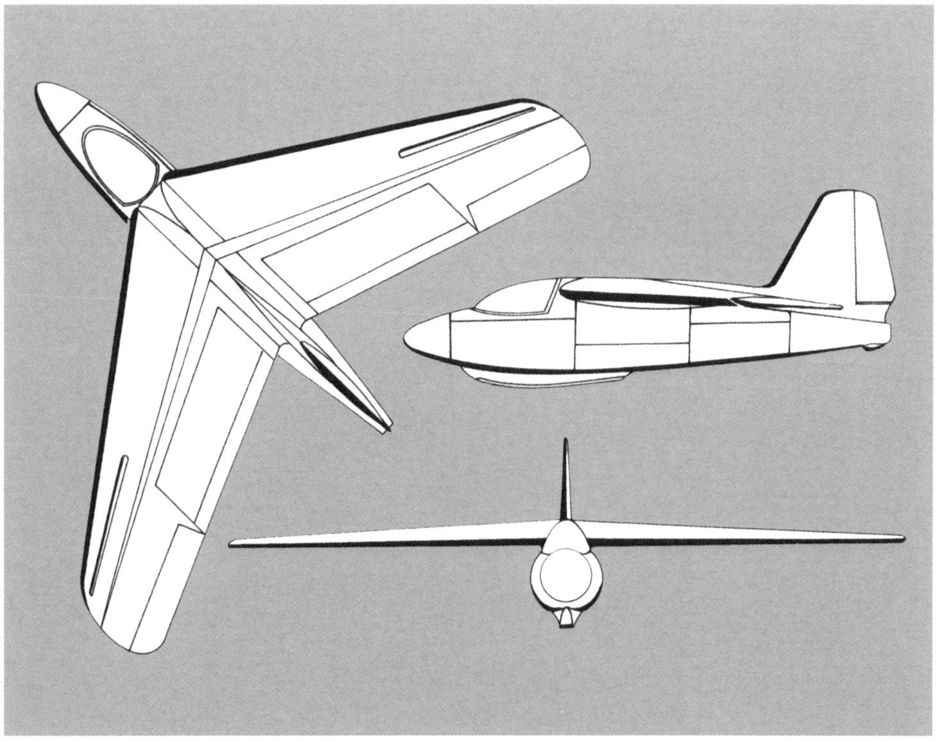

Dimensions

Span	9.00m
Length	6.50m
Height	2.70m
Wing area	18.00m^2

Weights

Empty weight	890kg
Loaded weight	2,250kg

Li P 01-115 (02.07.1941)

This project shows clear similarities to the later Me 163, but was a hybrid-powered aircraft. The dorsal air intake fed the BMW P 3302 or P 3304 turbojet, beneath which was a 1,500kp thrust HWK rocket motor.

Dimensions

Span	9.00m
Length	6.75m
Height	3.00m

Armament

2 x MG 151/20

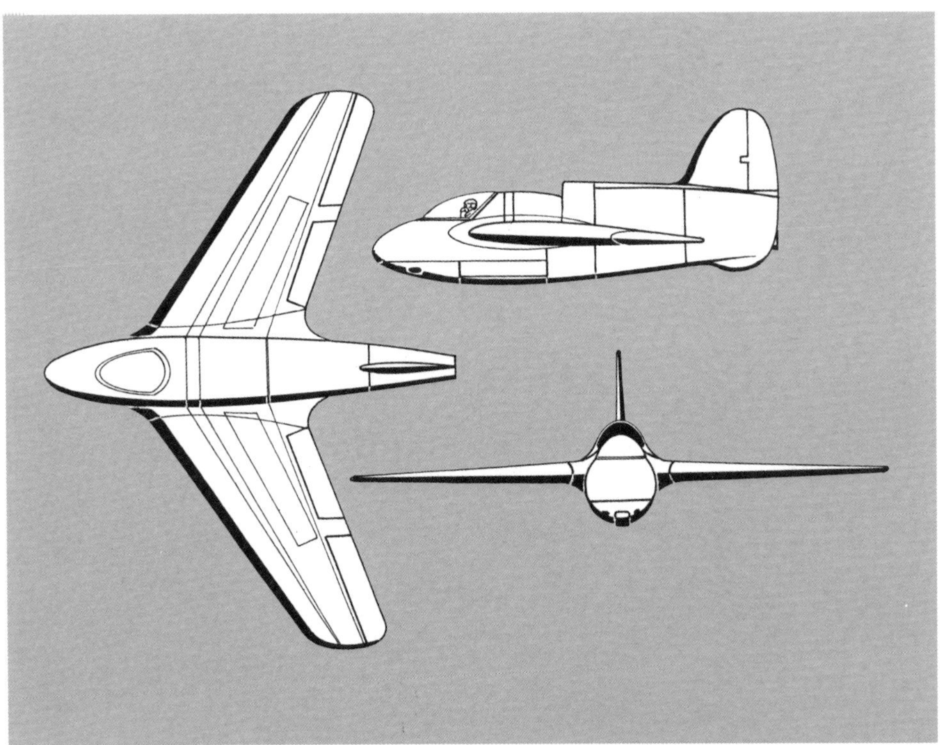

Li P 01-116 (12.06.1941)

Dimensions

Span	9.00m
Length	7.06m
Wing area	18.00m^2

Powerplant
BMW P 3302 or P 3304 turbojet + 1,500kp thrust HWK rocket motor

Armament
2 x MG 17 + 2 x MG 151/15

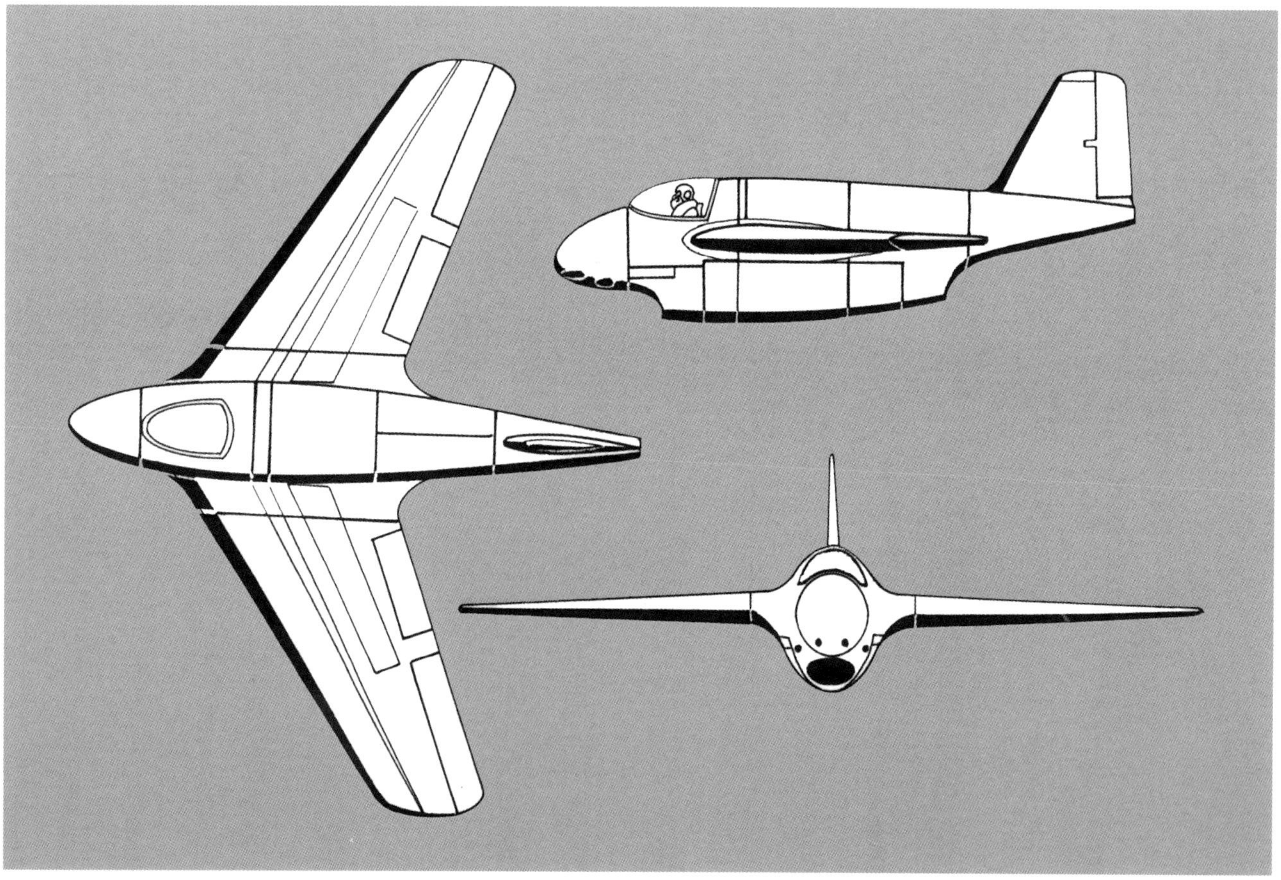

Li P 01-116 (16.07.1941)

With this proposal Lippisch temporarily departed from the realm of turbojet-powered designs. With a span of 9.00m, length 6.75m and height 3.00m, the fighter closely approached the dimensions of the Me 163 B; powerplant was a 1,500kp thrust HWK rocket motor plus an auxiliary cruising chamber, and the armament consisted of 2 x MG 151/20.

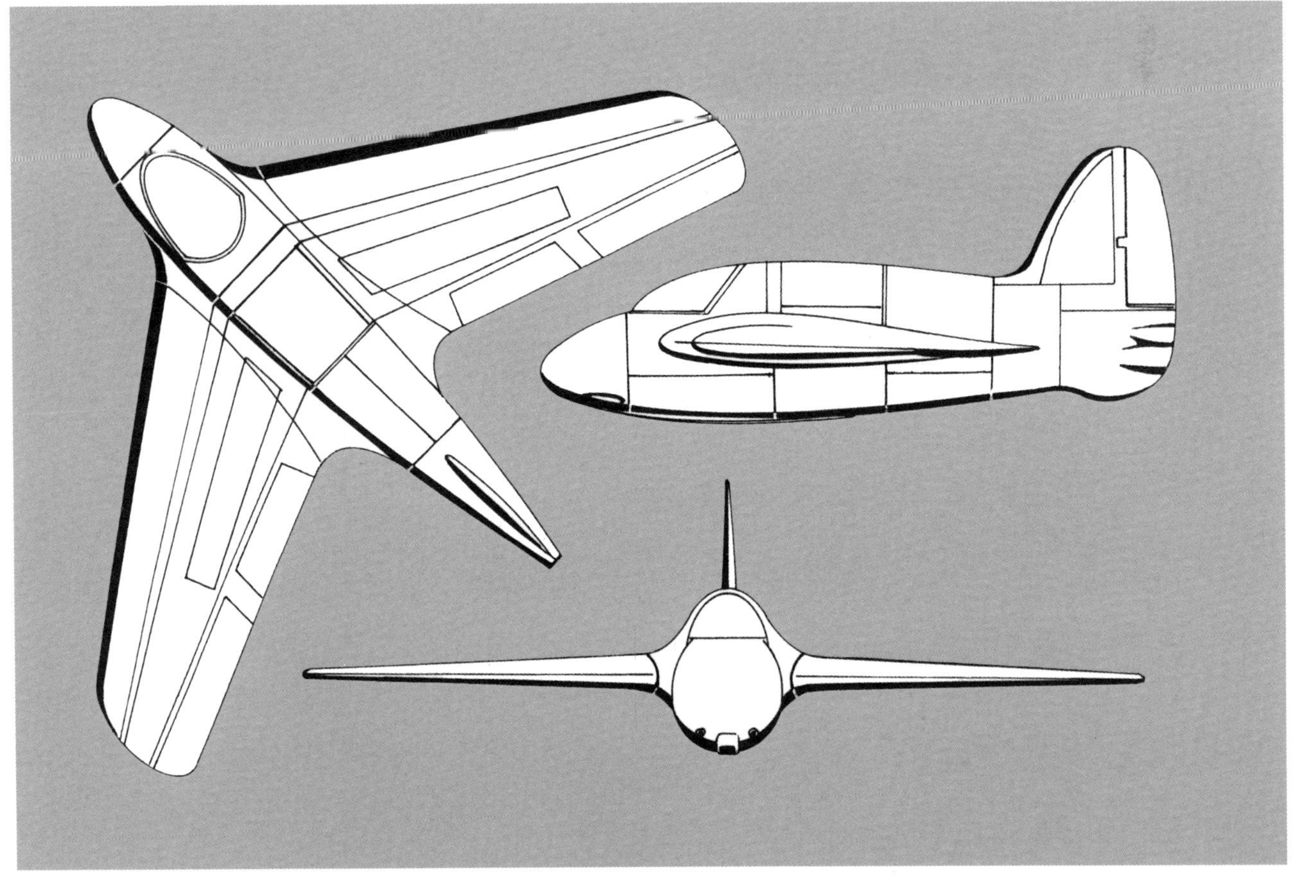

Li P 01-117 (22.07.1941)

Dimensions

Span	9.00m
Length	
fuselage	7.65m
overall	8.10m
Height	3.40m
Fuselage	
max diameter	1.50m

Armament
4 x MG 131 and
2 x MG 151/20s

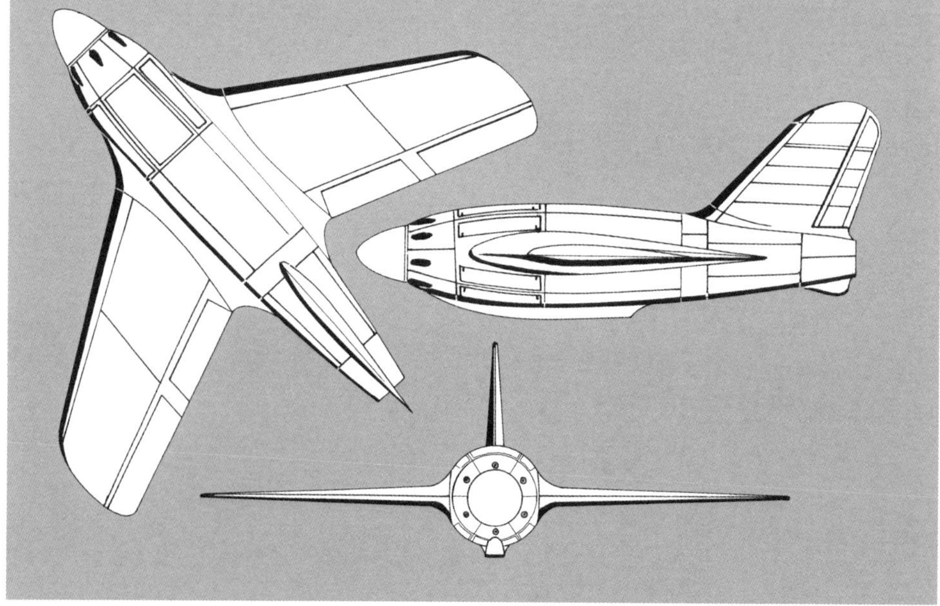

The P 01-117 served primarily for thoughts in relation to the number and arrangement of the weapons carried. The pilot was situated in the prone position, and because the guns and their ammunition were arranged symmetrically around the cockpit, had to enter and exit via the Plexiglas nose. Although it provided good vision, it offered little protection against enemy fire, added to which was the difficulty of egress in an emergency. The fuel tanks for the rear 1,500kp thrust HWK rocket motor were located amidships in the fuselage.

Li P 01-118 (03.08.1941)

This project featured an aerodynamically further developed configuration, the pilot (again) seated in a forward-reclining position with a good field of vision in the Plexiglas cockpit which, together with the lower vision panels, blended into the fuselage contours.

Dimensions

Span	9.00m
Length	7.20m
Height	3.00m

Powerplant
1 x 1,500kp thrust HWK rocket motor

Armament
2 x MG 151/20

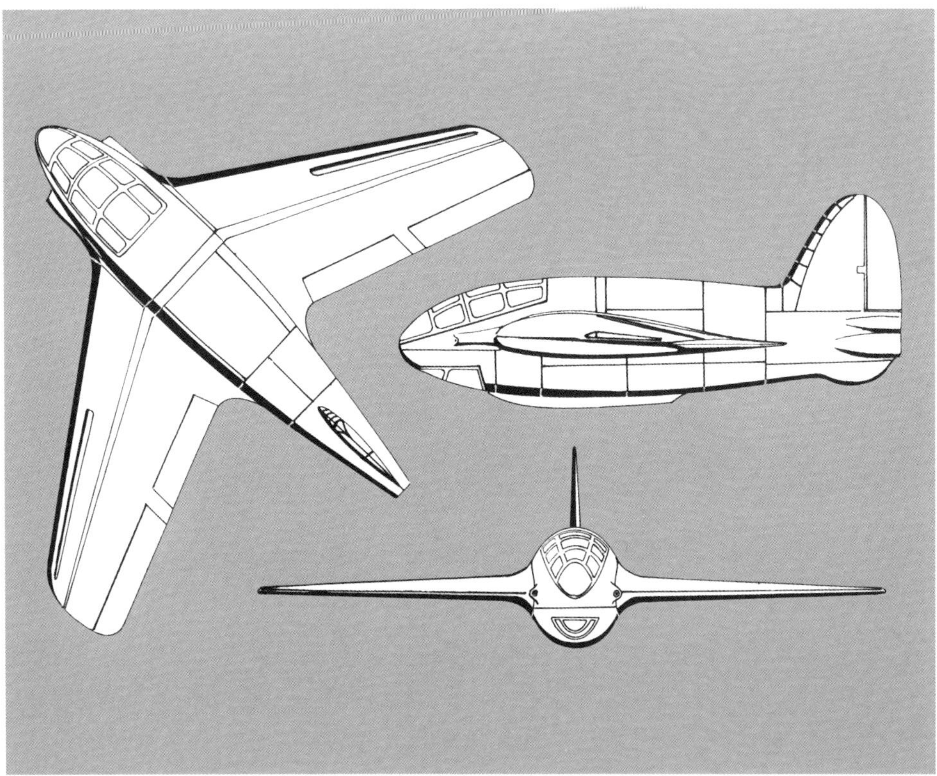

Li P 01-119 (04.08.1941)

The last of the projects known in this series, it was essentially similar in layout to the P 01-118 with the exception of the stepped cockpit and normal seating for the pilot.

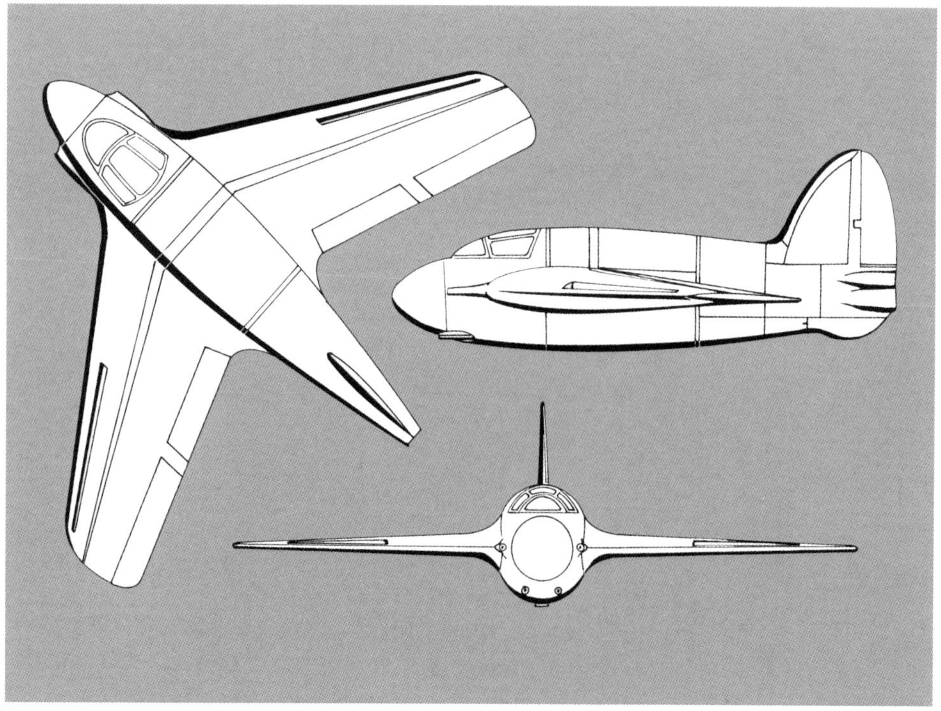

Dimensions

Span	9.00m
Length	7.20m

Armament

4 x MG 151/20

Powerplant

1 x 1,500kp thrust HWK rocket motor

Messerschmitt Flugzeugbau

Me 163 A

A total of 10 Me 163 A (V4 to V13) prototypes were built by Messerschmitt at Augsburg and corresponded to the Me 163 AV4 first prototype, these were eventually powered by the HWK RII-203b 'cold' rocket motor. When flown as a glider, it carried water ballast and was towed-off by a Me 110 C. To help pilots get the feel of the Me 163 and high landing speeds, the DFS Habicht (Hawk) glider had its wingspan progressively reduced form 10.00m to 8.00m and finally 6.00m, known in the latter form as the Stummel-Habicht (Stump-Hawk). Although all were unarmed, one prototype was experimentally fitted with 24 x R4M underwing rockets.

Dimensions

Span	8.85m
Length	5.60m
Height	2.16m
Wing area	17.50m^2
Max weight	2,400kg

Performance

Max speed	1,004km/h

Powerplant

1 x 750kp thrust HWK RII-203b rocket motor

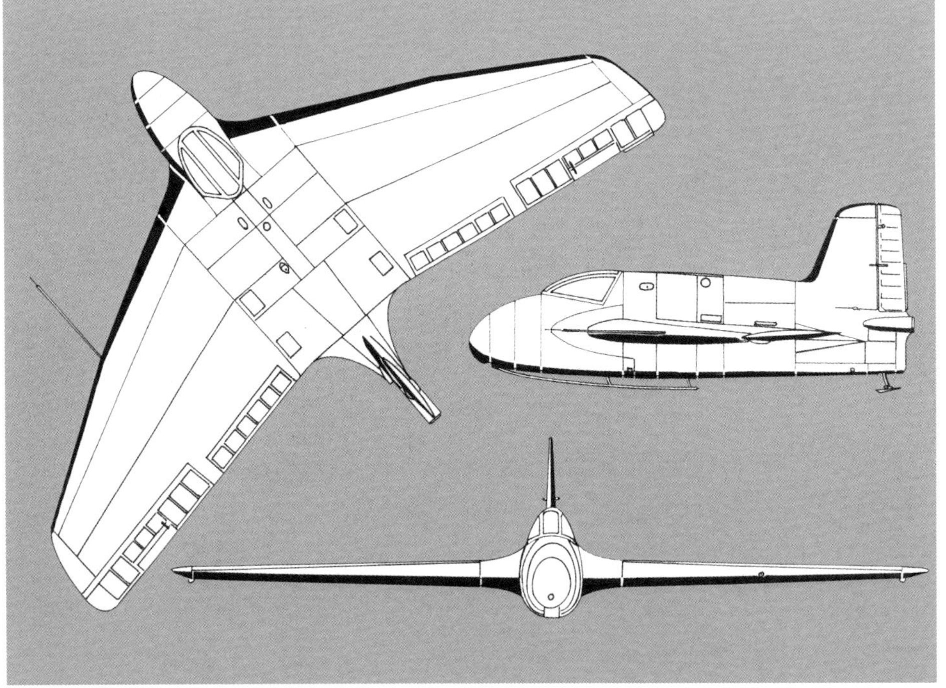

Me 163 A V8

For this Me 163 A trainer and the operational Me 163 B production aircraft that followed, no descriptions are necessary as both versions have been adequately described in various publications.

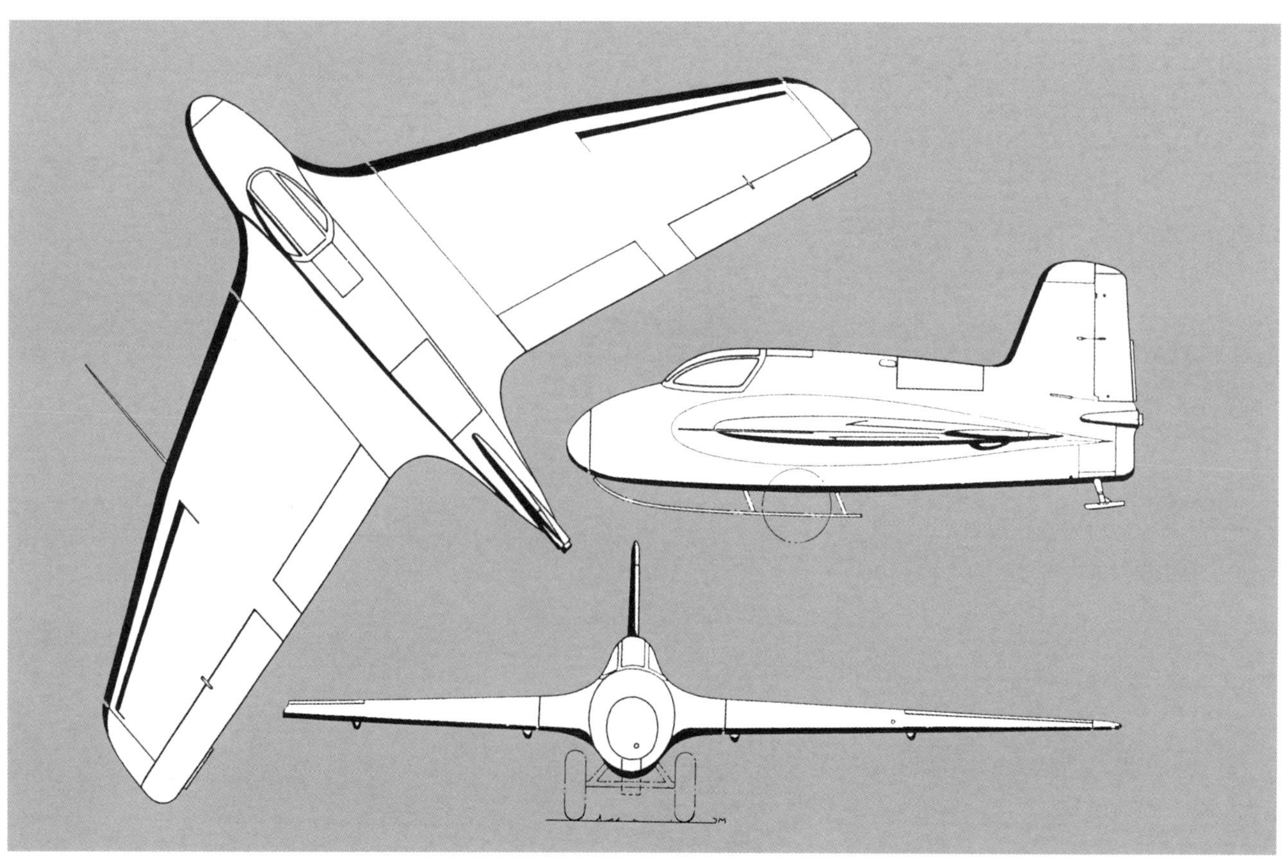

Me 163 B-1

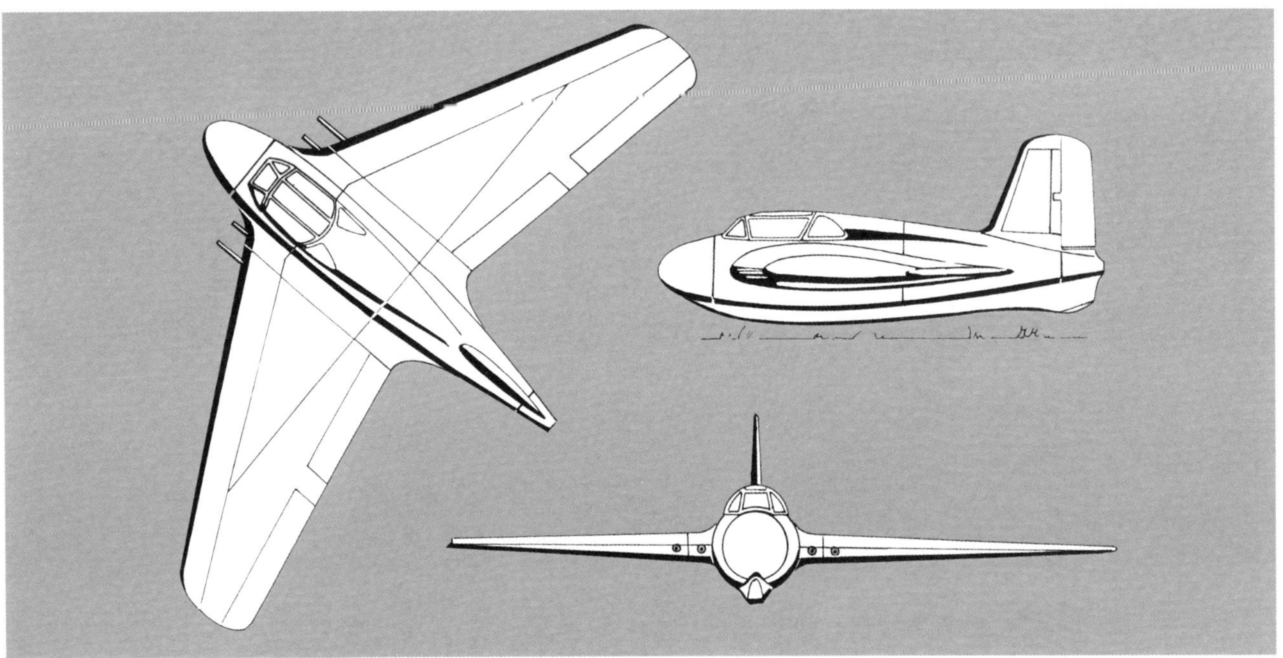

Dimensions & Weights (Sept 1944)

Span	9.30m
Length	5.92m
Height	2.75m
Wing area	17.30m^2
Empty weight	1,777kg
Take-off weight	3,950kg

Performance

Max speed	900km/h

Armament

2 x MK 108 or 2 x MG 151/20

Me 163 C / Me 163 D

In addition to the main combustion chamber regulable from 1,700-200kp thrust, the Walter HWK 509A-2 rocket motor had an auxiliary 300kp thrust cruising chamber. In climbing flight both chambers were used, the cruising chamber thereafter employed to increase the powered endurance from 8 to 12 minutes. First tested in the Me 163 BV6, this powerplant was intended for the Me 163 C-1a, of which a few pre-production aircraft with pressurised cockpit and full-view canopy were built.

Dimensions and Weight

Span	9.80m
Length	7.04m
Height on trolley	3.20m
Wing area	20.50m²
Max weight	5,000kg

Performance

Max speed	880km/h
Ceiling	14,000m
Range	130km

Armament
4 x MK 108

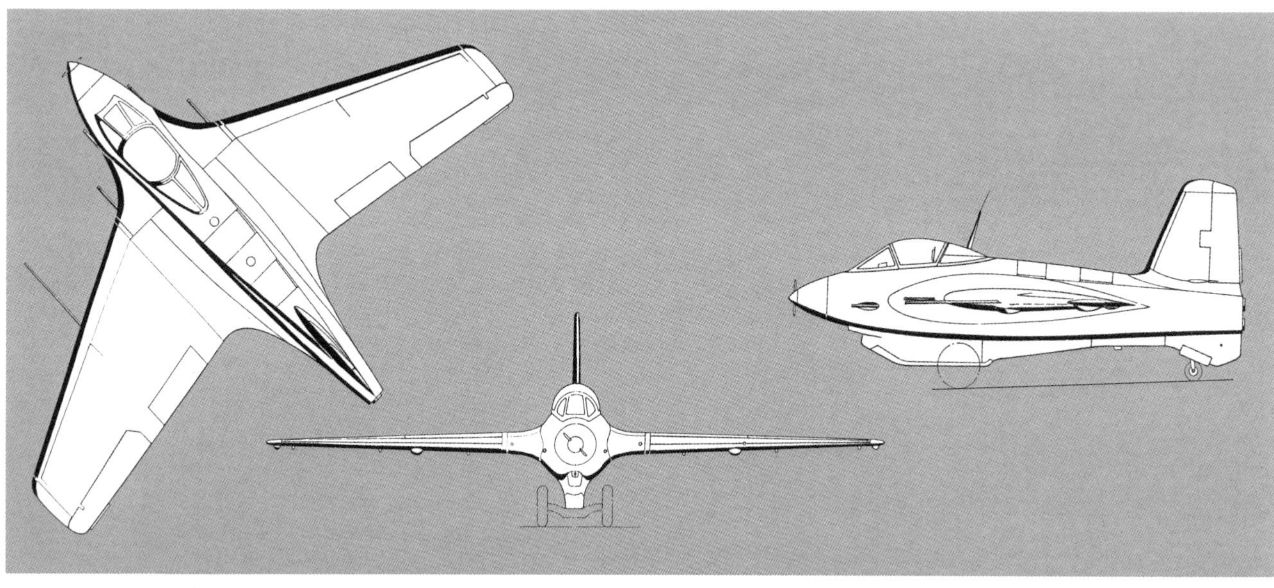

Me 163 D
A further development of the Me 163 B with tricycle undercarriage and fuselage length increased from 5.92m to 6.82m.

Armament
1 x MK 108 or 1 x MK 213 and 2 x MG 151/20

Li 163 S (14.09.1941)

The Messerschmitt Li 163 S is not to be confused with the similarly-denoted production Me 163 B as the S stood for Schulflugzeug (trainer) and was distinguished by the raised rear canopy for the second crew member.

The aircraft shown here, the Li 163 S (for Serienflugzeug) was derived from the Lippisch P 01-series and was the last proposal prior to the Me 163 B. Powerplant was 1 x 1,500kp thrust HWK 509A; span was 9.20m, length 5.70m, and four long-barrel guns were to have been installed in the wing roots.

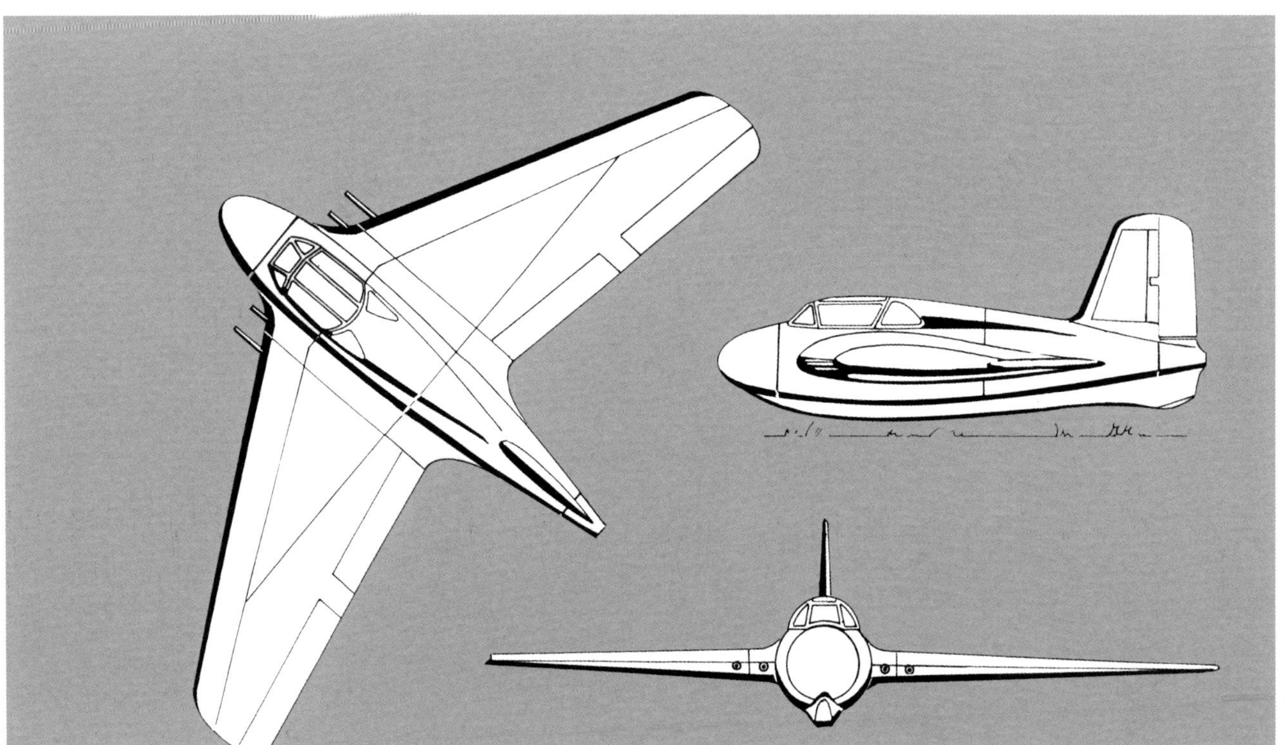

Me 263

The deficiencies inherent in the Me 163 had already been taken care of in 1943-1944 when the Me 263 project was laid out. A new rocket motor with cruising chamber increased the operational endurance and range, and instead of the take-off trolley, it was to have had a robust retractable undercarriage. In order to relieve the Messerschmitt firm, the project was handed over to Junkers. Here, it ran under the designation Ju 248, was given a circular fuselage, larger trailing-edge flaps and automatic wing nose flaps, but the RLM insisted on the Messerschmitt configuration. For various reasons, the 2,500kp thrust BMW 708 rocket motor was to have been installed at a later date, and an enormous amount of development work was performed on it. The aircraft was equipped with a pressure cabin and the 2,000kp thrust HWK 509 C rocket motor. Following extensive tests as a glider (still with fixed undercarriage) and first flown on 08.02.1945, the Ju 248 reverted to Messerschmitt where it was again accorded the designation Me 263.

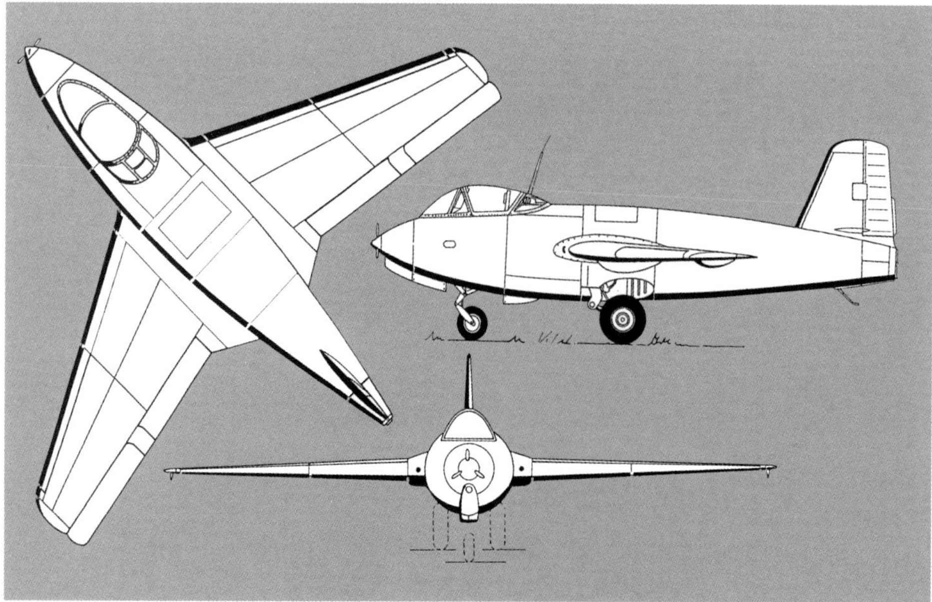

Dimensions and Weight
(December 1944)

Span	9.50m
Length	7.88m
Height	3.17m
Wing area	17.80m^2
Flying weight	5,113kg

Performance

Max speed at 14,000m	880km/h
Climbing time to 14,000m	3 mins
Range at 10,000m	220km

Armament
2 x MK 108 in wing roots

Me 263 Swivel-Wing Studies

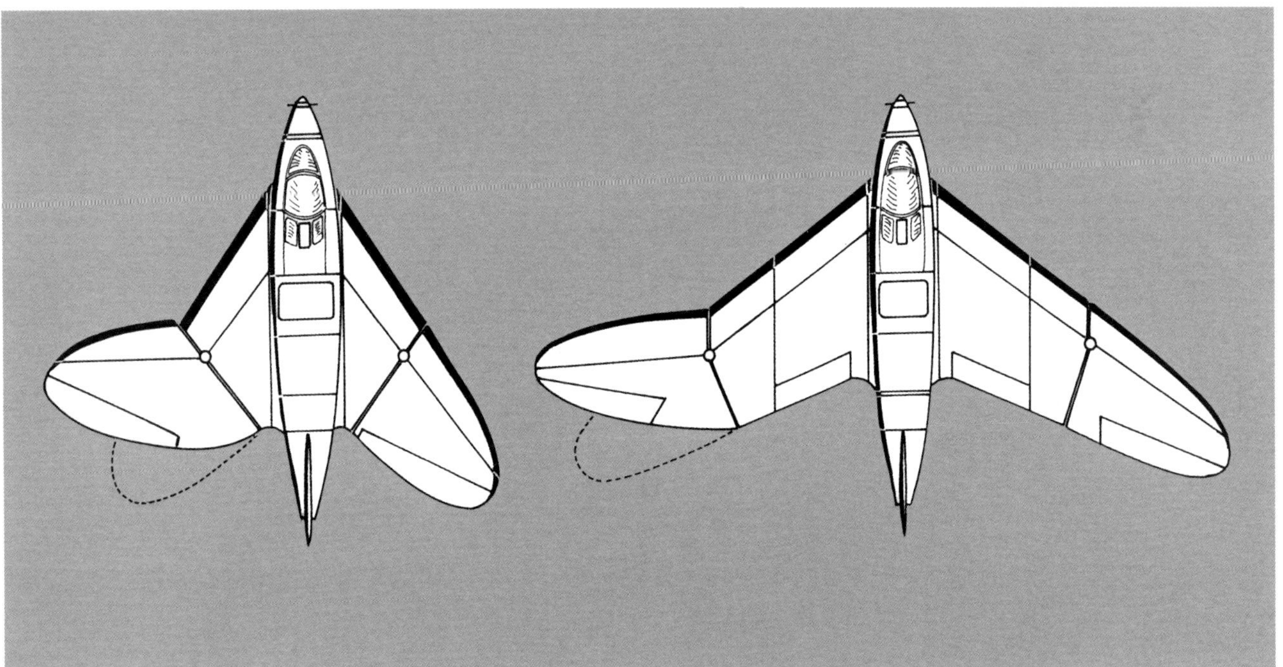

(Lippisch) Me 263 Swivel-Wing Studies

In these proposals, with a similar fuselage and fin and rudder as the Me 263, Dr. Lippisch considered how the outer wings could partially be made movable. Exactly how serious these ideas were and how far they were pursued is not known. The upper plan view shows a sharply-swept relatively short-span wing, the lower one with less sweep and of longer span.

Li P 04-108 (08.12.1939)

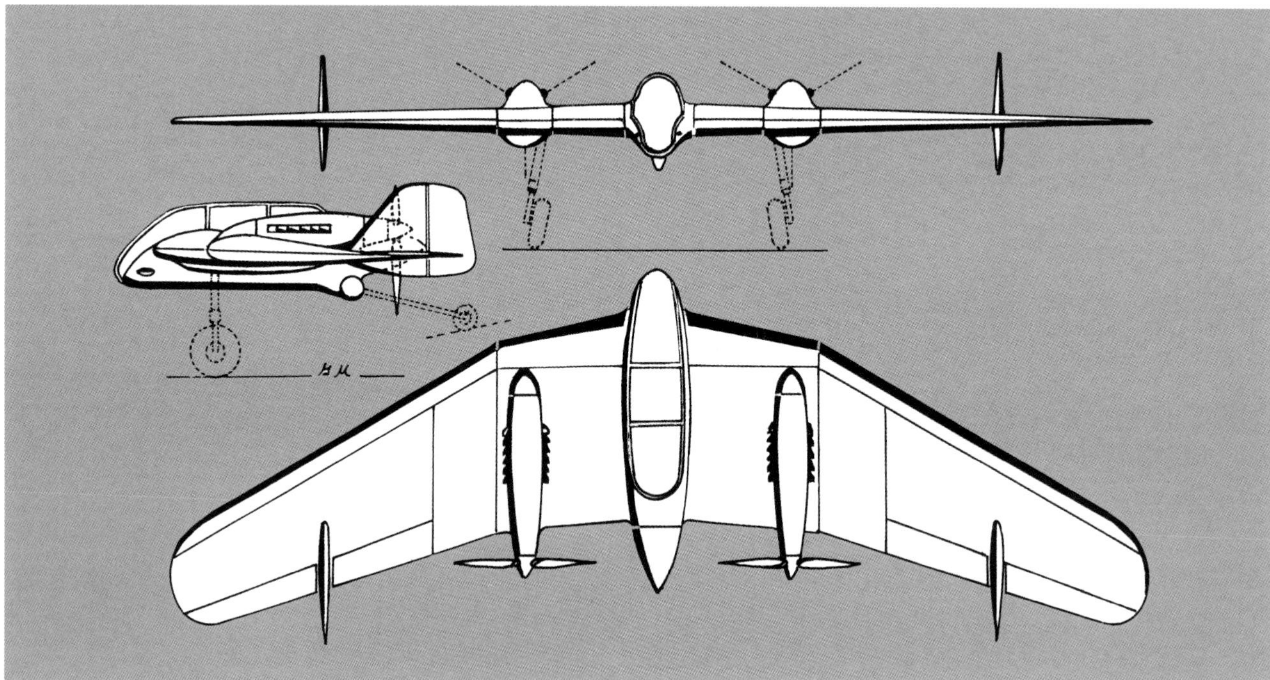

This design study for a Zerstörer/Bomber in a tailless layout was drawn up in 1939, after Lippisch had begun his activities at the Messerschmitt AG. For centre of gravity reasons each 1,200hp DB 601E engine, housed far forward in the wings, was to have driven pusher propellers via an extension shaft, the propellers protected from damage at take-off and landing by the telescopic-extension tailwheel. Calculations indicated a maximum speed of 510km/h and hence made it an internal rival to the Me 110. The rearward-firing MG 131 defensive armament housed in blisters near the fuselage tailcone was remotely controlled. Forward-firing armament consisted of four fixed MG 151s in the fuselage. Dimensions were: span 16.00m, length 5.83m and height 3.15m.

Li P 05 (25.08.1941)

The P 05 fighter represented an alternative proposal to the Me 163 B, which was unsatisfactory because of its short endurance. The 3 x 1,500kp thrust HWK 509 rocket motors and their fuel called for an airframe that had almost twice the wing area and loaded weight.

Dimensions

Span	12.80m
Length	7.60m
Height	3.10m
Wing area	36.00m^2

Armament

4 x MG 151/20

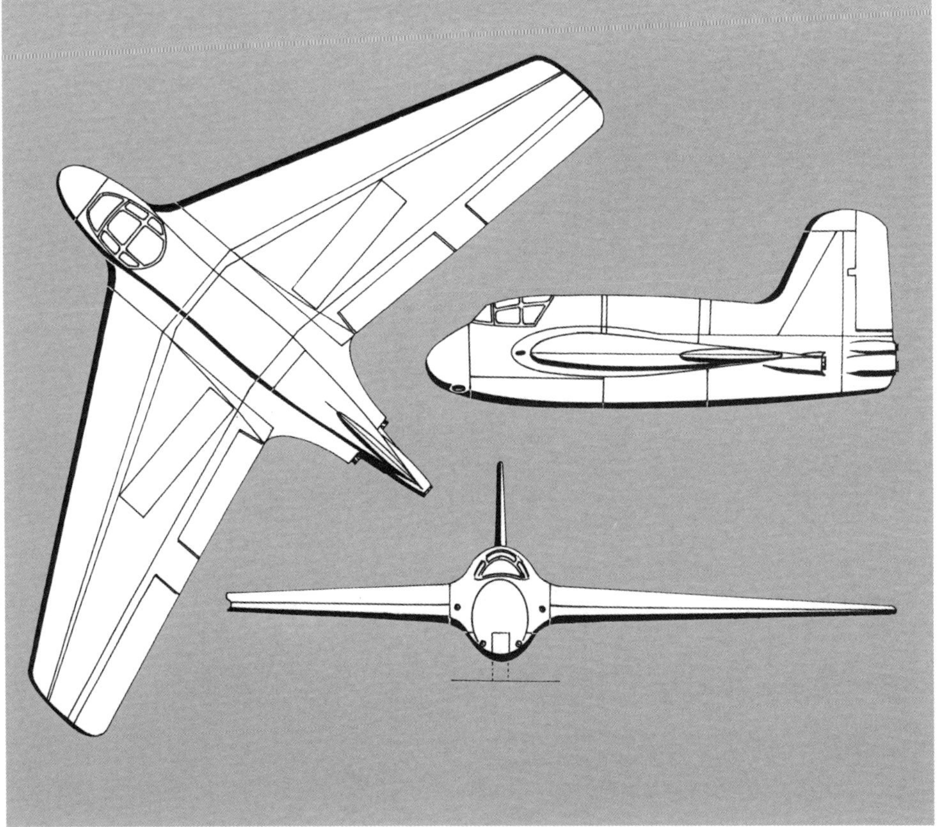

Li P 09 (28.10.1941)

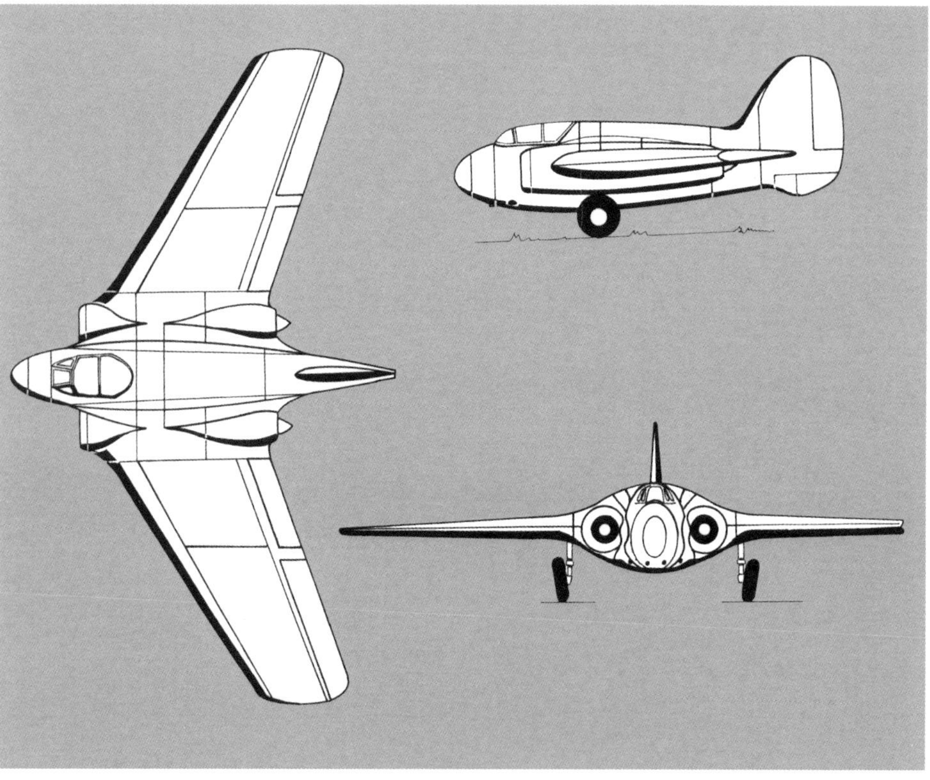

Dimensions	
Span	11.60m
Length	7.10m
Height	3.45m

Performance	
Max speed	975km/h
Range	5,000km
Ceiling	12,000m

One of the P 09 designs was a twin-jet fighter whose large oval fin and rudder is reminiscent of several of the P 01-series of projects. Powerplants were two Jumo 004A turbojets in the thickened wing roots. The wide-track undercarriage mainwheels retracted outwards and rearwards into the wings and the tailwheel was also retractable. The four-gun armament was housed beneath the pilot's cockpit in the lower fuselage and wing roots. At that time, the turbojets were still in the early development stage.

Li P 010 (26.11.1941)

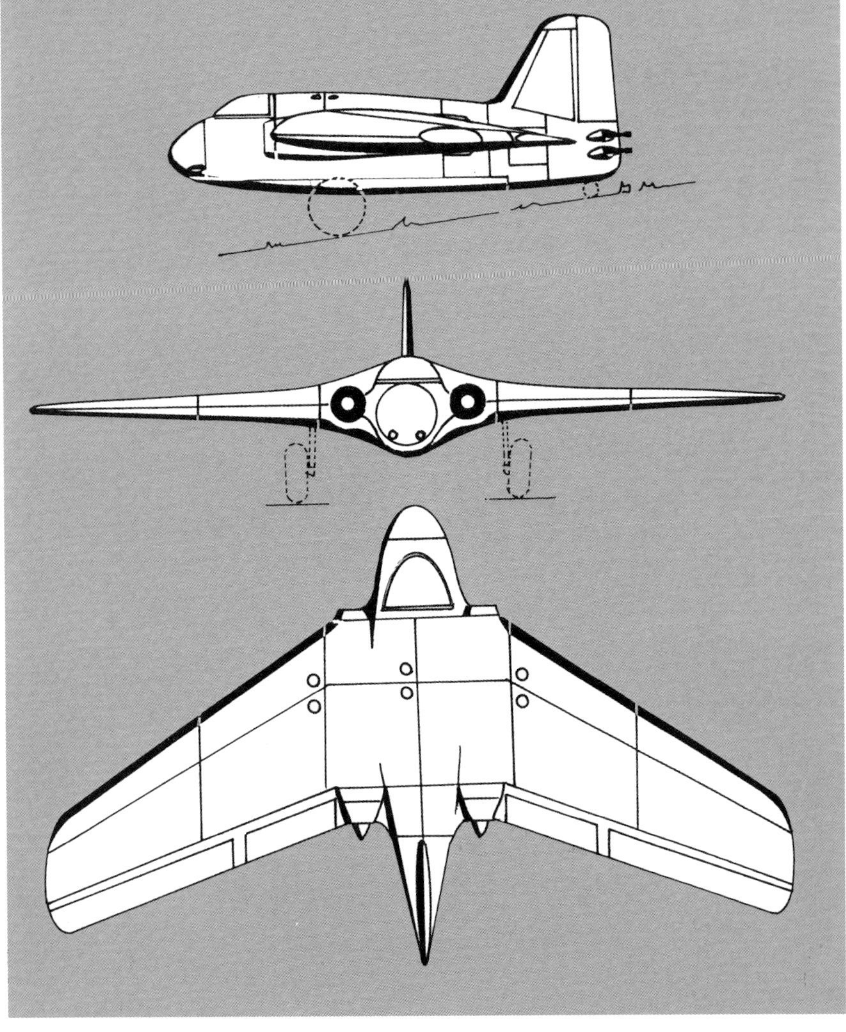

Dimensions

Span	13.40m
Length	8.15m
Height	3.80m

Performance

Max speed	850km/h

Powerplants

2 x Jumo 004A turbojets

Armament

2 x MG 151/20 in nose
2 x MG 151/20 in tail

The external appearance of this Schnellbomber and Zerstörer resembles both the P 09 and that of the Me 163, and housed the 1,000kg bomb in the fuselage beneath the fuel tanks. All three undercarriage members were retractable. The armament consisted of two forward- and two rearward-firing fixed guns, the latter operated via a periscope.

Li P 10-108 (20.05.1942)

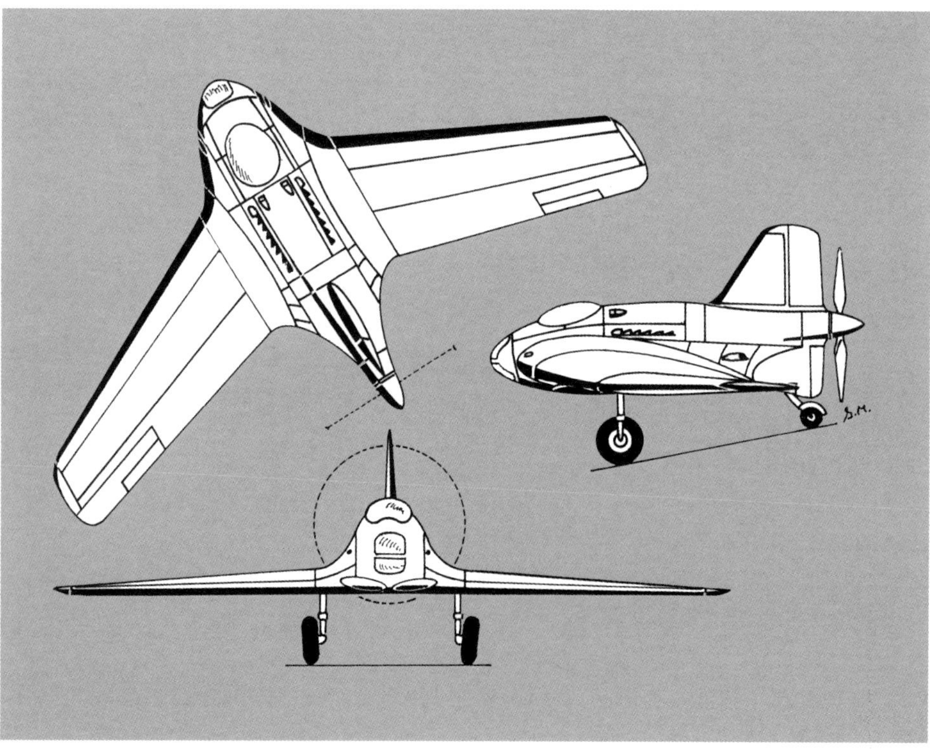

Dimensions

Span	18.00m
Length	9.85m
Height	5.90m

Armament
2 x MG 151/20

Bombload
1 x 1,000kg bomb

With the P 10-108, Lippisch reverted to the piston engine, but otherwise retained his tailless swept-wing concept. The 2,700hp coupled DB 606 was located at the centre of gravitiy and drove 4-bladed pusher propellers via an extension shaft. It remained a project only, as funds to build a model were not available. Designed by Dr.-Ing. Hermann Wurster; no performance data available.

Li P 11-92 (13.09.1942)

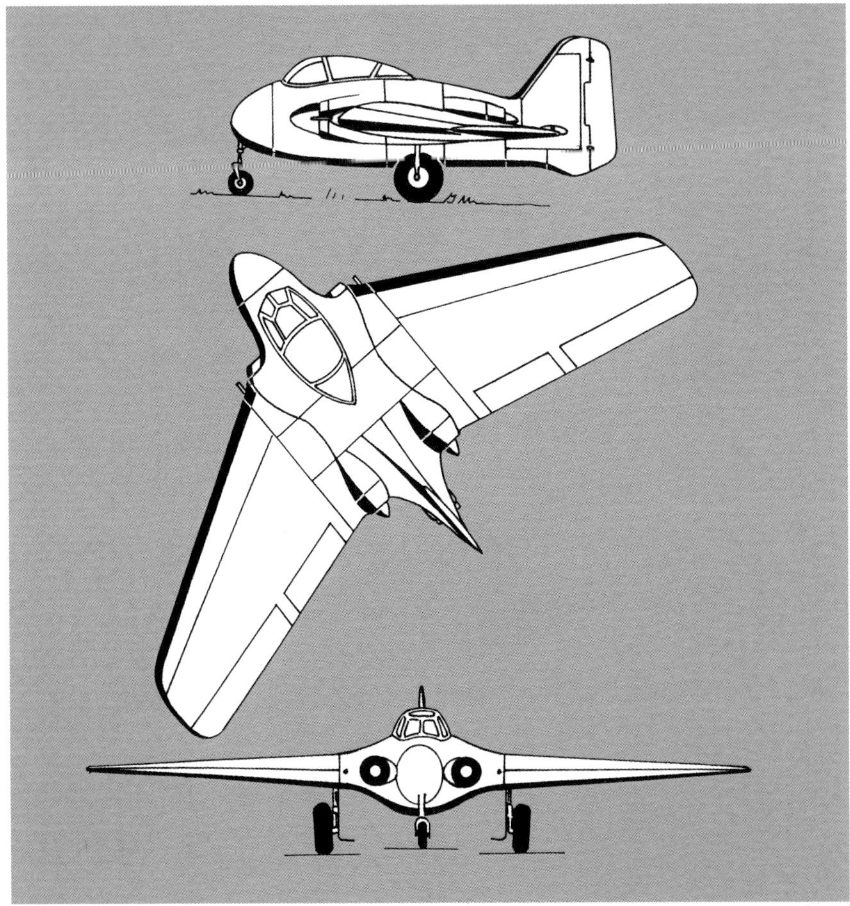

Dimensions

Span	13.00m
Length	7.50m
Height	3.00m

Powerplants
2 x 750kp thrust Jumo 004A turbojets + 2 x Schmidding 109-553 RATO units

Armament
2 x MG 151/20 in wing roots

With the exception of the nosewheel undercarriage, in this Schnellbomber and Zerstörer project Lippisch retained the features of the P 09 and P 010. New, however, was the raised and pressurised cockpit for the crew of two. The 1,000kg bombload was housed in an internal bomb-bay.

Li P 11-105 (01.12.1942)

The design principle here was very similar to that of the preceding project having moderate sweepback but of deeper wing chord, the taller fin enclosing two surfaces which could be hydraulically lowered through 90° into a horizontal tailplane to increase the maximum lift coefficient as the moment arm was greater due to the longer fuselage. Whereas the project study of 13.11.1942 housed a crew of two, this was reduced to one in this Schnellbomber on 01.12.1942. Like the earlier proposal, the mainwheels retracted outwards into the wings, the bombload again being housed internally in the lower fuselage, a drawing showing fixed forward- and rearward-firing weapons. An alternate variant with a V-tail was also drawn up (q.v.) but no details are available.

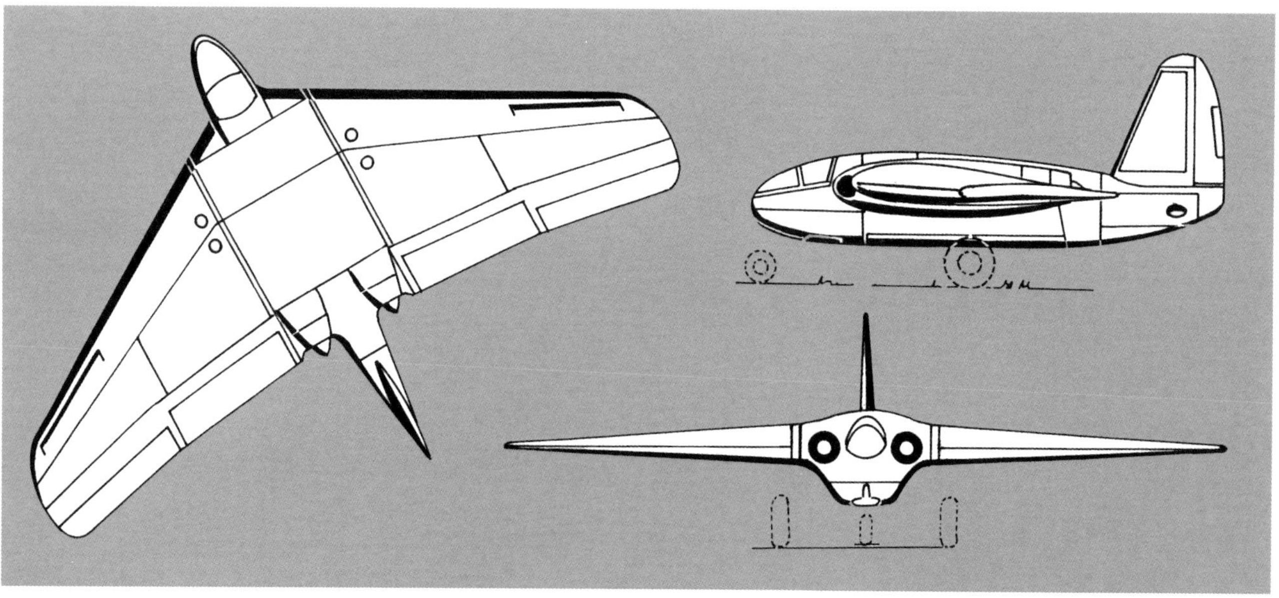

Dimensions

Span	12.65m
Length	8.14m
Height	4.00m
Wing area	37.30m^2

Weights

Empty weight	4,005kg
Fuel weight	2.200kg
Flying weight	7,500kg
Bombload	1,000kg

Performance

Max speed	900km/h

Powerplants

2 x 760kp thrust Jumo 004B +
2 x Schmidding 109-553 RATO units

P-11 (V-tail variant)

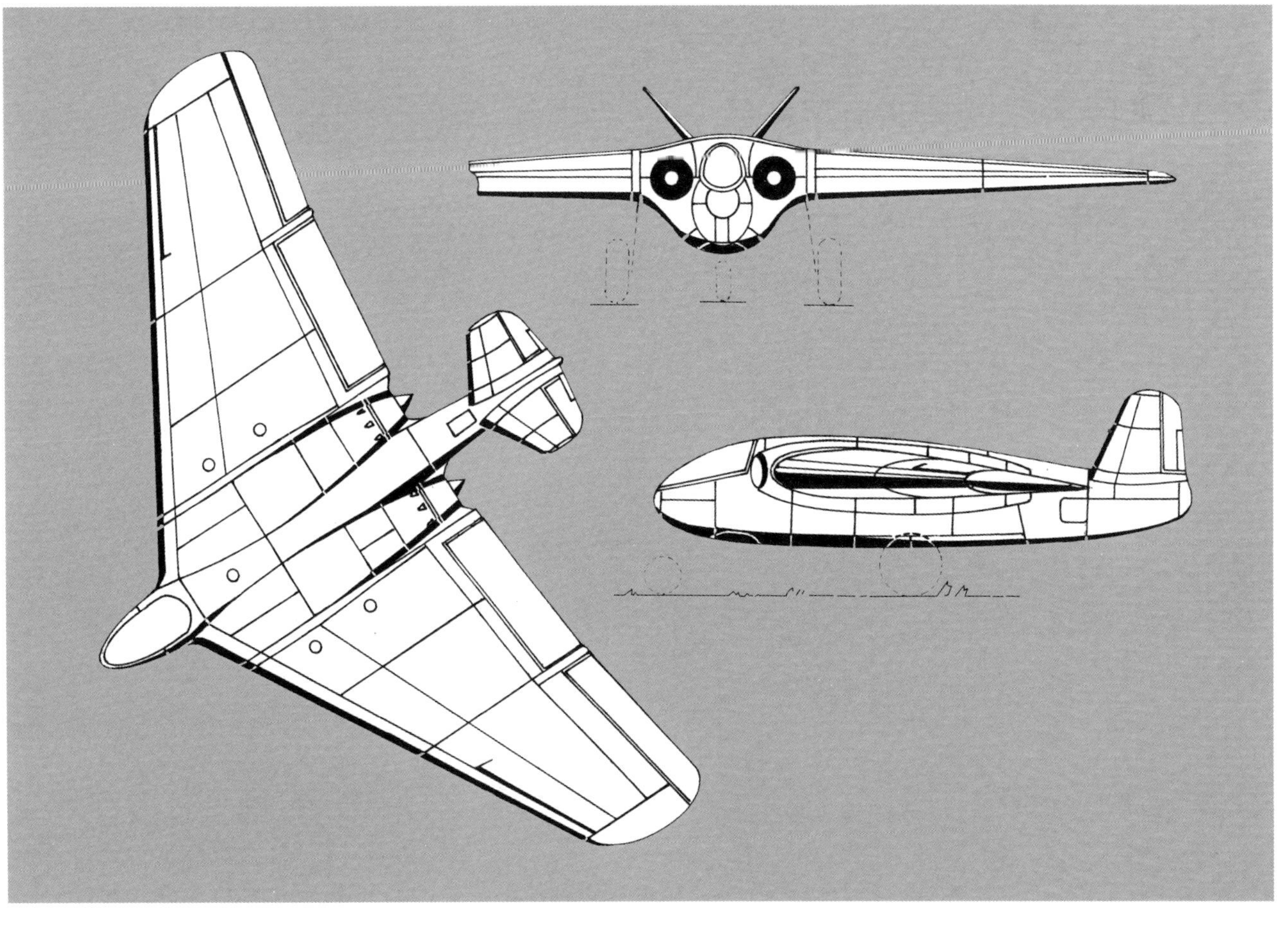

Li P 12 (30.09.1942)

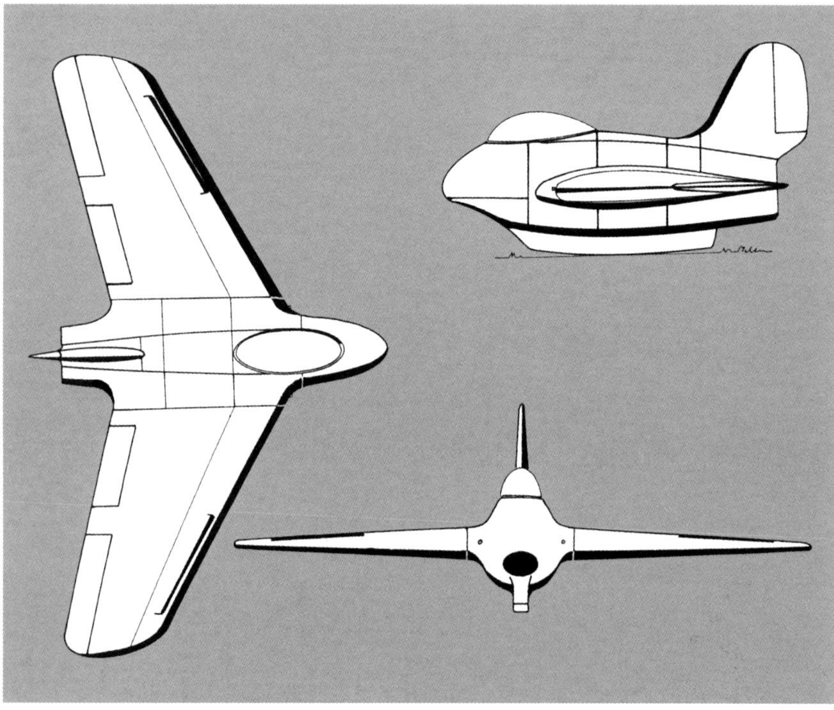

Dimensions	(small)	(large)
Span	11.00m	14.10m
Length	7.00m	7.60m
Height	3.90m	3.90m
Wing area	30.00m^2	50.00m^2

Armament
2 x MG 151/20

One of the first projects designed to utilise the large BMW P 3303 turbojet eventually developed into the 109-018, the P 12 was designed by Lippisch's aerodynamics expert Dipl.-Ing. Josef Hubert, based largely on the overall configuration of the Me 163 B. In the two variants, each with a different wingspan and area, provision was made for a redesigned fin and rudder on the larger variant that increased the overall length of the fuselage, both variants retaining the central underfuselage skid. The P 12 and P 13 project numbers were used again in 1943 and 1944 for a series of ramjet-powered projects. The 3-view drawing depicts the small-span variant.

Li P 13 (25.11.1942)

This P 13 project, also designed by Hubert, was for a tailless Schnellbomber powered by 2 x 1,475hp DB 605 B engines fore and aft of the cockpit driving tractor and pusher propellers. The wing featured compound sweep on the leading and trailing edges, the mainwheels retracting inwards into the wing roots ahead of the main spar, the tailwheel extending below the rear propeller for take-off and landing. Span was 12.80m, length 9.40m, height (wheels down) 5.10m, and estimated max speed 750km/h. Four fuel tanks holding 1,220 litres of fuel were housed in the inner wings beside the cockpit and a fifth with 260 litres ahead of it, beneath which was the external bomb.

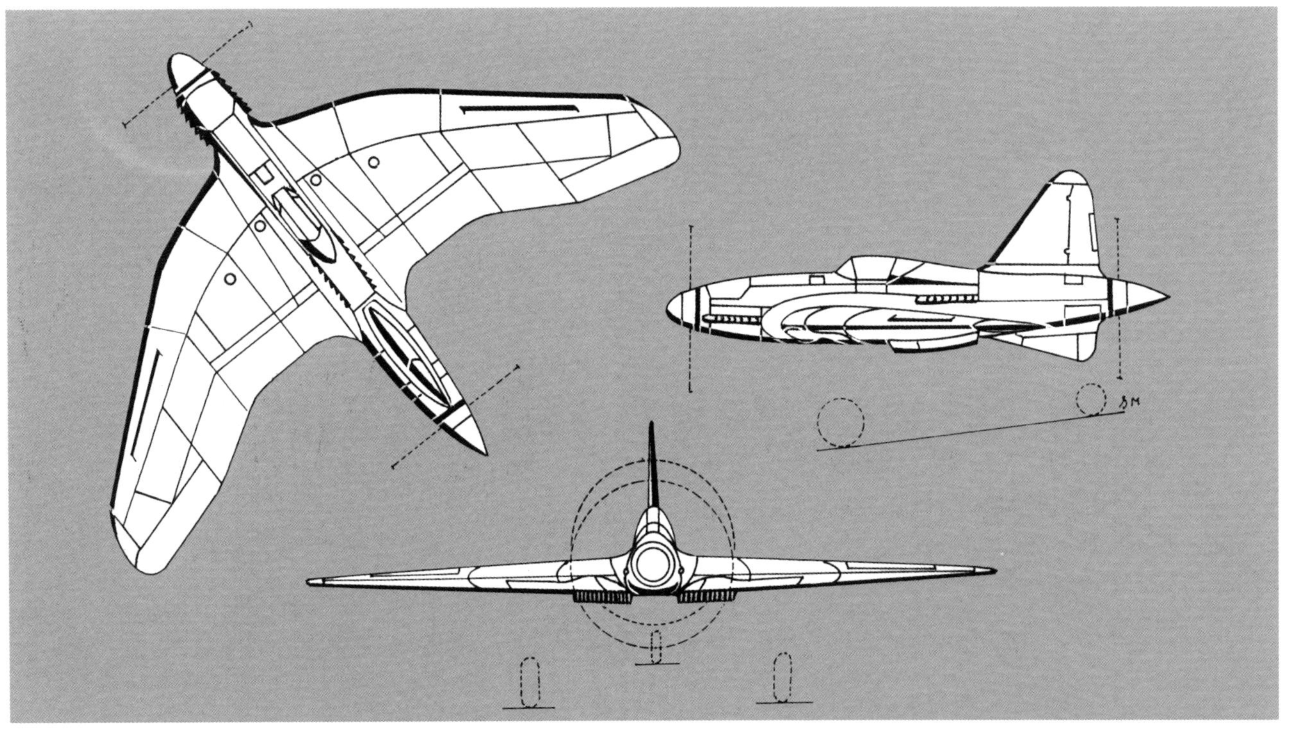

Li P 15 'Diana'

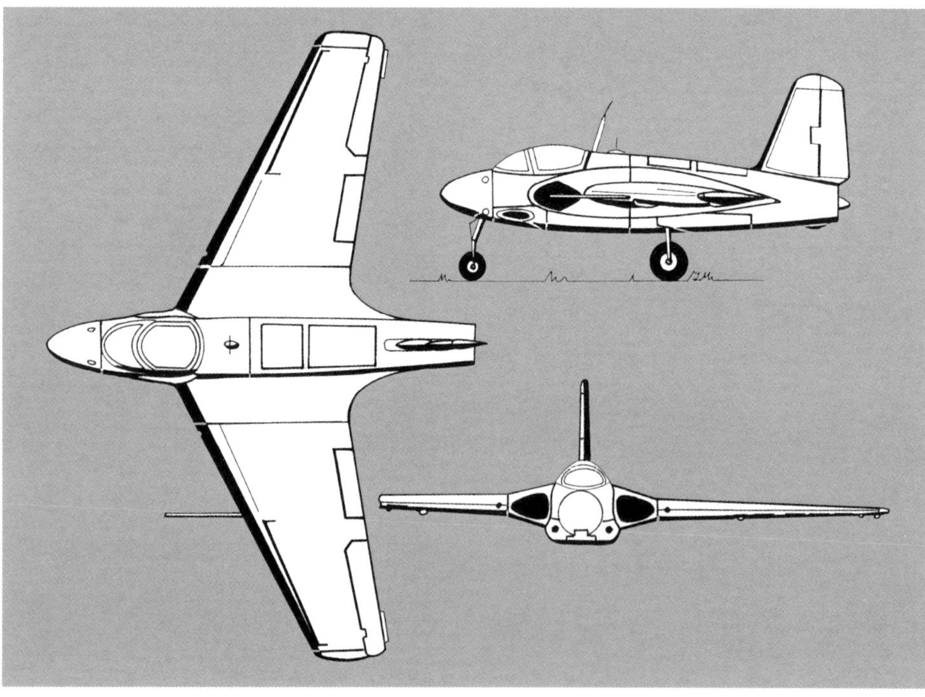

Dimensions and Weight

Span	10.00m
Length	6.40m
Height	3.00m
Wing area	20.00m²
Flying weight	3,600kg

Performance

Max speed	1,000km/h
Endurance	45 mins

Armament

2 x MK 108 in fuselage
2 x MK 108 in wingroots

At the beginning of March 1945, Oberstleutnant Siegfried Knemeyer, the Chief of Aircraft Development at the RLM, visited Dr. Lippisch in Vienna. The problems inherent in the short range and endurance of the He 162 led to the design of a hybrid fighter incorporating parts of the Me 163 B, Ju 248 and He 162. The resulting P 15 'Diana' thus used the nose and cockpit of the He 162 but with the fuselage of the Ju 248 to house the HeS 011A turbojet and the wings of the Me 163 B expanded to house the wingroot intakes. The project, tested in model form in the wind tunnel, promised to have good take-off and landing characteristics but was not complete at the end of the war.

Li P 20 (16.04.1943)

Problems experienced with the Me 163 B rocket motor led to Lippisch considering other forms of propulsion without foregoing the excellent aerodynamic characteristics of that aircraft. Besides the piston-engined Me 334, he also worked on the P 20 whose ancestry is clearly visible. Powerplant was a 1, 015kp thrust Jumo 004 C turbojet.

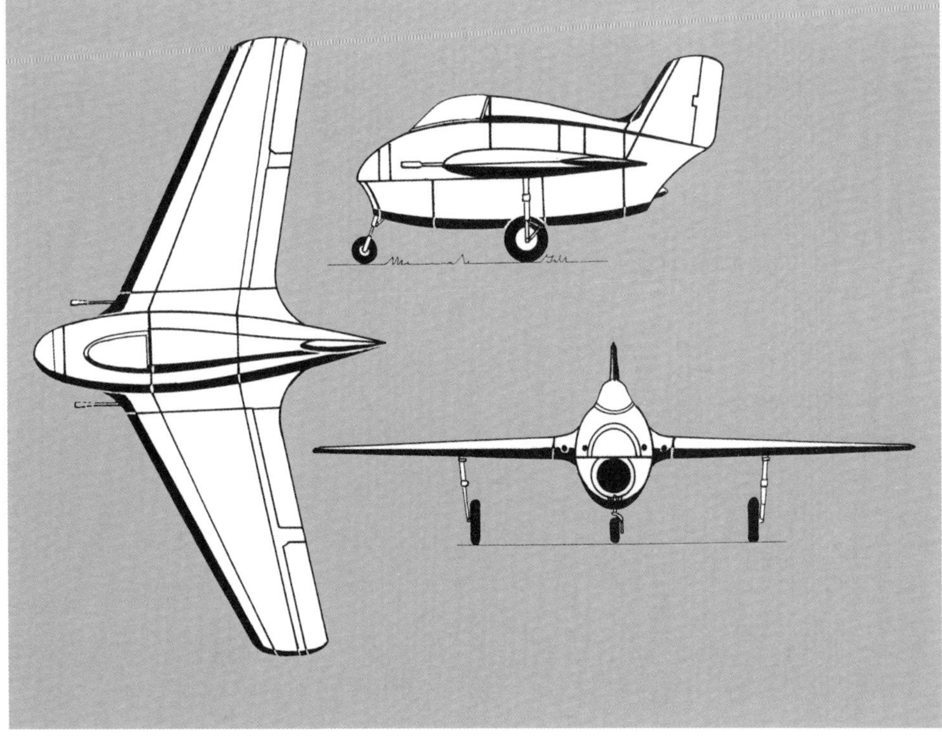

Dimensions and Weights

Span	9.30m
Length	5.73m
Height	3.02m
Wing area	17.30m^2
Empty weight	2,419kg
Flying weight	3,383kg

Performance

Max speed at 6,000m	905km/h
Max range at 11,000m	940km
Max endurance at 11,000m	1.53 hrs
Ceiling	11,600m

Armament

2 x MK 108 in fuselage
2 x MK 103 in wingroots

Me 109 TL

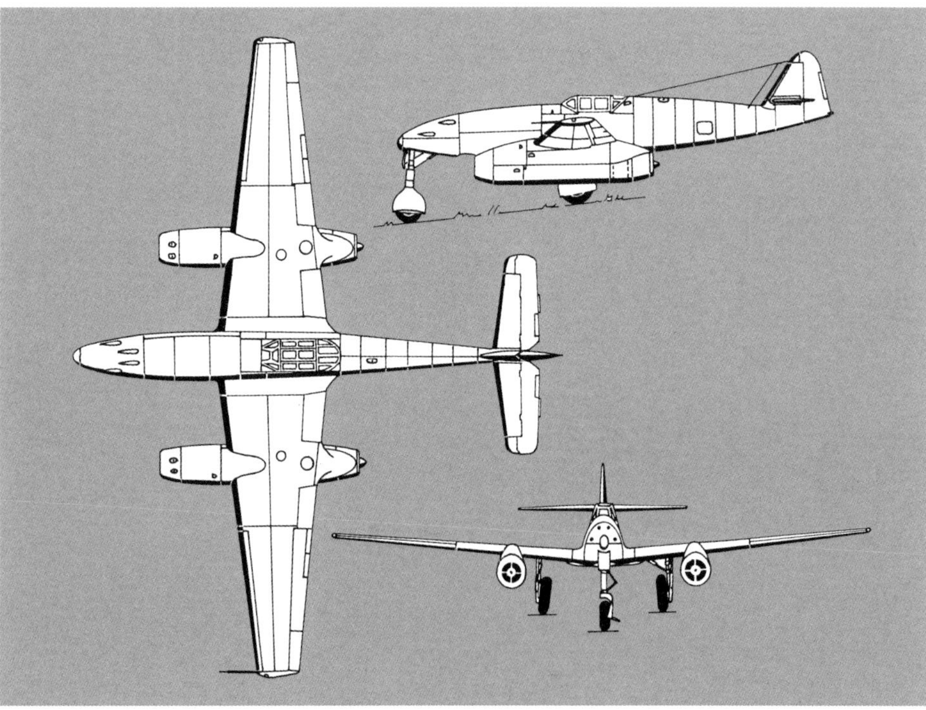

Dimensions and Weight

Span	13.00m
Length	9.20m
Height	2.60m
Wing area	19.50m^2
Fuel capacity	1,500 litres
Flying weight	4,750kg

Armament
2 x MG 151/20 +
2 x MK 108 in fuselage

Just as had transpired with the Fw 190 TL and the later P 15 'Diana' to evolve a TL-powered aircraft out of components of existing machines, this interim patchwork proposal, although technically interesting, would have turned out to be structurally just as time-consuming as the Me 262 whose flight trials were already far advanced (by 20.01.1943). Incorporating the tricycle nosewheel of the Me 309, two Jumo 004 turbojets and the wing of the Me 155 B, the tail surfaces, mainwheel undercarriage, fuel tanks and fuselage nose weapons bays all had to be redesigned. Performance was expected to approximate to that of the Me 262.

Me 265 (Li P 10)

Dimensions and Weight

Span	17.40m
Length	10.00m
Height	3.20m
Wing area	45.00m^2
Flying weight	11,000kg

Performance

Max speed	675km/h

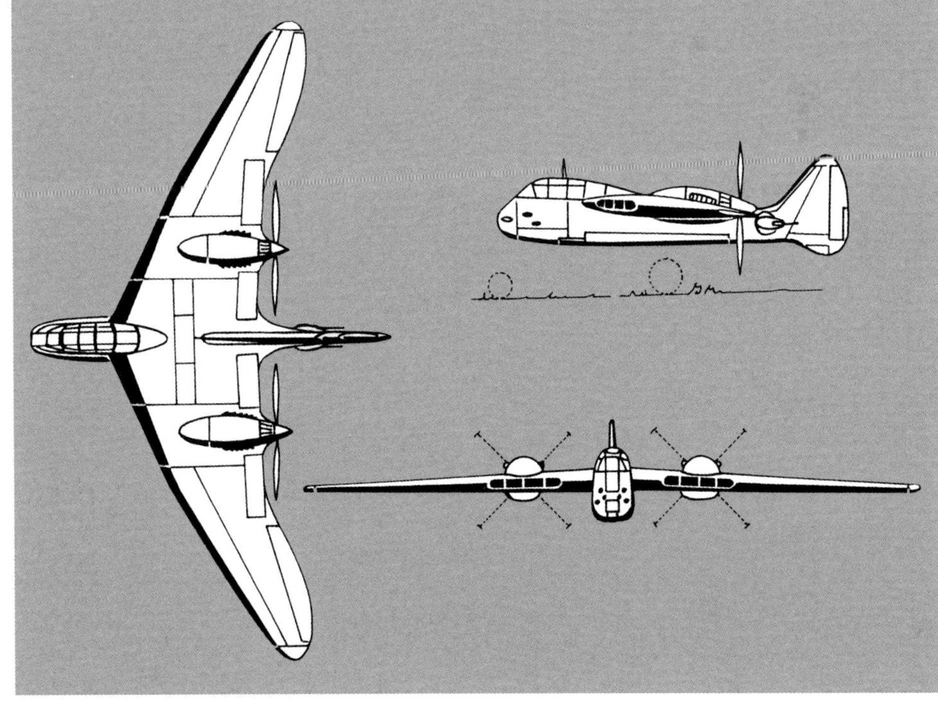

When it was established that the Me 210 had turned out to be a failure, it was decided to close the gaps that resulted. In the autumn of 1942, Lippisch's designer Stender worked on a tailless Zerstörer which embodied much of the Me 210 fuselage together with its rearward-firing remote-controlled fuselage barbettes and to which a new wing was attached – a similar planform having been adopted for the later Li P 13. Powerplants were 2 x 1,750hp DB 603 engines driving **3**-bladed pusher propellers. In order to remove the faults in the Me 210, however, Messerschmitt had worked it into the improved Me 410, whereupon the Me 265 became superfluous.

Me 328 A-1

Dimensions and Weight
(Me 328 A-1 of 31.03.1942)

Span	6.40m
Length	6.83m
Height	2.10m
Wing area	7.50m²
Flying weight	2,200kg

Performance

Max speed*	
at sea level	755km/h
Ceiling	12,000m

*with 2 x 300kg thrust pulsejets

Armament and Bombload
2 x MG 151/20 (as A-1 fighter)
1,000kg bomb (as B-1 bomber)

The Me 328 (P 1079) has been so well documented that it is difficult to keep the text short, hence reference should be made to other published accounts.

The first flights of this aircraft, evolved as a cheap but high-performance fighter and bomb-carrier, commenced as an unpowered glider on 01.08.1942 [Rudolf Ziegler of the DFS claimed he first flew it on 23.07.1941]. Since these demonstrated favourable results, this Bordjäger suggested itself in 1944 for use as a Sturmsegler (attack glider) like the Bv 40 or else as a piloted bomb for suicide missions. The Me 328 B was fitted with two Argus VSR-7 pulsejets, but vibrations transferred to the airframe by these forerunners of the As 014 resulted in the destruction and crash of the prototypes. When one takes into account the date when the first gliding flights were undertaken and knows that well-functioning mass-produced pulsejets came to be employed operationally, it makes one wonder why the machine never came to be so used. In the meantime, other priorities must have existed, so that the programme simply dragged on.

Ever since its inception, a whole series of variants with various powerplants were drawn up and at the beginning of 1945 the Porsche 109-005 expendable turbojet was even considered. The data above stems from 31.03.1942.

Me 328 A-2

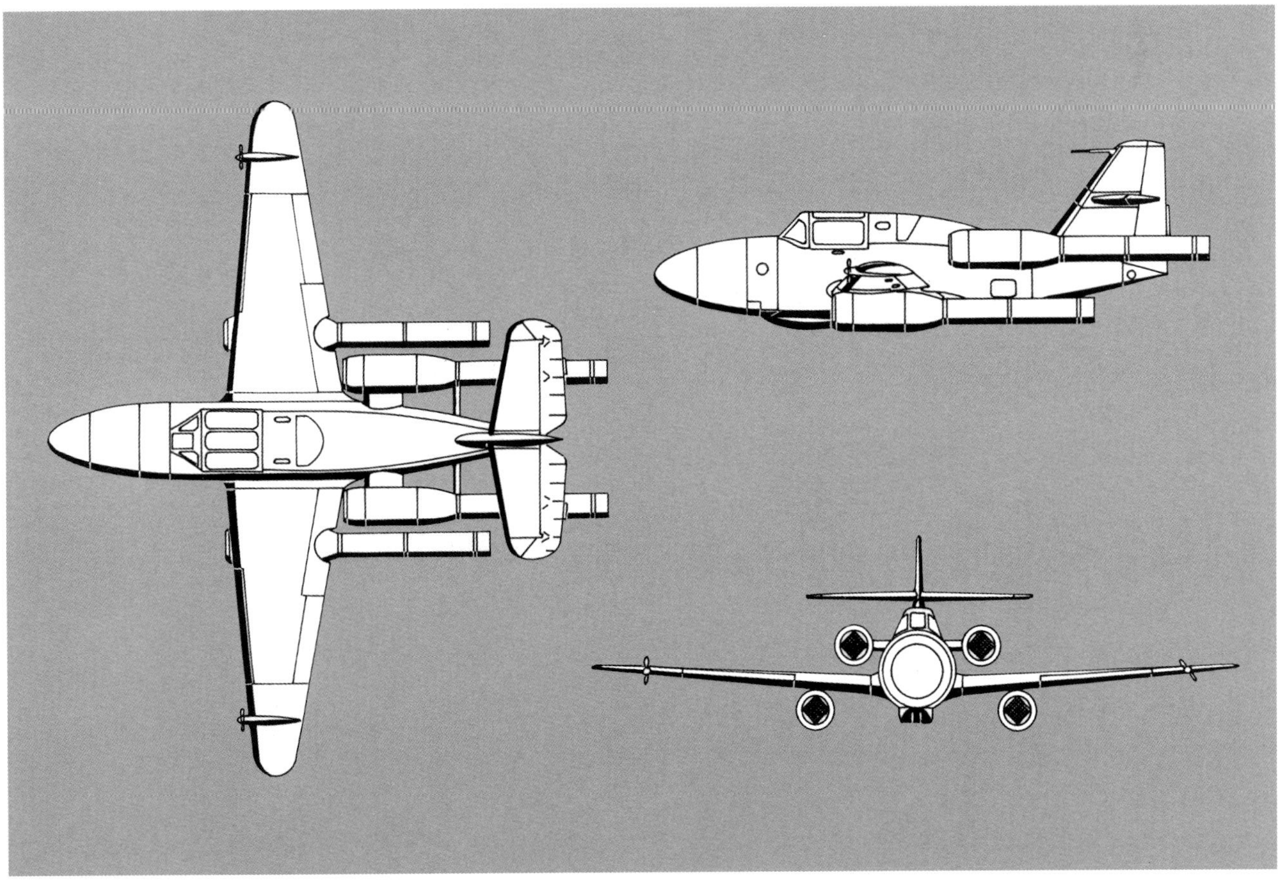

Me 328 B-0 / B-1

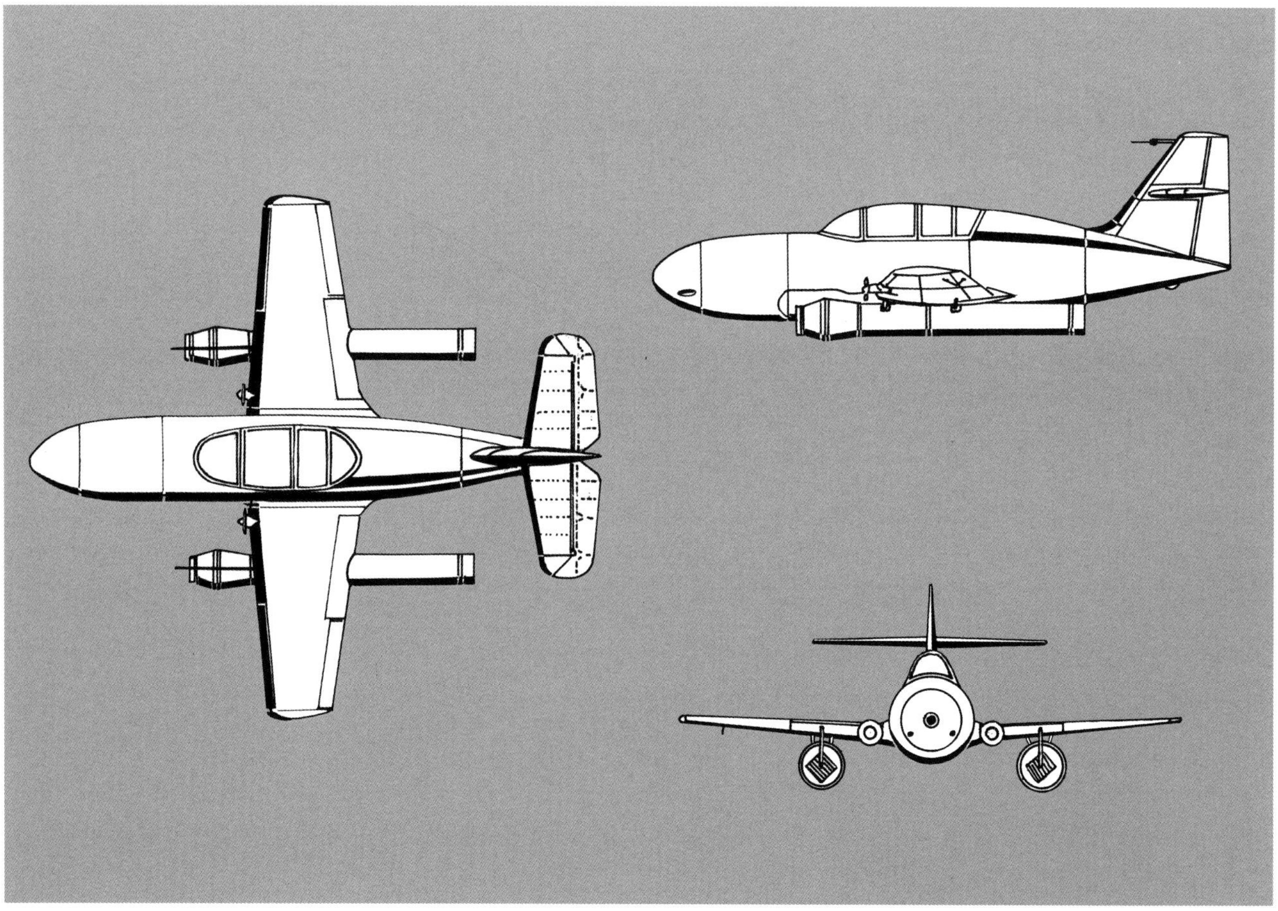

Me 328 B

This variant corresponded to the A-1, but (supposedly) was to have had small wingtip ramjets.

Me 328 C

Turbojet-powered, it had a fixed mainwheel undercarriage and a nosewheel that retracted rearward into the fuselage. All other proposals featured landing skids.

Messerschmitt Me 328 Bordflugzeug

Variant 1 has a rectangular short-span wing that can be extended by lateral sliding sections. Variant 2 has an almost circular wing that can also be extended in span via sliding sections.

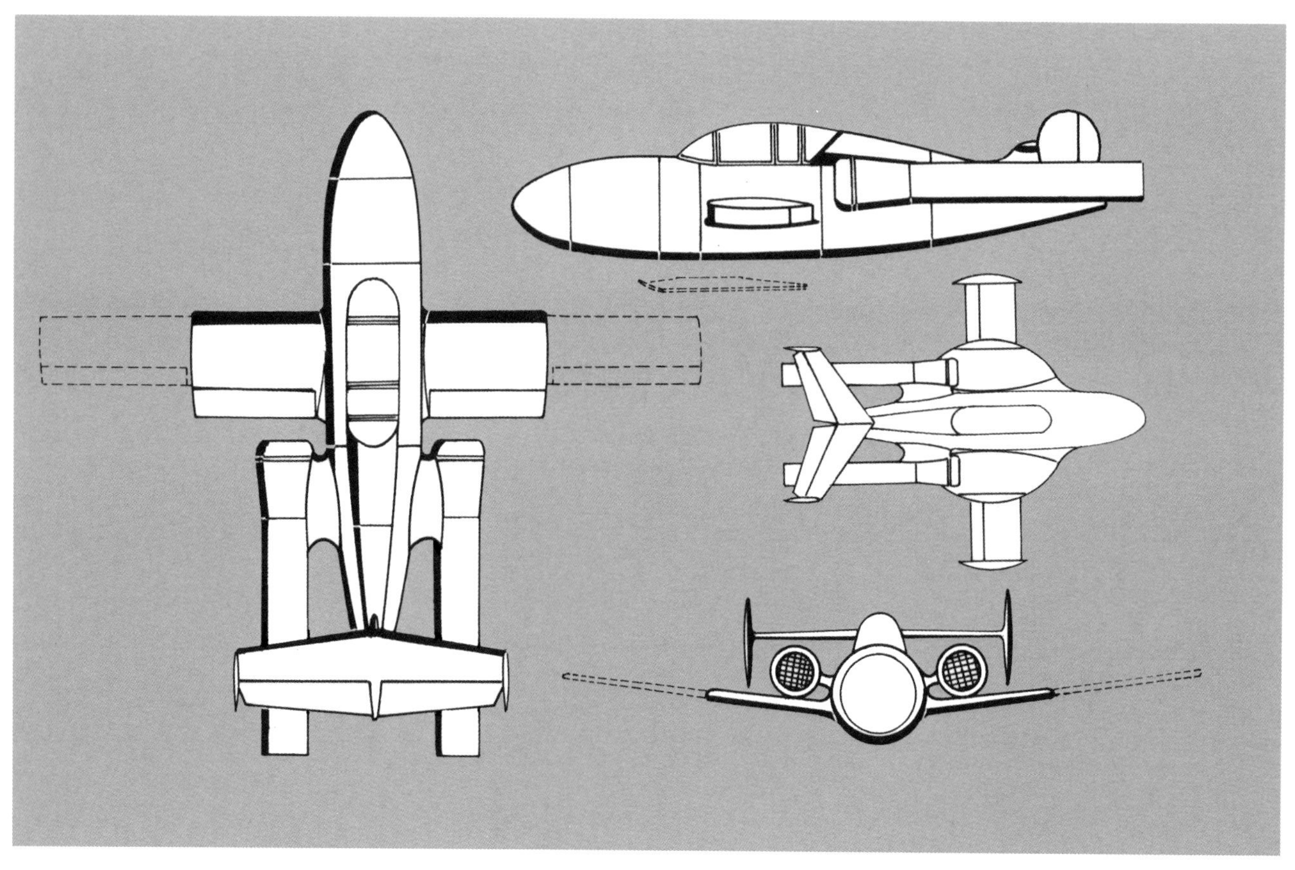

Me 328 (Porsche 109-005)

This variant was to have been powered by a 500kp thrust Porsche 109-005 turbojet.

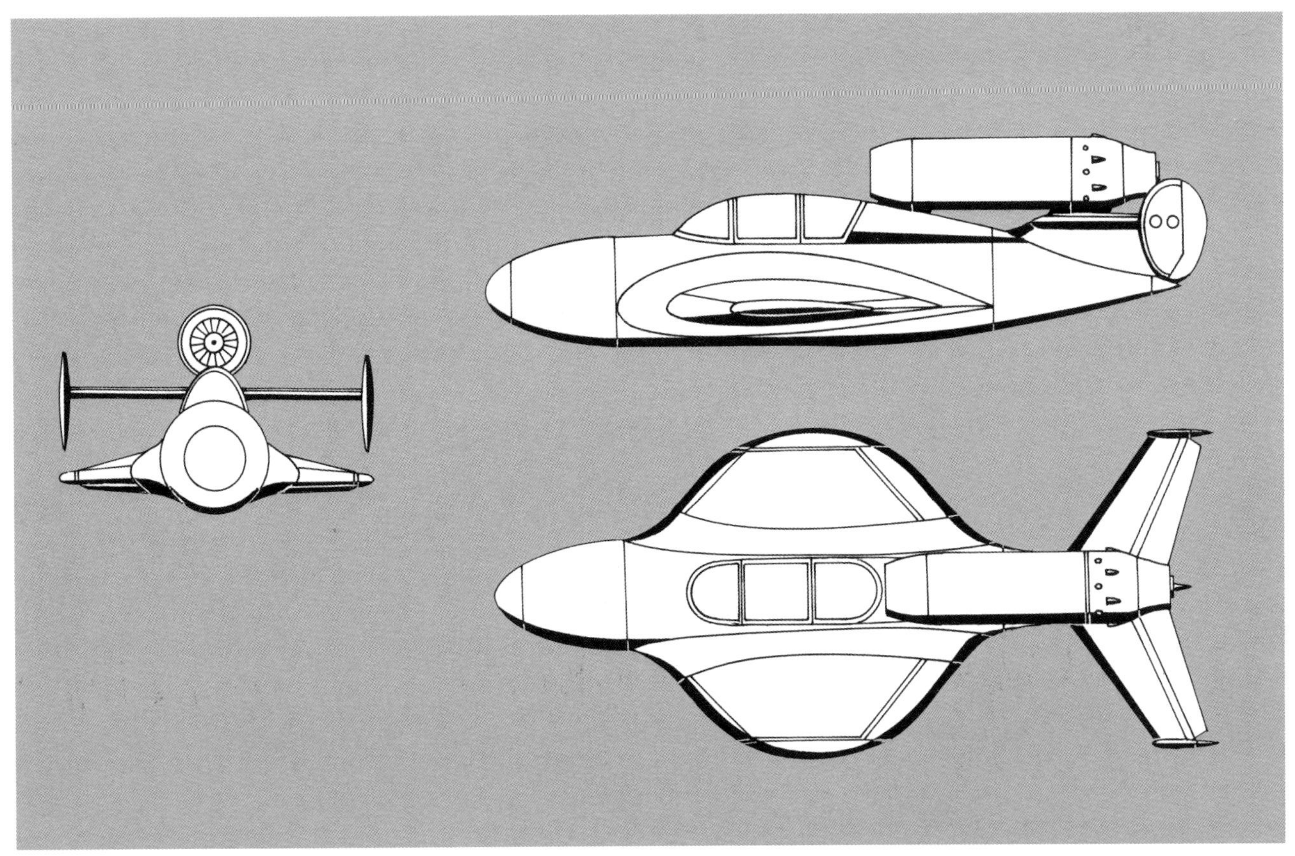

Me 329 (March 1942)

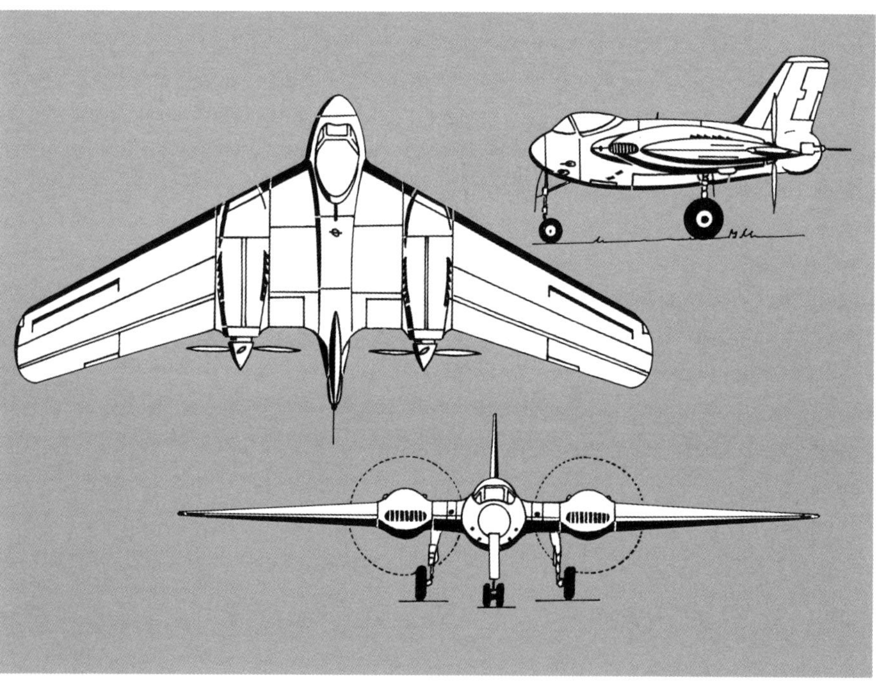

Dimensions and Weights

Span	17.50m
Length	7.715m
Height	4.74m
Equipped weight	6,950kg
Max bombload	2,500kg
Take-off weight	12,150kg

Performance

Max speed	730-750km/h
Ceiling	12,500m

Amongst all the projects which became bogged down in theoretical considerations, the 2-seat Me 329 Zerstörer of March 1942 shows how serious the engineers were, as it had even advanced to the full-scale wooden mock-up stage and to being tested in the wind tunnel. This tailless aircraft with its large fin and rudder was to have been powered by two DB 603 G engines driving 3-bladed 3.40m-diameter pusher propellers, the tail armament consisting of an MG 151 whose angle of fire could be traversed through 90° via periscopic sighting control, the 4 fixed forward-firing MG 151/20s at the sides of the cockpit being located ahead of the internally-housed SC 1000 bomb. It was given up in favour of the Me 410.

Me 334

Dimensions and Weight

Span	9.30m
Length	7.00m
Height	3.72m
Wing area	17.30m²
Flying weight	2,800-3,000kg

Armament

2 x 13mm MG 131

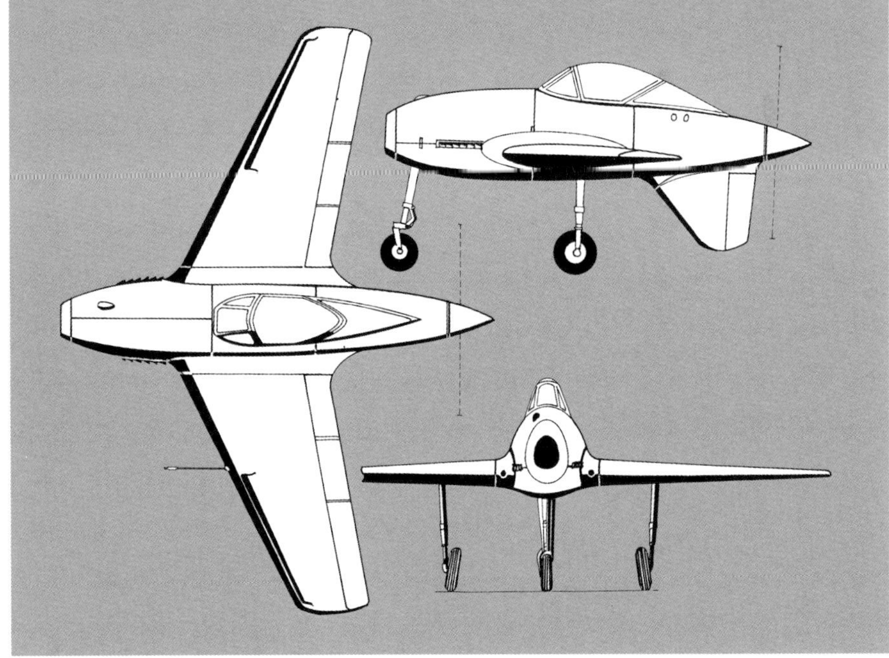

The problems with the rocket-powered Me 163 B also led to this design being drawn up in 1943. Whereas the P 20 was powered by a turbojet, this proposal was to have been powered by a 1,475hp DB 605A to C (a DB 603 is also mentioned in literature) driving pusher propellers of 3.0m diameter. Maximum speed would have been rather more than that of the Me 109G-6.

The Me 262 Family

Me P 65 (05.06.1940)

In order to portray the development phases of the Me 262, it is depicted here in the form of illustrations and drawings only. The project began with unswept tapered wings and calculations as to how the two early turbojets of rather small dimensions should be placed in the wings – either above or below or through the wing main spar; likewise, whether the cockpit would be placed forward near the nose, or at mid-fuselage.

The final configuration gradually crystallised starting from the P 65 (1939) via the P 1065 (1940). As the development of this aircraft has been thoroughly documented by several writers, the reader is referred to the appropriate literature. Out of this development series appeared the P 1070.

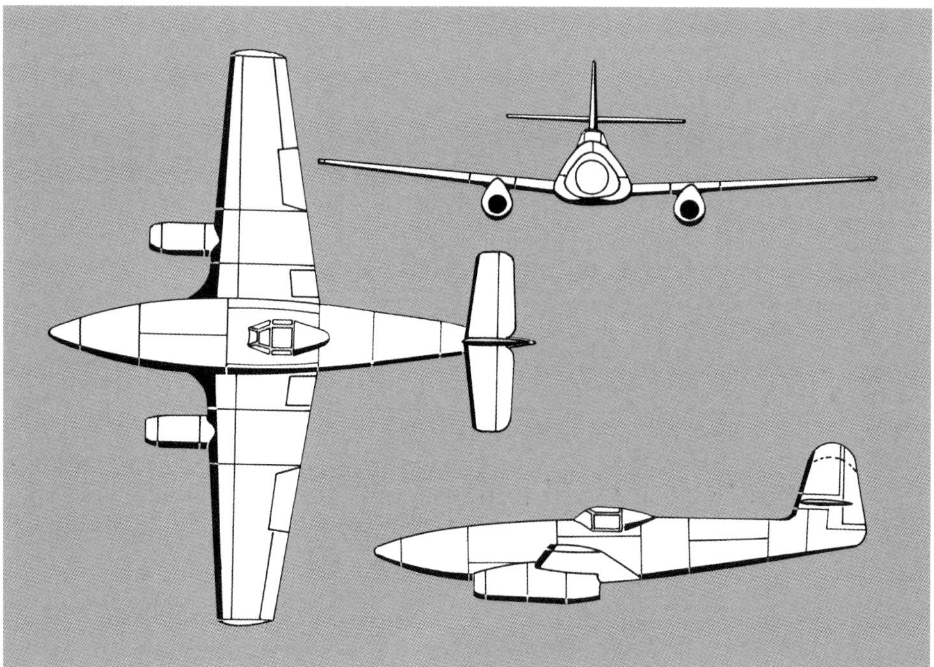

The initial proposals that led to the Me 262 were clearly conventional. Easily recognisable is the triangular fuselage cross-section to allow the undercarriage wheels and more fuel to be accommodated.

Me P 1065

For centre of gravity reasons the outer wings were given moderate sweepback as in the plan view below. That wing sweep at high speeds produced less drag, was gradually discovered.

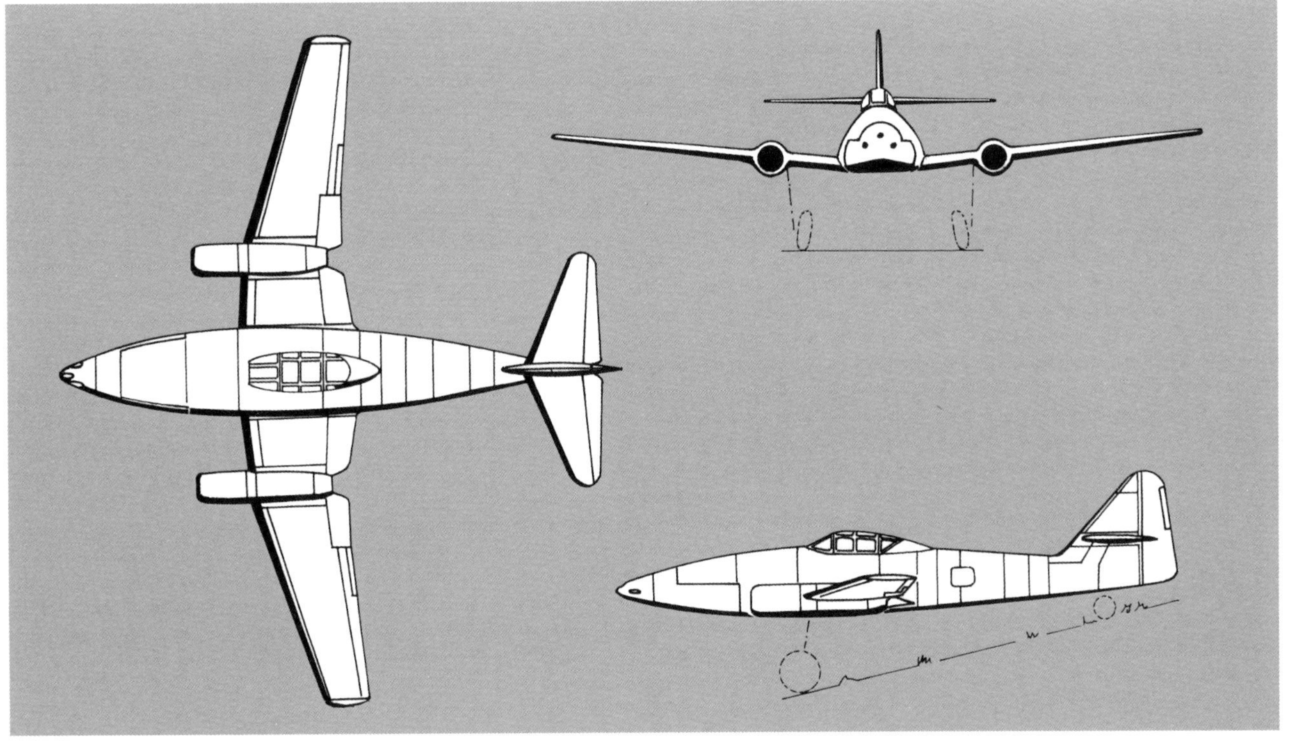

Me P 1065

Two Me 262 variants with differing cockpit locations, showing a mid-positioned cockpit (upper) and with forward cockpit near the nose (lower).

Me P 1070 (P 70)

During its development, the Me 262 exceeded by a large margin the dimensions to be expected from the concept of a 'lightweight' fighter. The P 1070 project therefore sought to reduce the weight of a twin-jet aircraft and reduced the overall drag by reason of its smaller overall dimensions and surface area, incorporating at the same time the known advances in aerodynamics. Planned powerplants were two 600kp thrust BMW turbojets but in the end, the manufacturing effort would have been almost as much as that required for the Me 262, hence the project was not pursued further.

Dimensions and Weight

Span	8.30m
Length	8.10m
Height	2.90m
Wing area	13.00m^2
Flying weight	2,800-3,200kg

Performance

Max speed, estimated	1,100km/h

Armament

2 x 13mm MG 131
2 x 15mm MG 151

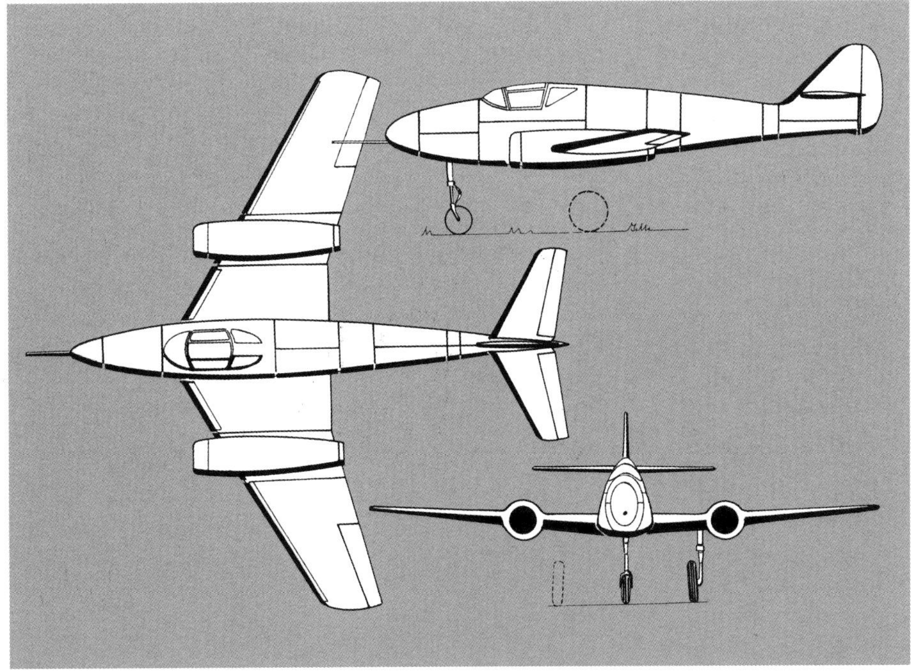

Me 262 V1 Phase I

The Me 262 V1 flown with nose Jumo 210G only.

Me 262 V1 Phase II

The Me 262 V1 flown with nose Jumo 210G and two early BMW P 3302 turbojets.

Me 262 A-1a

The Me 262 A-1a as a fighter with JG 7.

Me 262 Schnellbomber Ia / II

The Me 262 Schnellbomber Ia variant with forward-positioned cockpit.

This Schnellbomber variant had a deepened fuselage to accommodate the bombload internally to reduce the loss in speed that occurred with the underslung external bombs.

Me 262 HG I

The HG here stood for Hochgeschwindigkeit (high-speed). The performance boundaries of the Me 262 were to be raised in stages that progressively incorporated the latest results of swept-wing research. As a first step, the wing sweep and wing area between the fuselage and engines was increased by a triangular addition together with a swept tailplane and a lowered, more streamlined cockpit canopy. Flight trials were conducted in January 1945 with the partially-modified Me 262 V9 prototype. The swept tailplane caused unexpected problems, but otherwise fulfilled expectations.

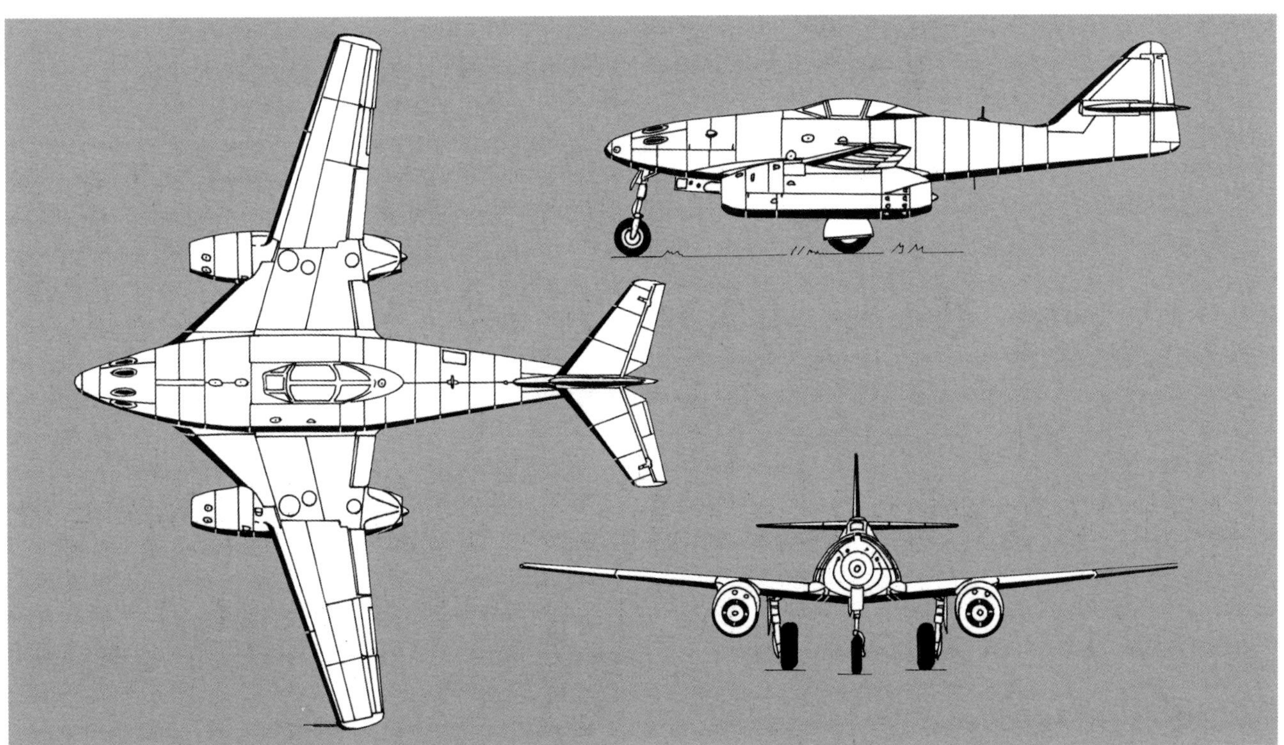

Messerschmitt Me 262 HG II

As part of the second step, the swept wing and lowered cockpit canopy were again featured, as well as aerodynamic improvements made at the wing leading-edge and engine nacelle junction. The Me 262 HG II prototype (c/n 111538) with a new 35° swept wing was readied for flight trials but, before these could commence, was badly damaged when another Me 262 landed on top of it. In the scene below, the forward Me 262 HG II is depicted with V-tail, the rear machine with normal tail surfaces.

Me 262 HG II Variants

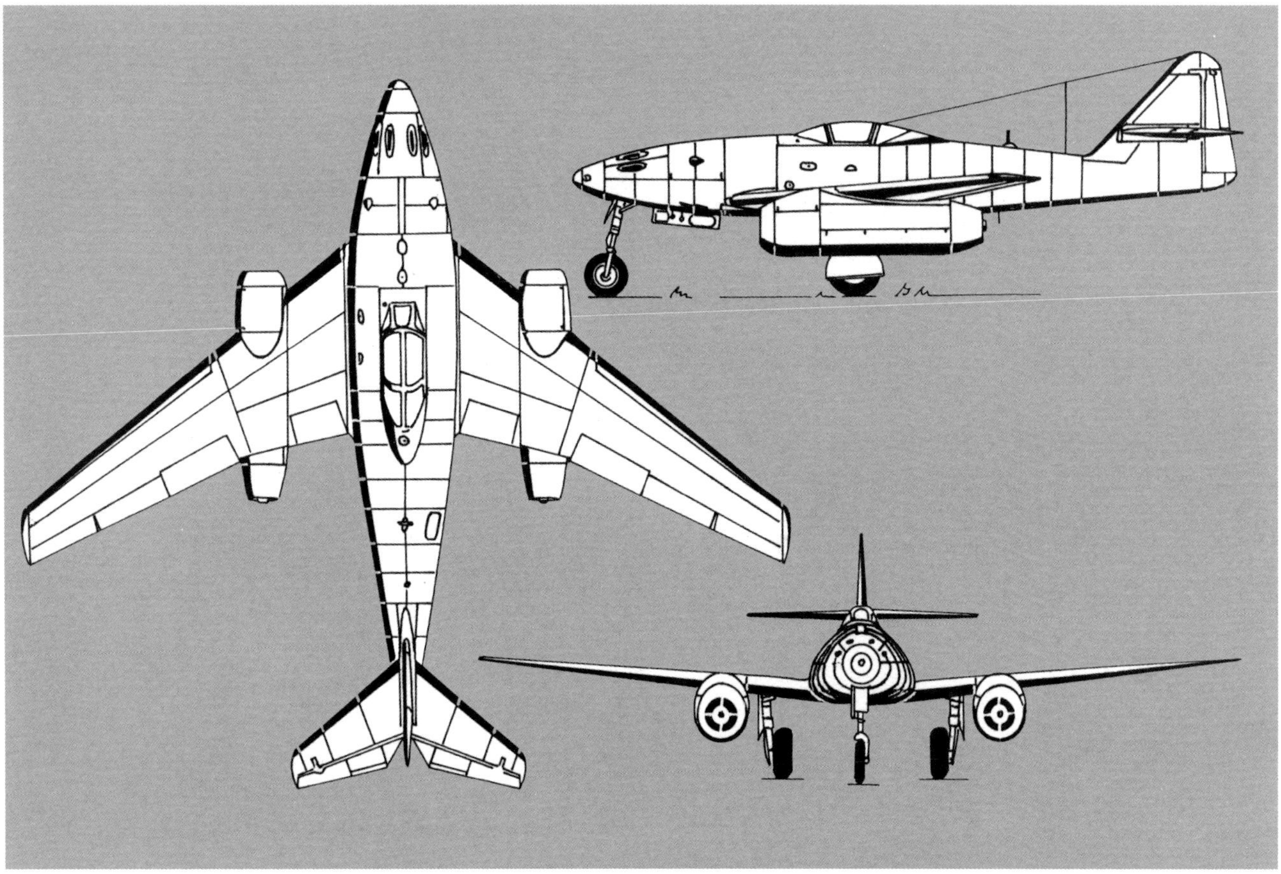

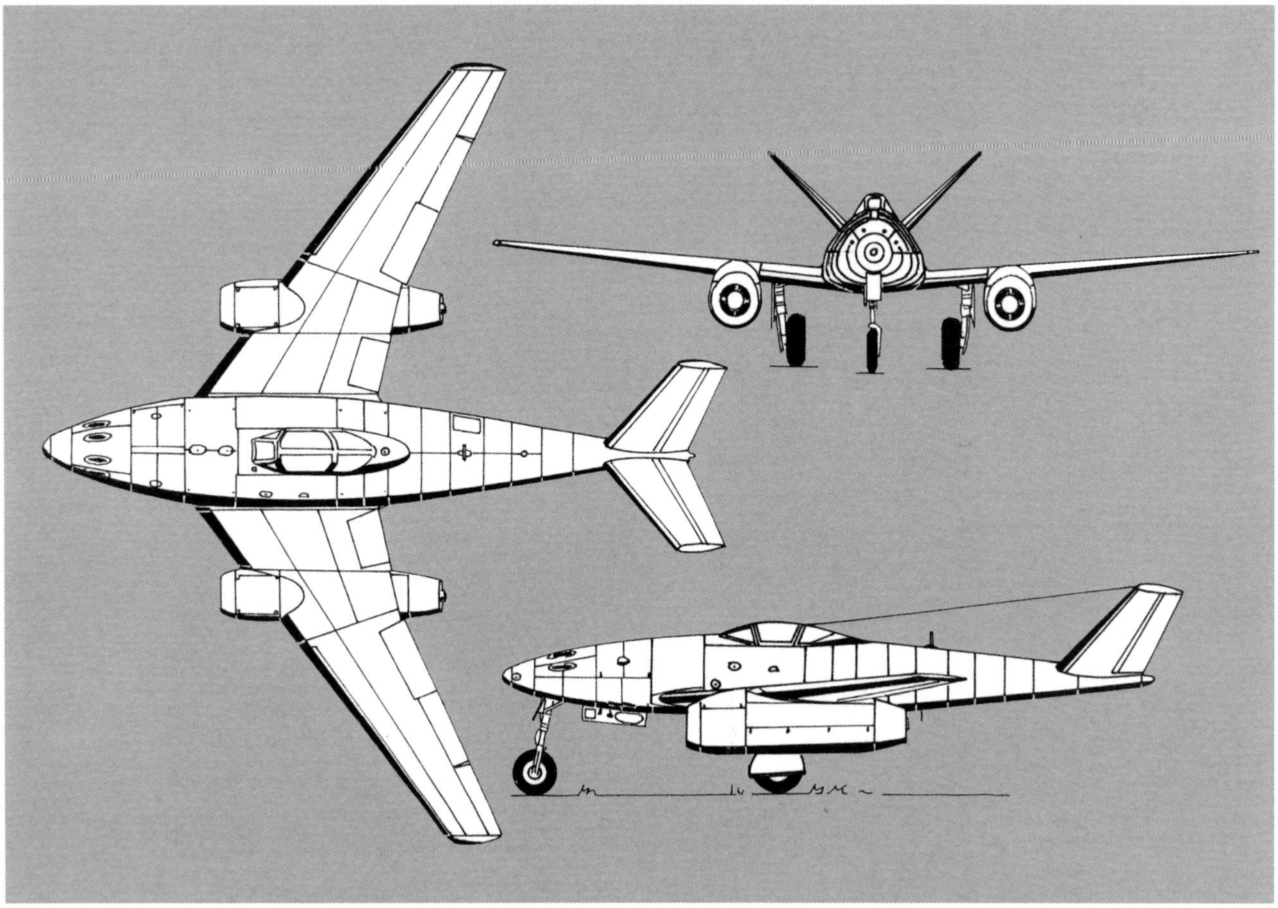

Me 262 HG III Entwurf I

The Me 262 HG III with flattened wing root air intakes.

The variant with geometrically-revised air intakes.

Me 262 HG III Entwurf I

The HG III here has a new 45° swept wing with the two HeS 011A turbojets located at the wingroots, the swept tailplane and lowered canopy being retained. The air intakes were a matter of conjecture: in one variant appearing as a flattened oval but more rotund in another. Although tests with wind tunnel models were undertaken, it consisted of an almost completely new aircraft for which structural modifications would have been insufficient, and was thus not completed before the war ended.

Dimensions & Weights

Span	11.08m
Length	10.60m
Height	3.78m
Wing area	28.50m^2
Equipped weight	4,323kg
Flying weight	6,451kg

Performance

Max speed at 6,000m	1,100km/h

Armament

4 x MK 108 in fuselage nose

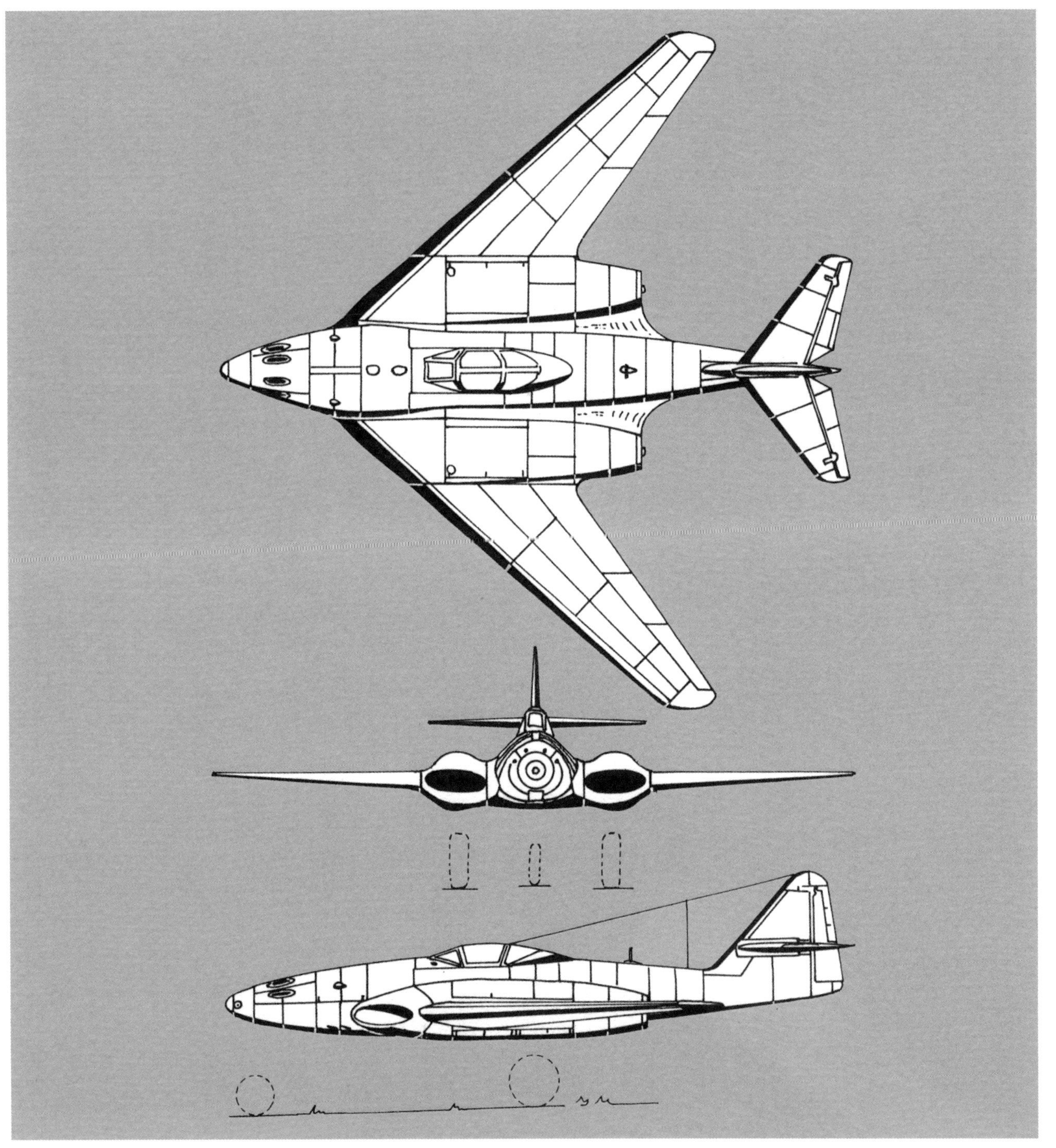

Me 262 HG III Entwurf II

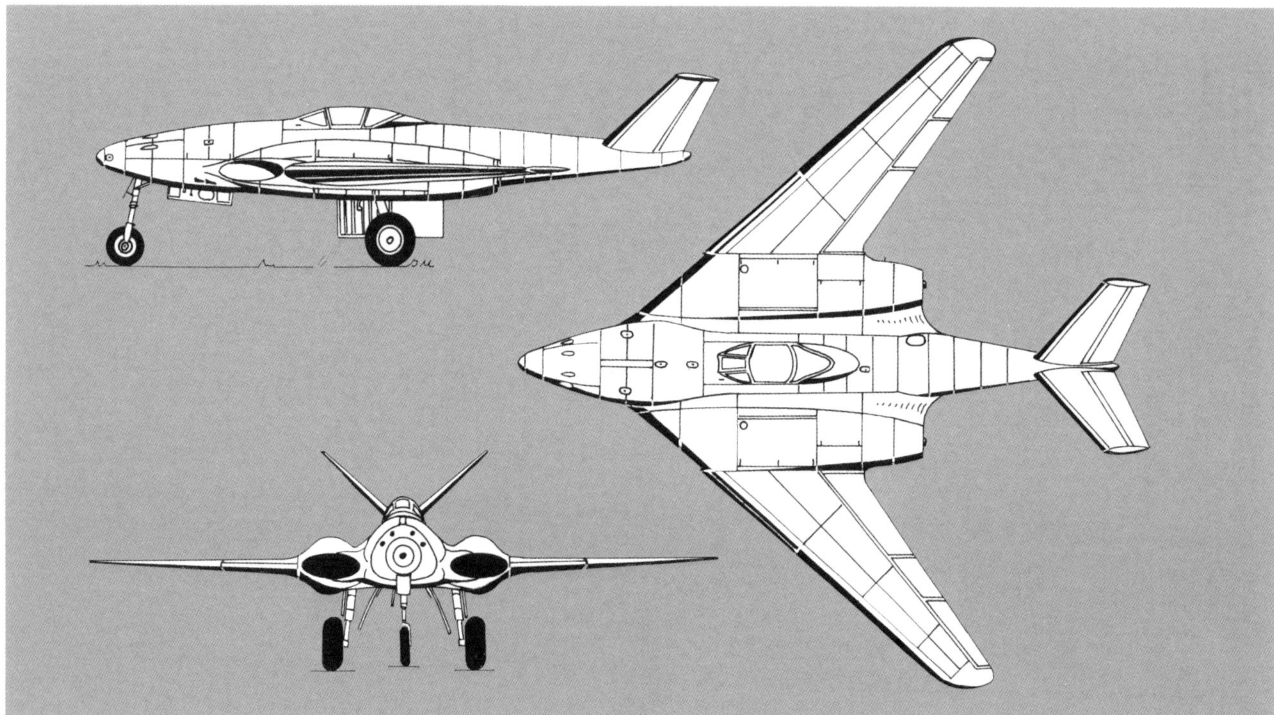

Me 262 HG III Entwurf II / Entwurf III

Two variants of the HG III are known which correspond to the original layout. The Entwurf II has a V-tail and uncanted oval air intakes, but otherwise corresponds to Entwurf I. The Entwurf II, however, is considerably altered in the fuselage region, where the cockpit is relocated at the rear and forms a part of the empennage group.

The HG III Entwurf I attained the highest state of fighter aircraft technology, which in the post-war period was only to be realised abroad after a passage of several years.

With regard to the HG IV, a photograph of a plastic model exists – not that of a wind tunnel model – which shows a 'normal' Me 262 with the cockpit canopy and empennage configuration of the HG III Entwurf III. How far the model is a realistic representation cannot be confirmed at the present time.

Me 262 HG III Entwurf III

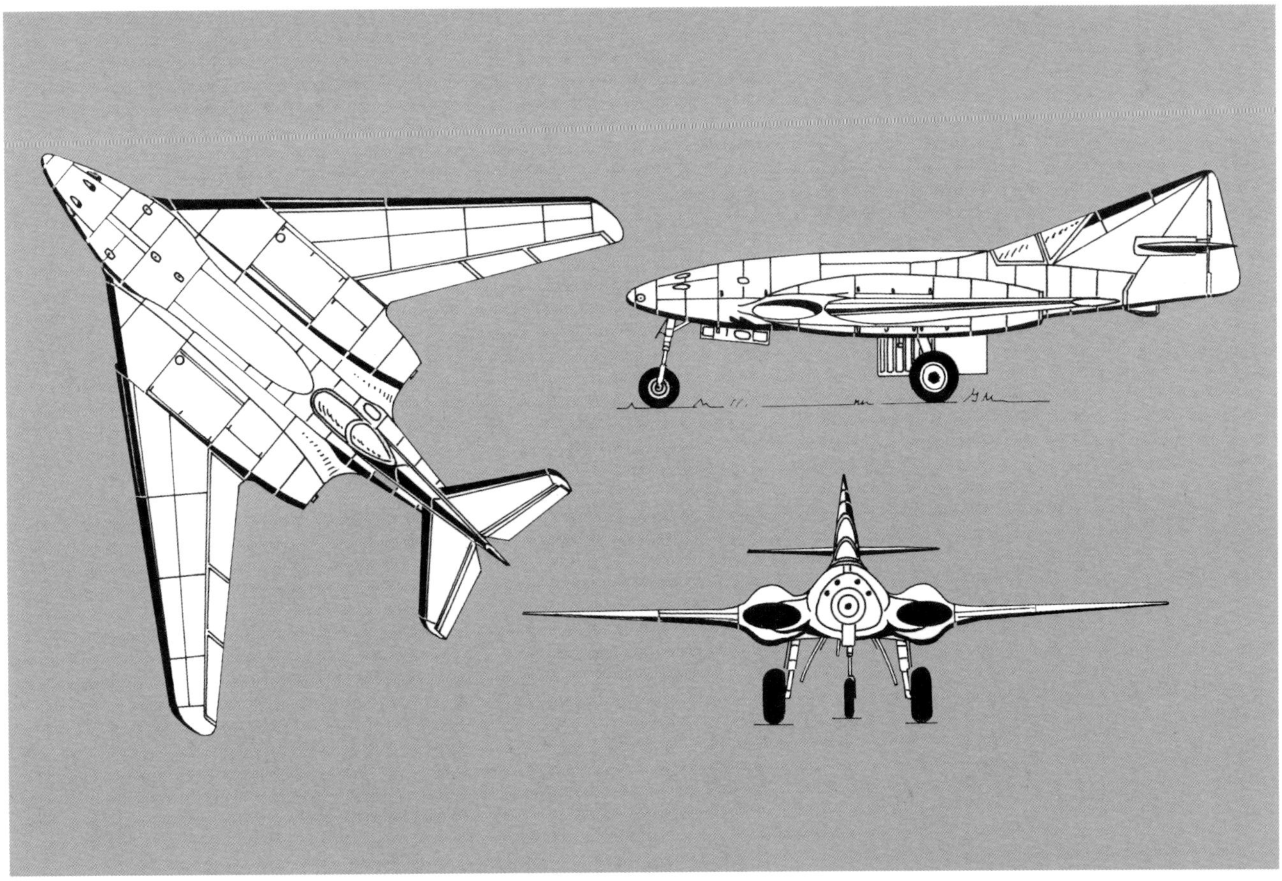

Me 262 HG IV

The Me 262 HG IV on take-off, prepared from an illustration of a plastic model. Other evidence for an HG IV has not been discovered.

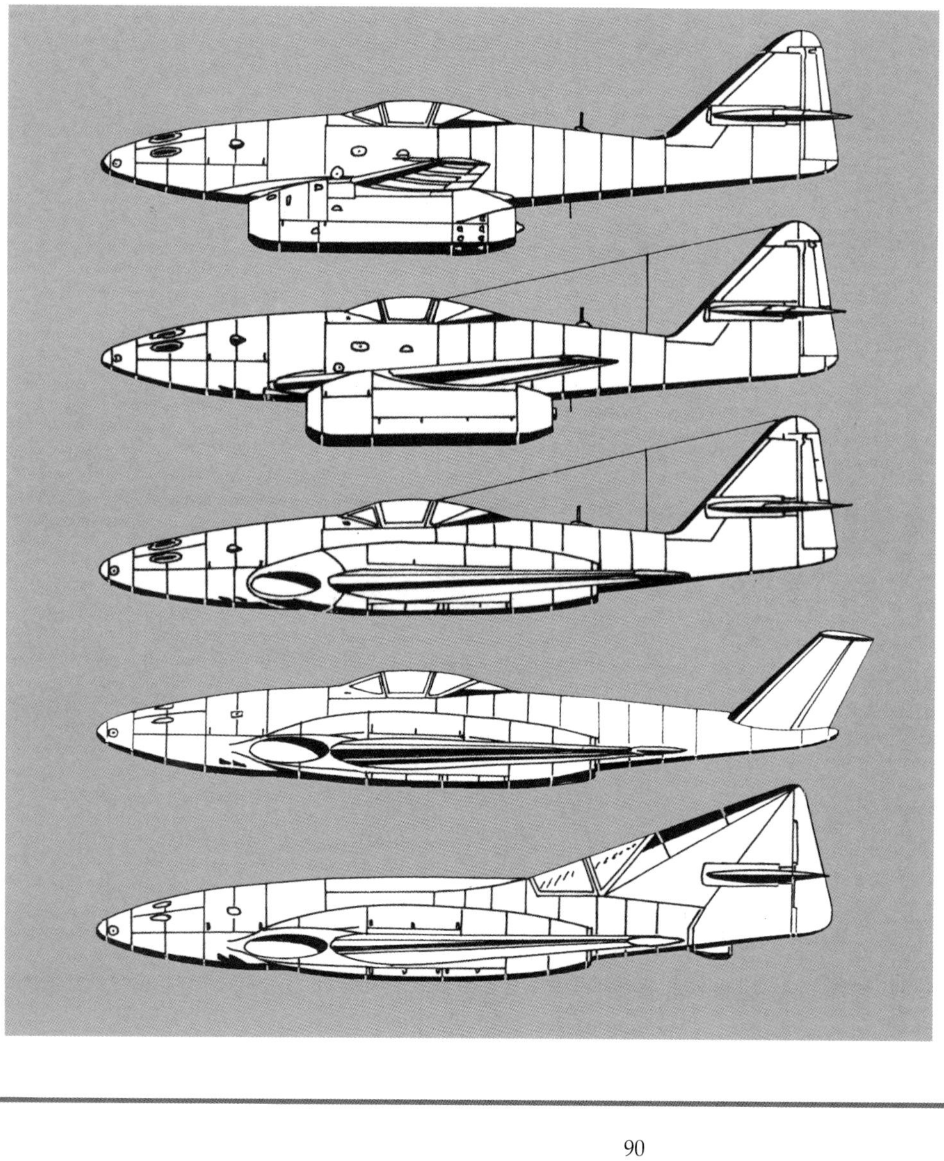

Me 262 B-1a/U1

The Me 262 B-1a/U1 has the Hirschgeweih (Stag Antler) of operational aircraft, then in great demand, and is clearly to be regarded as a precursor of the Me 262 B-2. For comparison, the side views show the difference between the flown Me 262 A-1a/U1 (upper) and the projected Me 262 B-1a/U1 (lower).

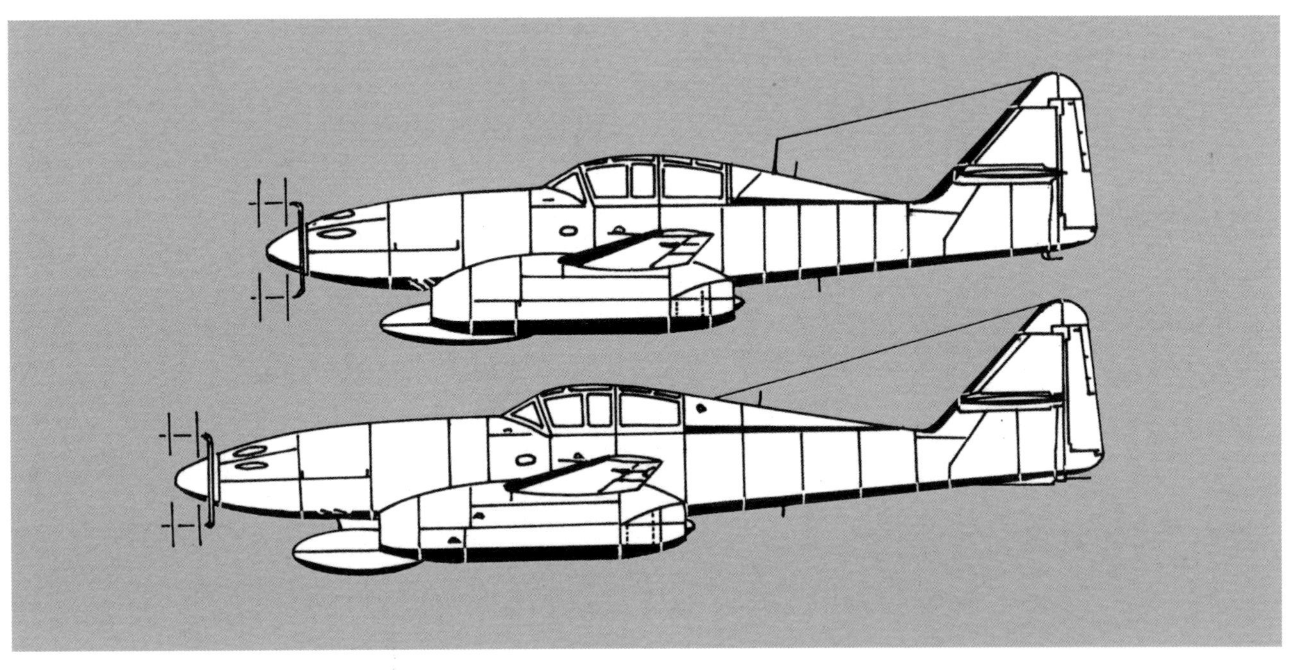

Me 262 B-2

To develop a night fighter out of the Me 262 was logical, and it is a fact that the Me 262 A-1a/U1 was flown operationally. It was followed by the Me 262 B-1a/U1, a lengthened variant of the A-1a/U1. The Me 262 B-2 then followed, which housed the second crew member in a lengthened aerodynamic canopy, and already on 07.12.1944, a mock-up inspection of it took place. In the initial phase, the external radar antenna probes were retained, but with refinement could reduce the loss in speed by 20km/h. However, installation of the Bremen-O radar with internal parabolic dish was then planned. In the proposal for the final Me 262 B-2, ready on 17.03.1945, powerplants were to have been 2 x 1,300kp thrust HeS 011As but were planned to be replaced by 2 x 1,500kp thrust HeS 011B turbojets when these became available; RATO units were also part of the take-off equipment.

Dimensions and Weights

Span	12.56m
Length	11.70m
Height	3.85m
Wing area	21.70m^2
Equipped weight	5,149kg
Flying weight	8,124kg

Performance (with HeS 011A-0)

Maximum Speed at 6,000m	930km/h
Ceiling	12,300m
Range	1,480-2,260km

Armament

4 x MK 108 in fuselage nose
2 x MK 108 *Schräge Musik*
2 x 24 R4M rockets or
2 x R100BS as Rüstsatz

Me 262 B-2 (13.02.1945)

The Me 262 B-2 as a turboprop night fighter (2 x 109-021) with longer range.

Me 262 B-2a (04.10.1944)

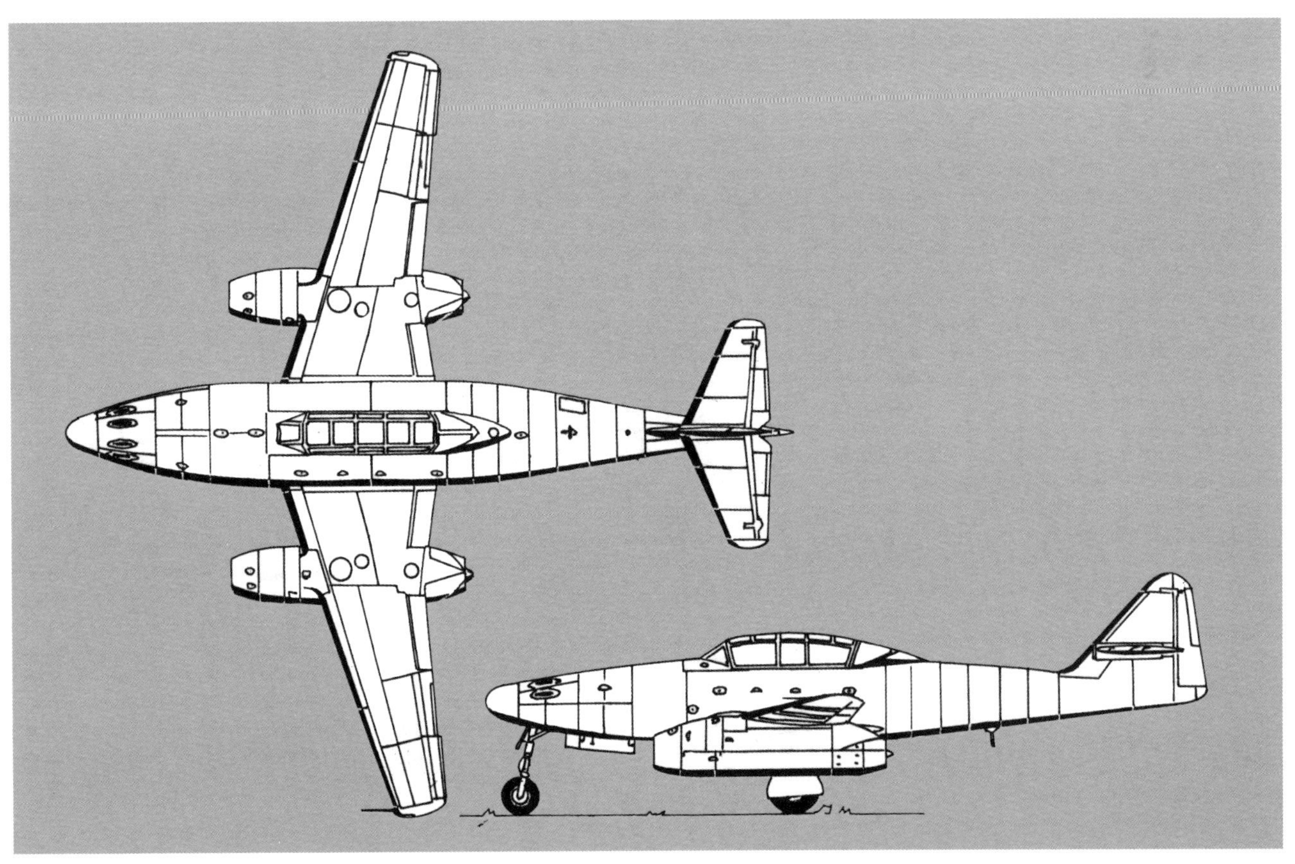

Me 262 Night Fighter (12.02.1945)

Further development of the day fighter led to the 2-seat Me 262 HG III night fighter variant.

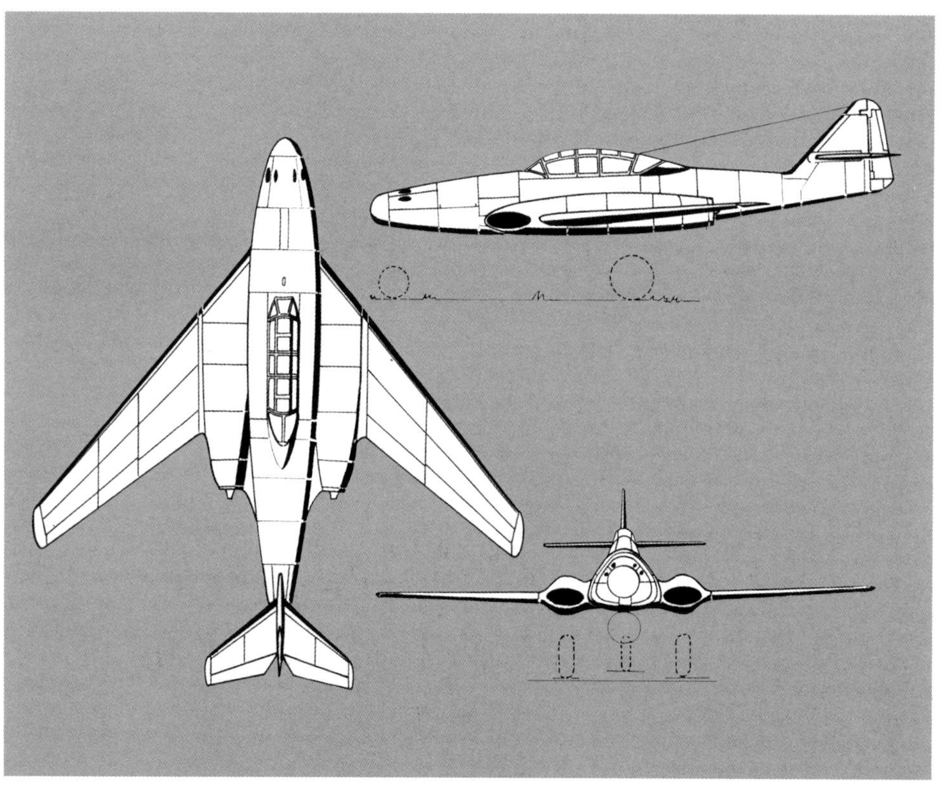

Dimensions and Weights

Span	11.20m
Length	11.70m
Height	3.58m
Wing area	28.70m²
Equipped weight	5,064kg
Flying weight	
normal	8,070kg
max	9,160kg

Performance
(with HeS 011A)

Max speed	
at 8,000m	965km/h
Ceiling	12,000m
Endurance	
at 10,000m	2.3 hrs
at 12,000m	c.4.0 hrs

Armament
4 x MK 108 in fuselage nose
2 x MK 108 as *Schräge Musik* Rüstsatz

Me 262 B-2 Variant I (17.03.1945)

Nightfighting became more complex and encompassed an ever greater sphere of operations, and besides the pilot and radar observer, space for a third crew member (the navigator) had to be made. In an interim step, the proposed HeS 011A or B turbojets were still placed beneath the wings, together with a new wing centre section. As flight trials of the Me 262 HG II were due to commence shortly, more precise data was expected from it.

Dimensions and Weights

Span	13.06m
Length	12.57m
Height	3.58m
Wing area	$28.00m^2$
Flying weight	
normal	9,176kg
max	10,316kg

Performance

Max speed	948km/h
Ceiling	12,000m
Endurance	
at 10,000m	2.5 hrs

Armament

4 x MK 108 in fuselage nose
2 x MK 108 as *Schräge Musik* Rüstsatz

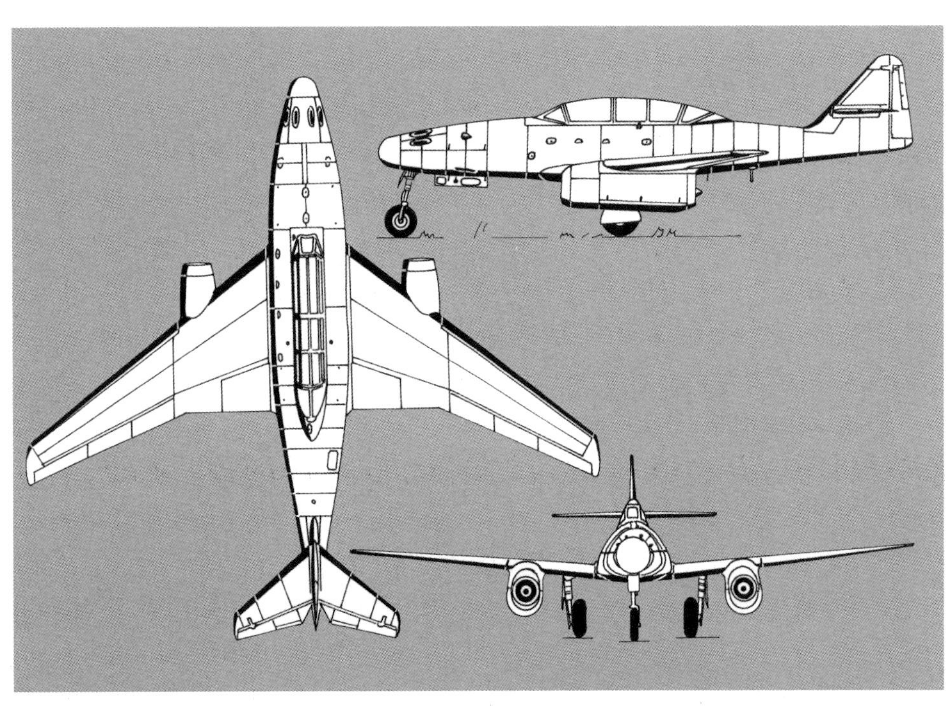

Me 262 B-2 Variant II (17.03.1945)

As a final step in the 3-seat night fighter proposal, the turbojets were relocated to the wing roots and thus altered the external appearance of the aircraft. Except for a higher maximum speed in excess of 1,000km/h, all other data remained unchanged.

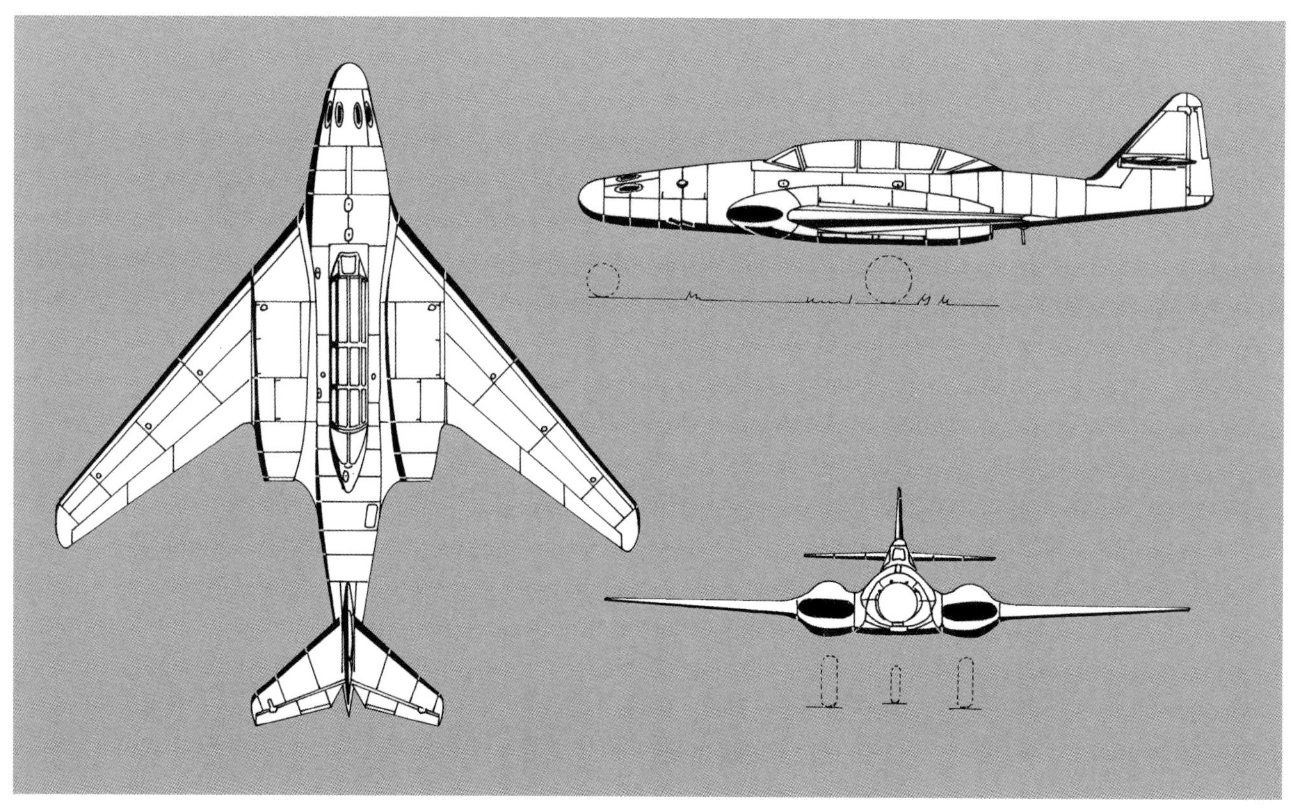

Me P 1073 B (13.08.1940)

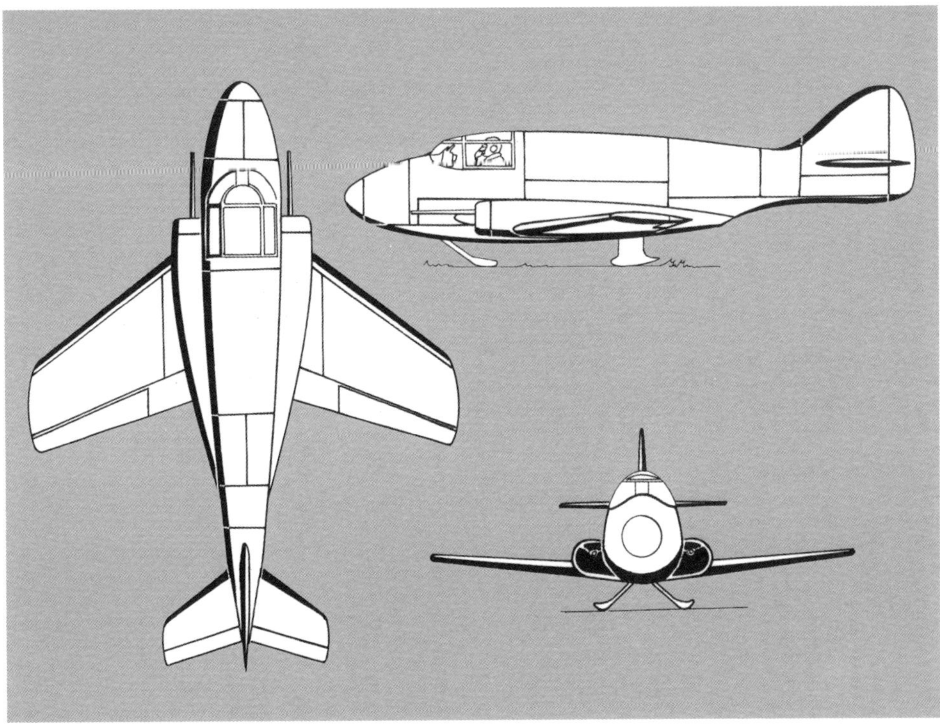

Dimensions

Span	4.40m
Length	5.90m
Height	1.72m
Wing area	6.50m²
Wing sweep	35°
Fuselage width	0.80m

Weight

Flying weight	1,620kg

Powerplant
1 x BMW P 3304 turbojet

Armament
2 x MG 151/20

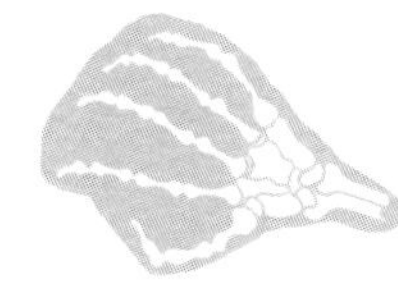

This proposal consisted of a small single-seat Bordjäger, of which three were to have been carried aloft and air-launched by the 8-engined P 1073A long-range mothercraft for operations over the Atlantic or the USA. Its powerplant was located in the centre of the fuselage and fed by lateral air intakes just ahead of the wing roots that also housed the armament. The swept wings were foldable and the tricycle landing gear consisted of short-stemmed sprung skids. Performance data is not known.

Me P 1079/1 (15.04.1941)

Long before work on turbojets began to be sponsored by the RLM in 1939, Dipl.-Ing. Paul Schmidt of Munich had as early as 1931 commenced work on pulsejet development, and by 1940 had progressed to the stage of having tested his SR 500 pulsejet. As pulsejet work by the Argus firm, begun only in November 1939, had not advanced to a unit of equivalent thrust, Messerschmitt considered use of the Schmidt duct for a whole series of design studies under the P 1079 designation. Although promising on paper, none of Schmidt's range of pulsejets ever flew as they proved to be unsuitable as flight engines. When the more successful As 014 pulsejet was eventually selected as the powerplant for the Fieseler Fi 103 flying-bomb in 1942, the series of projects was continued, but powered by Argus pulsejets instead. As will be seen on subsequent pages, all possible engine locations were considered, the common airframe features being a 40° swept wing and tailplane. Principally intended for the low-level Schnellbomber role, the single-seater was to have carried 2 x 500kg or 1 x 1,000kg or even 1 x 1,700kg underslung bomb. The early P 1079 swept wing and empennage variants were eventually reworked into the more orthodox Me 328 proposed for use in the coastal defence, fighter, and low-level bomber roles.

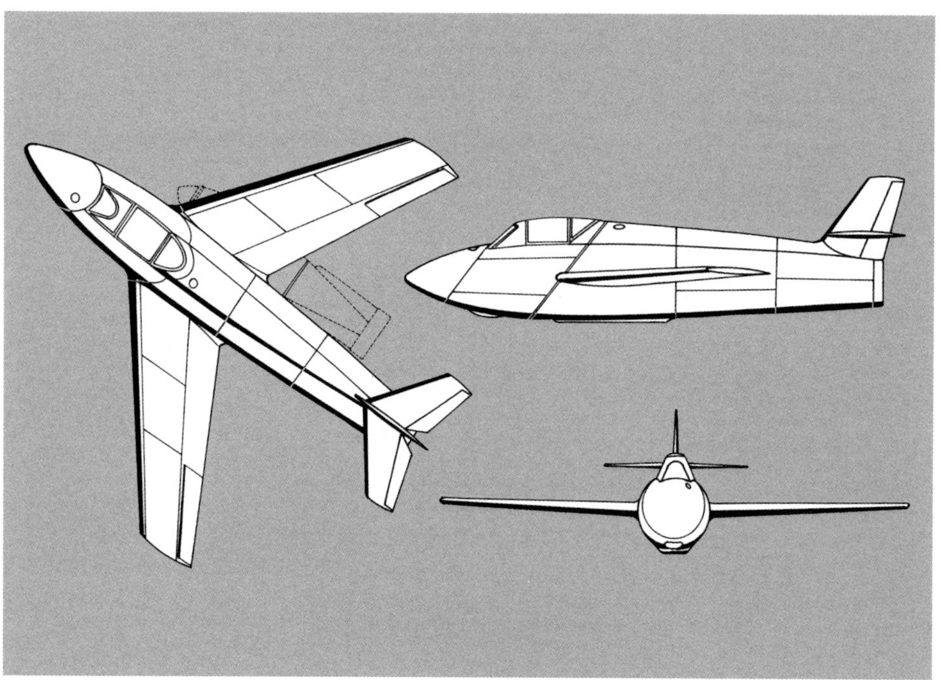

Dimensions

Span	6.32m
Length	6.40m
Height	1.67m

Performance

Max speed	760km/h

Powerplant

1 x 500kp thrust SR 500

Fuel load	905 litres

Bombload

up to 1,700kg

Me P 1079/2 (05.05.1941)

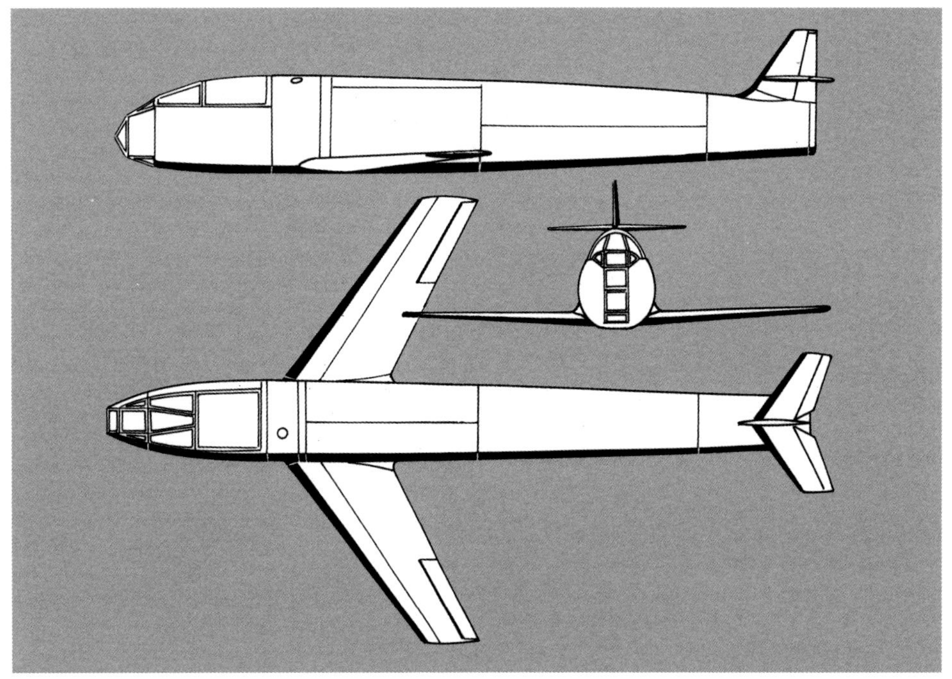

Dimensions

Span	5.00m
Length	8.10m
Height	1.65m

Powerplant

1 x 500kp thrust SR 500

Fuel load	1,200 litres

The P 1079/1 to P 1079/3 each had an unfavourable ventral fuselage air intake.

Me P 1079/3 (09.05.1941)

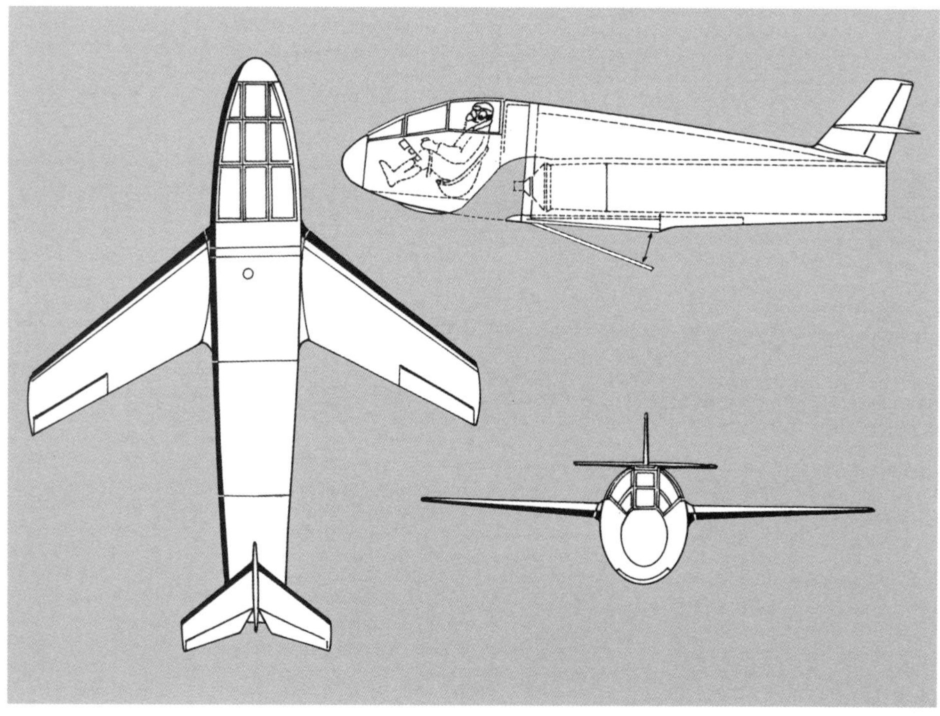

Dimensions

Span	5.00m
Length	6.28m
Height	1.67m

Powerplant

1 x 500kg thrust SR 500
Fuel load 1,200 litres

Me P 1079/5 (11.05.1941)

In the P 1079/5, with air intakes beneath the wing roots, various wingspan, tailspan and fin heights were drawn up. Wing areas ranged from 5.00 to 10.00m² and fuel load from 300 to 920 litres in the thickened wing profile.

Dimensions

Span	5.00m
Length	6.15m
Height	1.30m
Wing area	5.00m²

Powerplant

1 x 500kp thrust SR 500

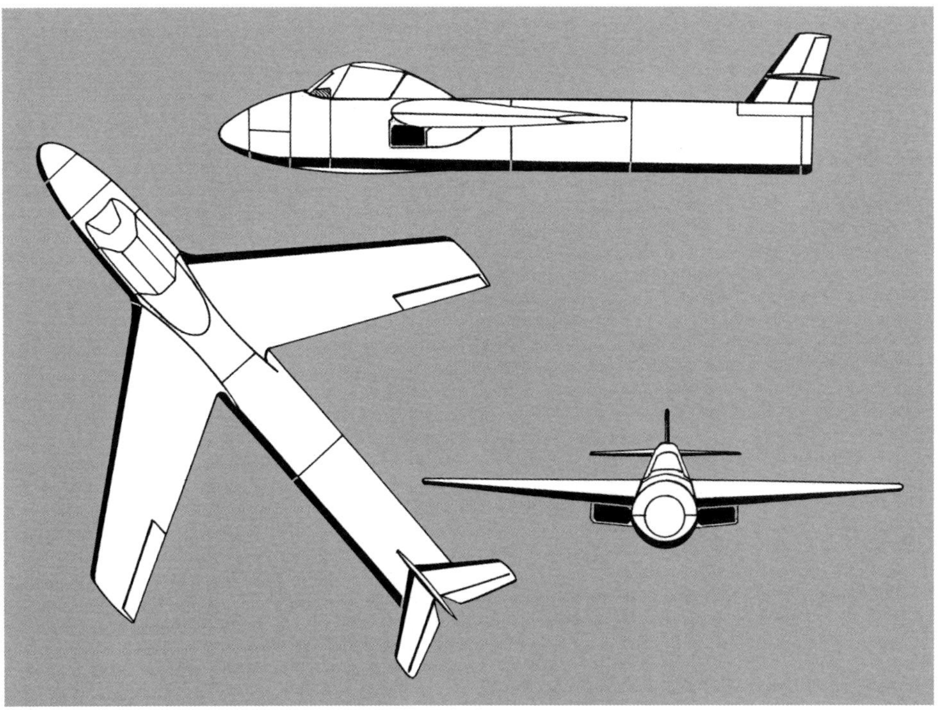

Me P 1079/7 (15.05.1941)

The SR 500 pulsejet, with a more favourable air intake, was now housed in a duct above the fuselage and supported the tail surfaces. The fuel load reverted to the fuselage, the swept wing returning to its thin profile.

Dimensions

Span	5.00m
Length	c.6.55m
Height	2.49m

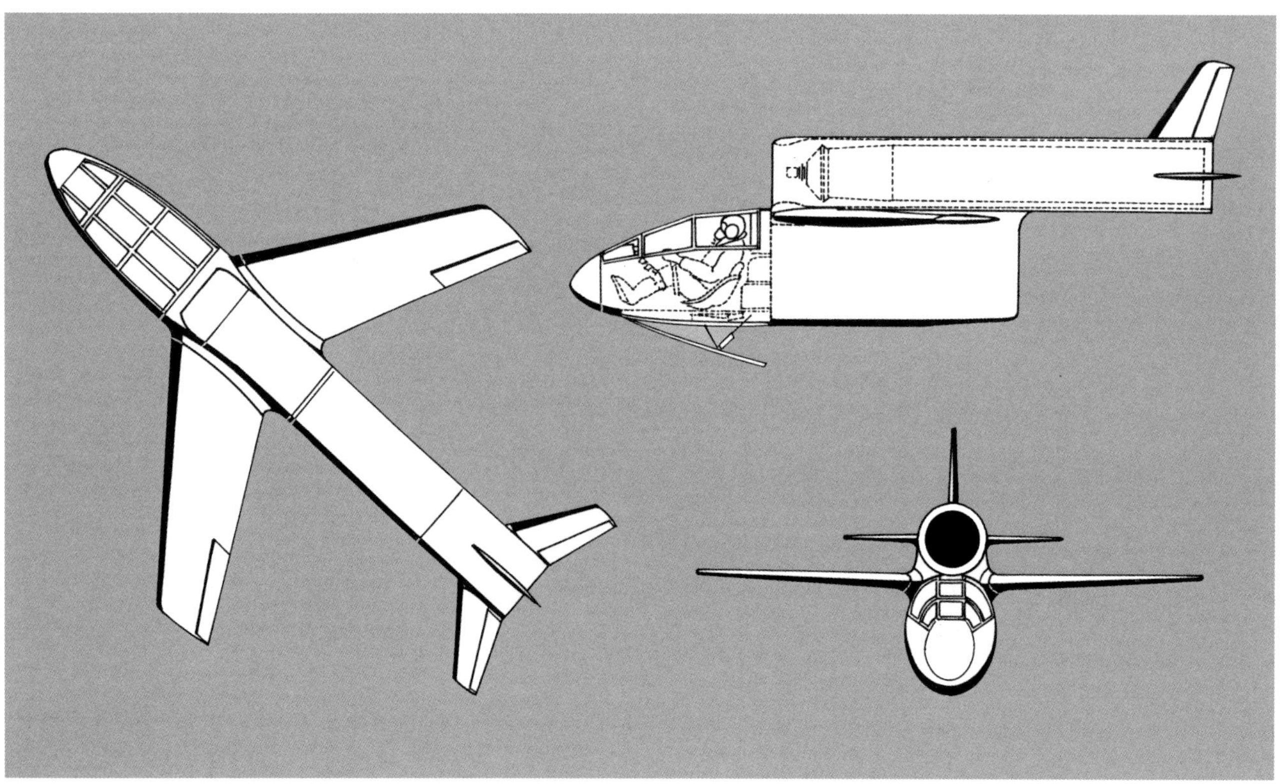

Me P 1079/10c (20.05.1941)

In this scheme, the SR 500 pulsejet projected some half its length beyond the fuselage, its air intake located on the dorsal fuselage. Span was 5.00m, length 7.20m, height 2.25m (?), fuel load 800 litres and armament 2 x MG 131s. One drawing showed a single underslung SD 1700 B bomb, whilst in another it was enclosed in an aerodynamic fairing.

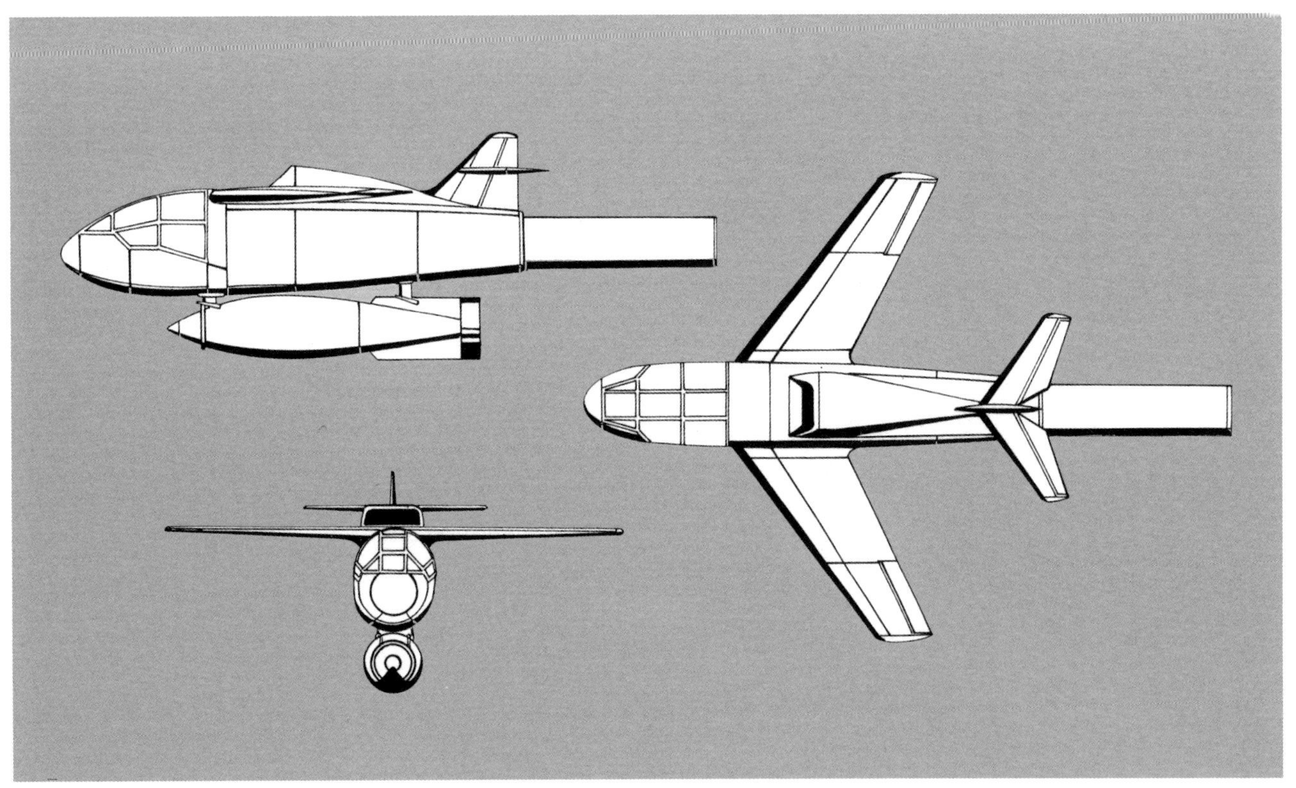

Me P 1079/13b (28.06.1941)

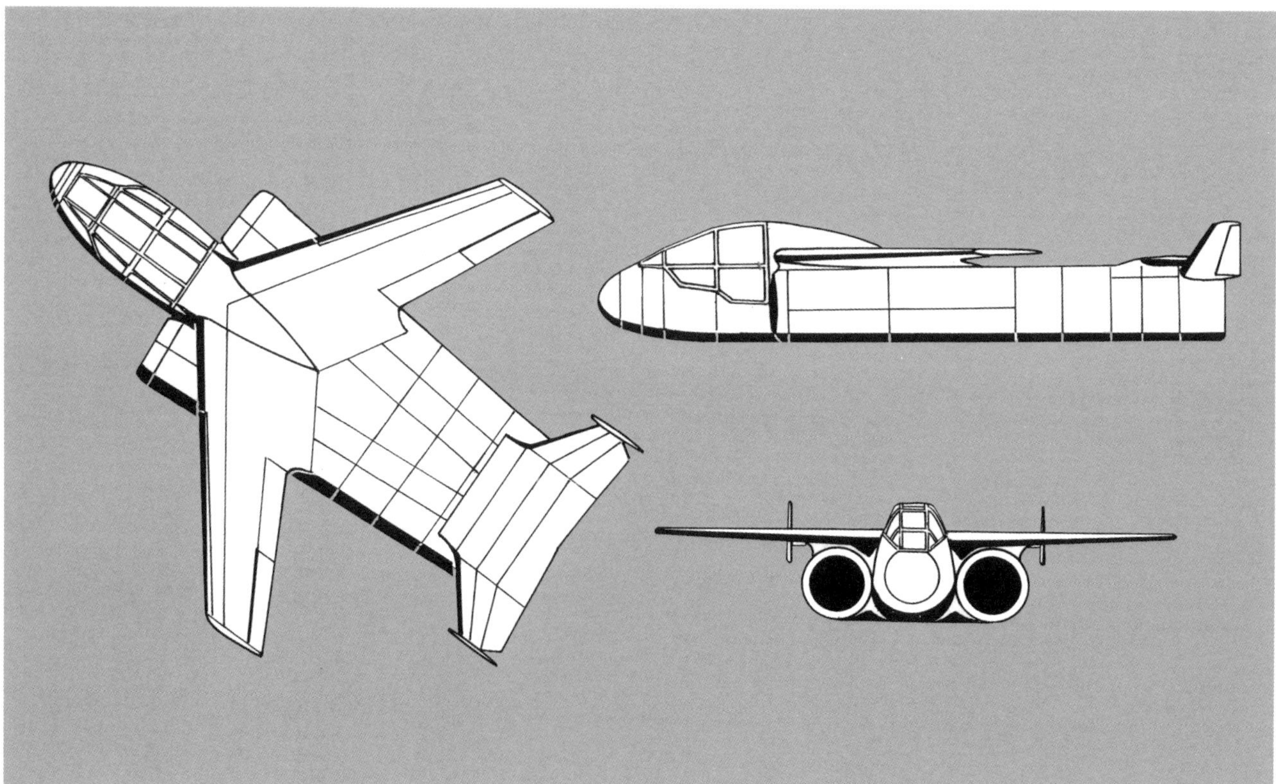

This proposal utilised two SR 500 pulsejets, which permitted an easier exchange and higher flight loads but less stability. The tailplane, whose centre section could function as a dive brake, now supported twin endplate fins and rudders. Span was 5.00m, length 6.15m, height 1.10m and fuel load 900 litres.

Me P 1079/15 (09.07.1941)

The powerplant here was a single Schmidt SR 1000 pulsejet on the fuselage axis, the space on either side accommodating the offset cockpit and fuel loads varying from 1,540 to 2,375 litres. Although the pilot had a poor view to port, space was available for payloads such as armament.

Dimensions	
Span	6.00m
Length	6.70m
Height	c.1.75m

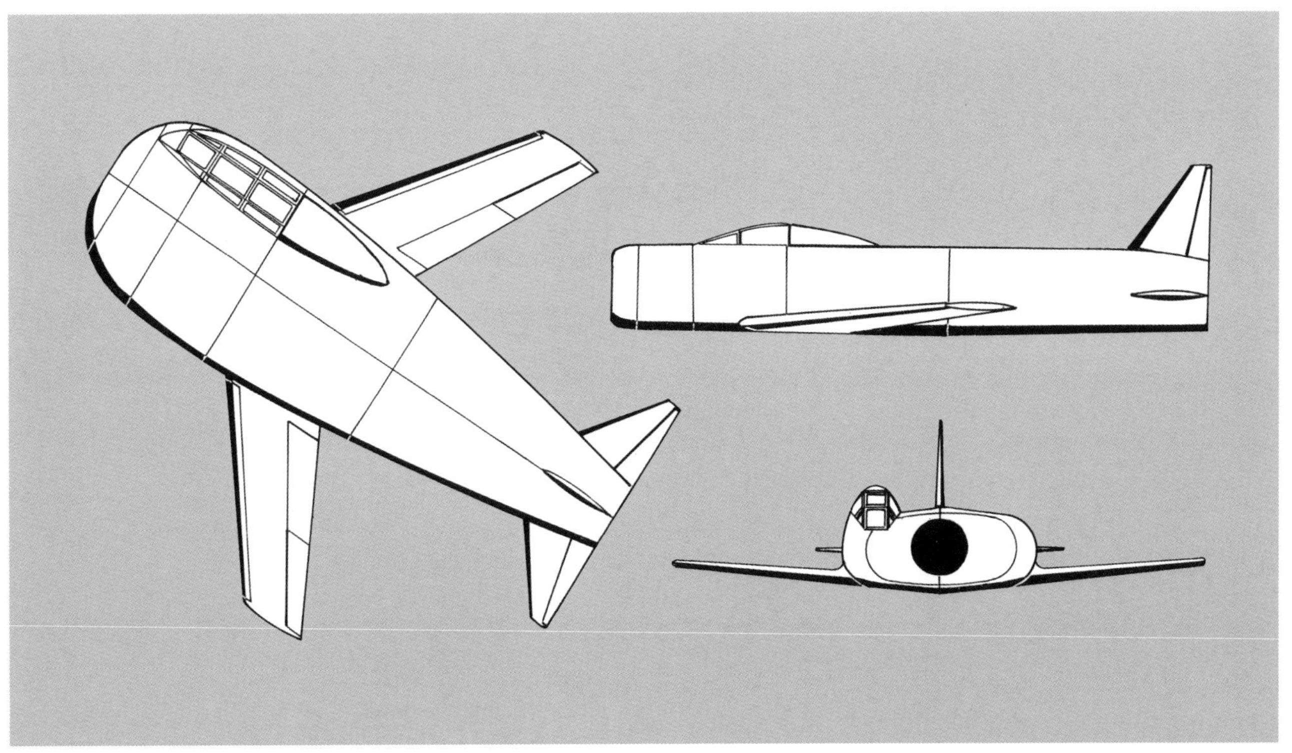

Me P 1079/16 (10.07.1941)

This was also powered by a single SR 1000 pulsejet, but in an asymmetrical arrangement that retained the offset cockpit to starboard. The tailplane and twin endplate fins and rudders were mounted on a stub fairing above the rear fuselage. Span was 5.00m and length 7.00m.

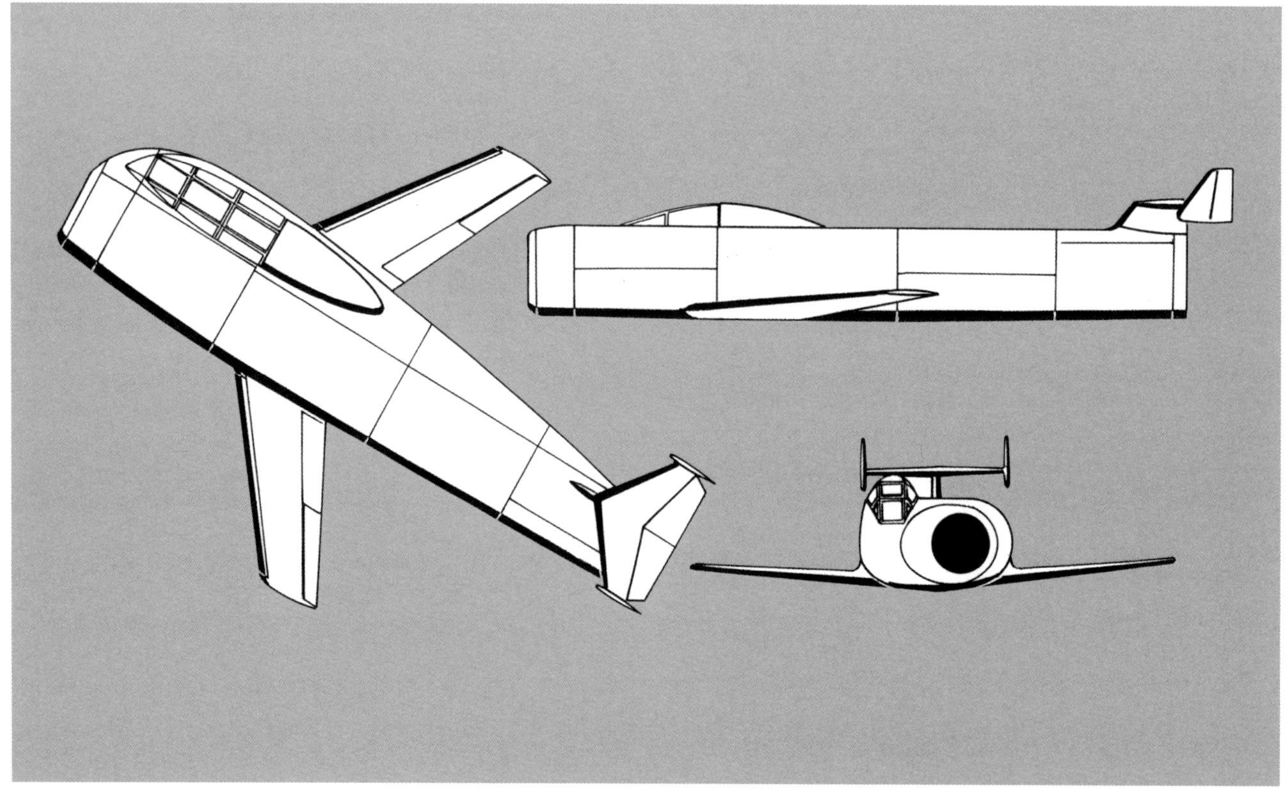

Me P 1079/17 (12.07.1941)

Powered by 1 x SR 1000 pulsejet, it was a derivative of the P 1079/16, where the fuselage was rotated through 90° and thus provided the pilot with good visibility, improved stability about its transverse axis, and enhanced the possibilities of carrying armament.

Since the possibility of carrying bombs was poor, the bomb-carrying concept was altered to that of a fighter.

Note: Except for the wingspan, the other dimensions are approximations. Some dimensions were only partially given, such as fuselage length but not overall length.

All of these design studies featured skid landing gear. Take-off with the aid of a trolley was a possibility, but with the heavy bombload (without aerodynamic fairing), would have been difficult. Almost certainly, hardly any thought was given to operationally practical usage, but more to flight characteristics and constructional issues.

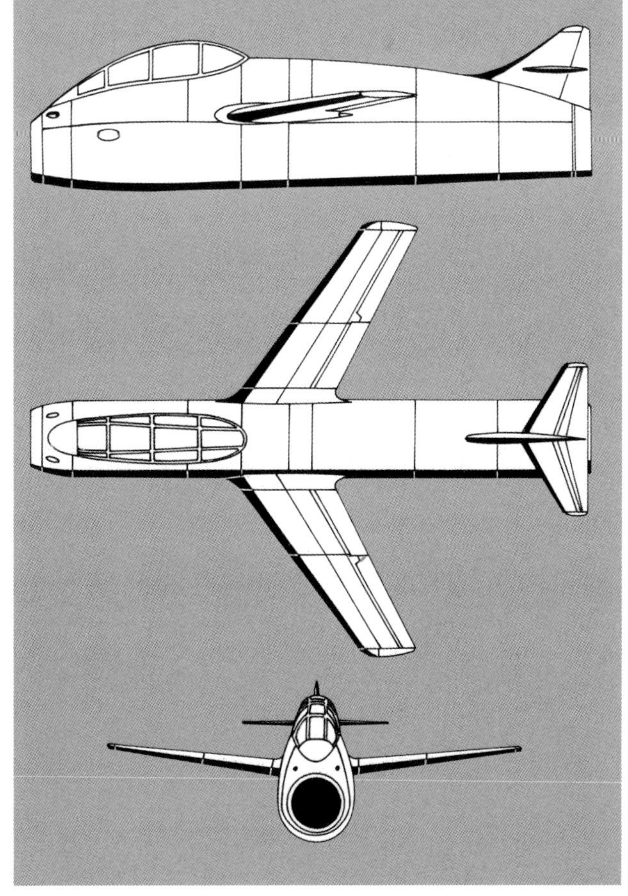

Dimensions

Span	5.00m
Length	6.70m
Height	1.73m
Fuel	800 litres

Armament 2 x MG 131s

The Me P 1092 Series

As with previous projects, the P 1092 studies encompassed a whole series of proposals, but with a much more realisable background. These involved the concept of a single-jet aircraft at a time when not all of the problems with turbojet propulsion had been resolved, but where the technology had clearly surpassed the teething stage. Whereas twin-jet aircraft such as the Me 262 were configured to be powered by the two of the early, weak powerplants, it is clearly apparent that only one turbojet, more powerful in the interim, was capable of powering the entire aircraft. The numbers of engines produced were still insufficient, and too few followed on the production lines. In order for a single-jet fighter to attain the optimum, a whole series of configurations had to be conceived and calculations made.

Me P 1092/A to P 1092/E

In a memorandum (beginning of 1943) Messerschmitt proposed to reduce the 51 aircraft types in series production to just five. One solution for this consisted of his developing the Me 262 into a universal weapons system with corresponding variants (see the Me 262 Family). The other consisted of a smaller and lighter, easy-to-build multi-purpose aircraft with common basic components, but with various types of propulsion unit and equipment, which would be capable of fulfilling all anticipated operational needs. The following thus appeared:

Me P 1092/A	Single-seat fighter with 1 x Jumo 004C turbojet
Me P 1092/B	Single-seat rocket interceptor with 1 x HWK 509A rocket motor
Me P 1092/C	Single-seat Schnellbomber with 2 x Argus pulsejets
Me P 1092/D	Single-seat long-range & high-altitude fighter, Schnellstbomber, Stuka and torpedo-carrier with 2 x Jumo 004C turbojets
Me P 1092/E	Two-seat night fighter with 2 x Jumo 004C turbojets

These designs were to have employed the outer wings of the Me 262, the fuselage being also largely standardised in layout.

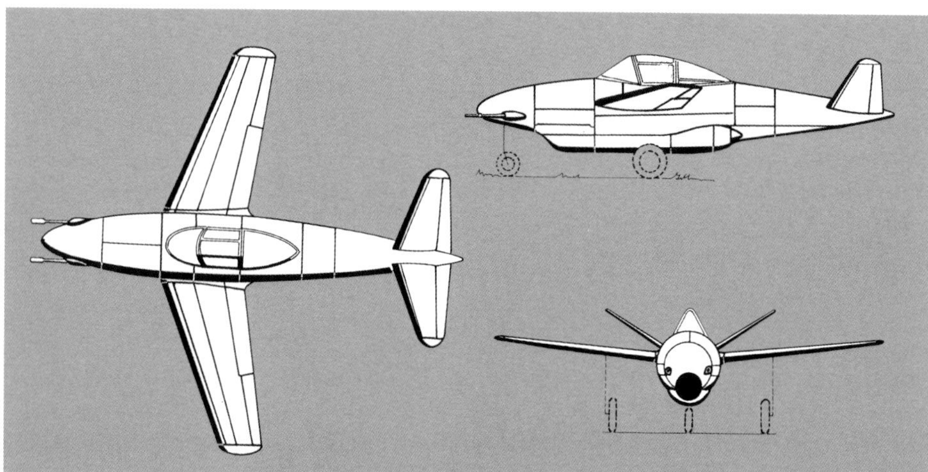

Me P 1092/A

Dimensions and Weight

Span	8.40m
Length	9.00m
Height	2.50m
Wing area	12.00m^2

Flying weight c.4,000kg with 1,200 litres fuel

Armament

2 x MK 103 in fuselage

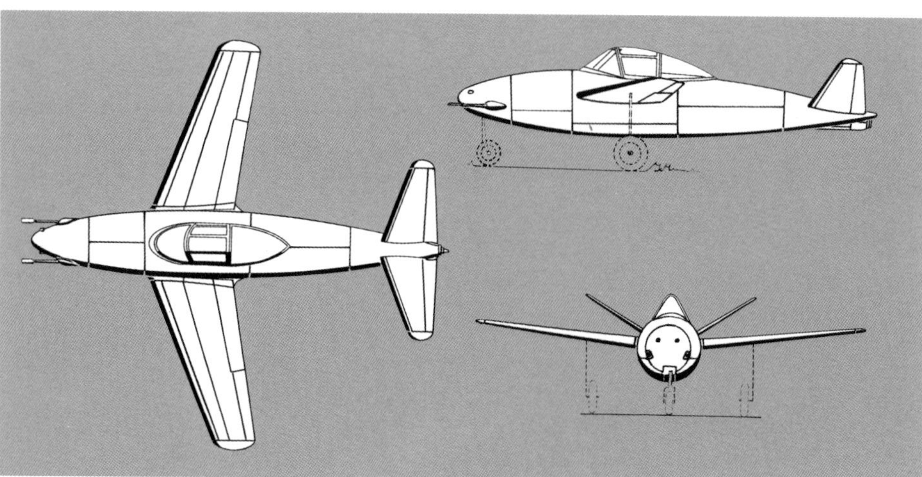

Me P 1092/B

Dimensions

Span	8.40m
Length	9.00m
Height	2.50m
Wing area	12.00m^2

Fuel load 2,730 litres in six fuselage tanks

Armament

2 MK 103 + 2 x MG 151/15

Me P 1092/A (25.05.1943)

Me P 1092/B (25.05.1943)

Me P 1092/C (25.05.1943)

This unarmed Schnellbomber, powered by two underwing Argus pulsejets, carried 3,130 litres of fuel in 5 fuselage tanks and an SC 500 in an internal bomb-bay beneath the pilot. Dimensions were as for the P 1092/A.

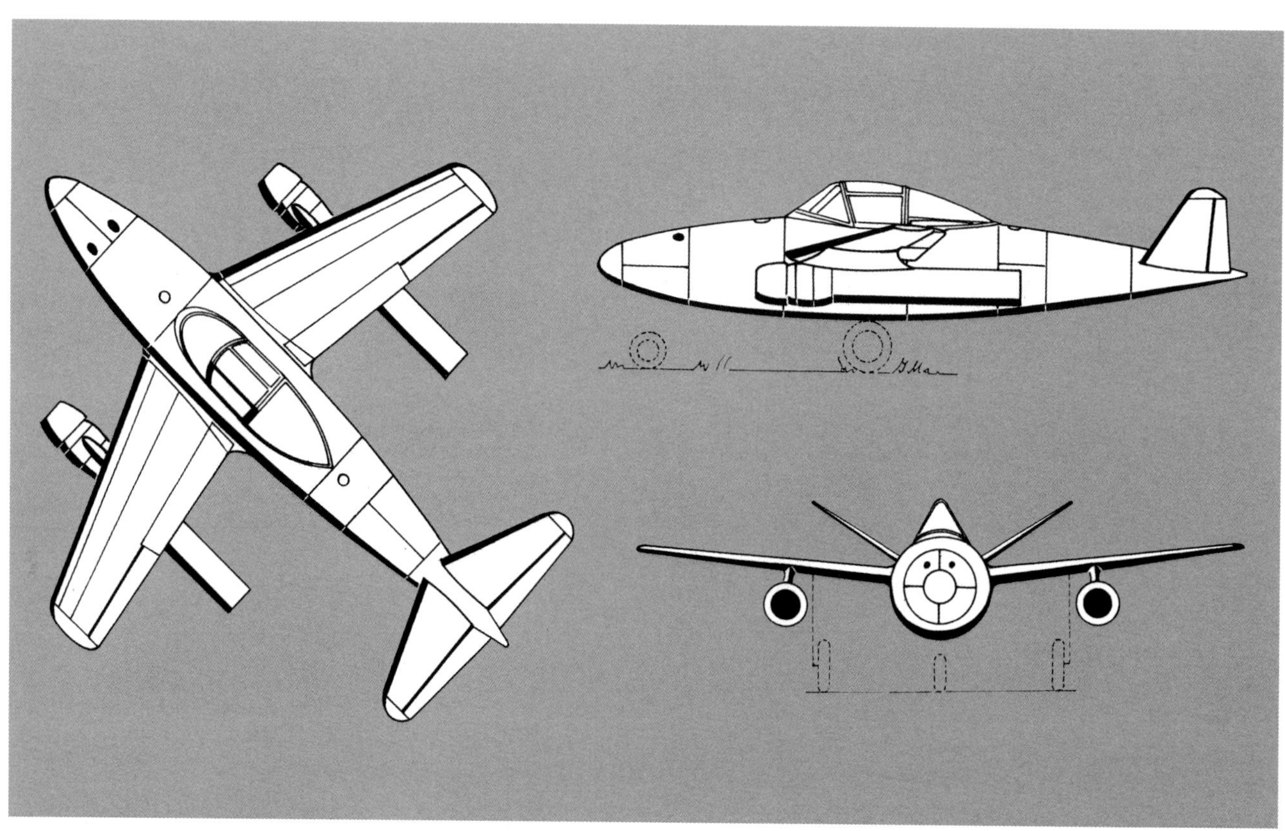

Me P 1092/D (25.05.1943)

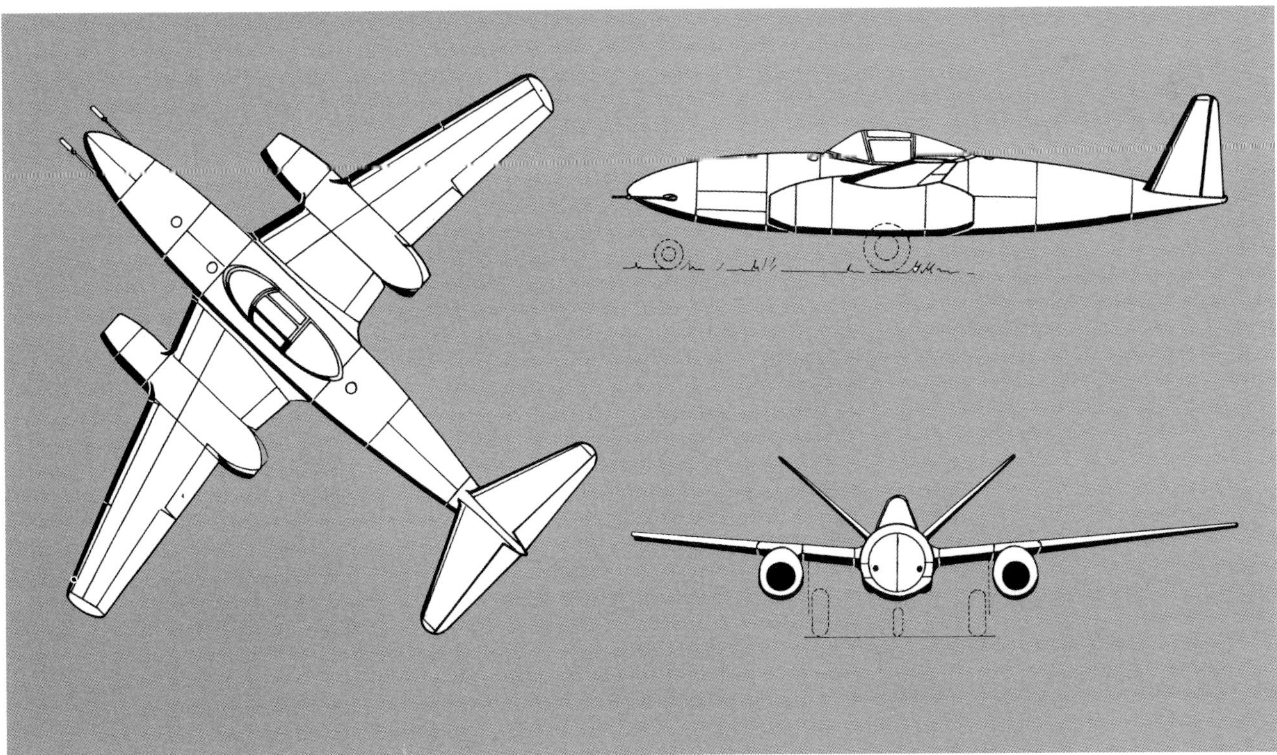

This basic single-seater, intended as a multi-purpose aircraft, was dimensionally noticeably larger, with span 12.56m, length 11.00m and height 3.20m. Powerplants were 2 x Jumo 004C, fuel 2,560 litres in 4 fuselage tanks, and standard armament 2 x MK 103. Further equipment could be added according to the mission to be performed. The entire Me 262 wing was adopted for this larger aircraft.

Me P 1092/E (25.05.1943)

This night fighter was an offshoot derived from the P 1092 D and had the same dimensions and engines. In addition to the second crew member (radar operator), it had more powerful armament. The 3-view shows four forward-firing unidentified weapons (but probably 2 x MK 103 and 2 x MG 151) as also two large-calibre cannon offset as *Schräge Musik* weapons in the fuselage nose. It had the complete wing of the Me 262.

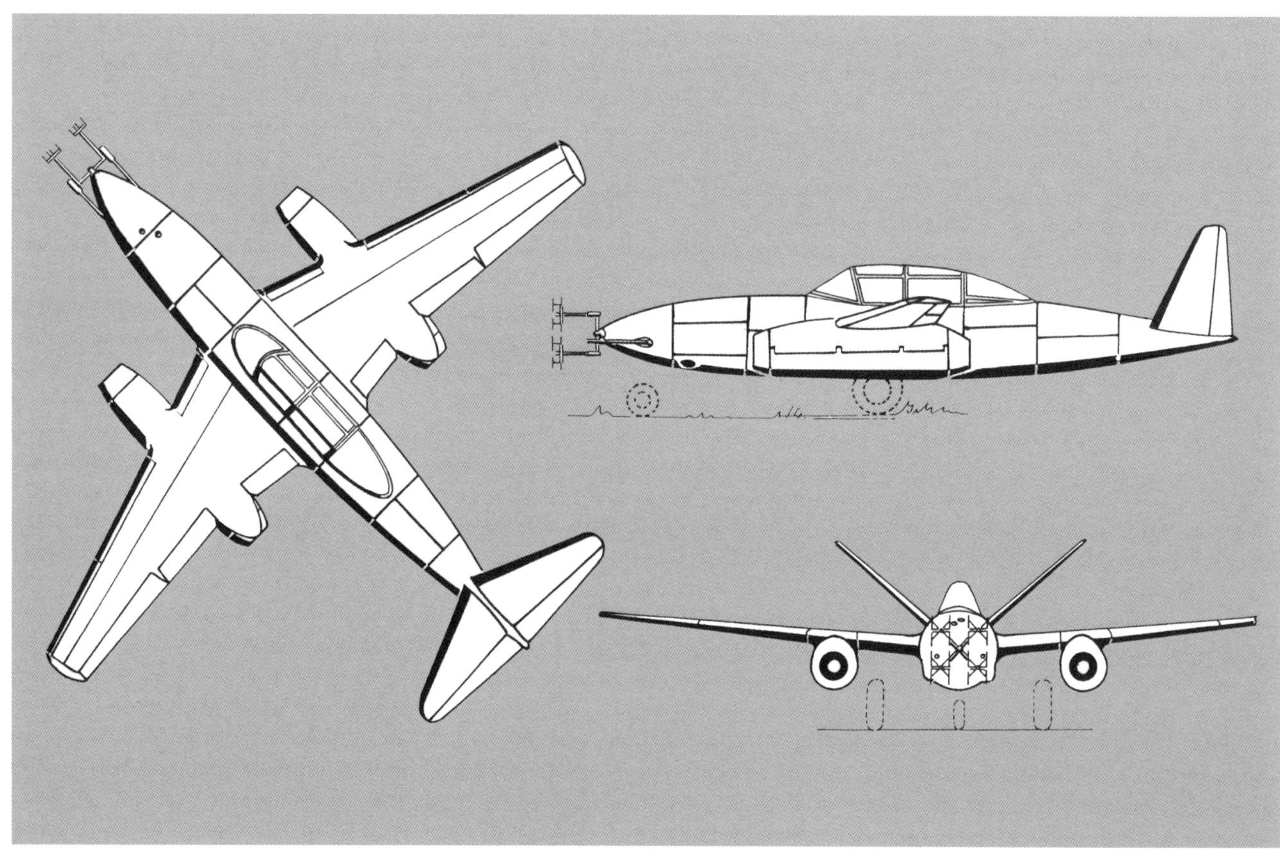

Me P 1092/1 (08.06.1943)

In the initial proposal the principle was clearly visible: the Jumo 004C turbojet was under-slung in the fuselage, the wing roots having an additional forward-swept area to house the wide-track mainwheels, with the cockpit canopy blending into the base of the fin. Because of the low air intake orifice there was little space for nosewheel stowage, the mainwheel stowage in the mid-positioned wing resulting in limited ground clearance.

Dimensions and Weight

Span	8.50m
Length	8.23m
Height	3.26m
Wing area	13.50m^2
Flying weight*	3,850kg

* with fuel 1,200 litres

Performance

Max speed at 6,000m	910km/h
Ceiling	11,600m
Max range	1,025km

Armament

2 x MK 103 + 2 x MG 151/15

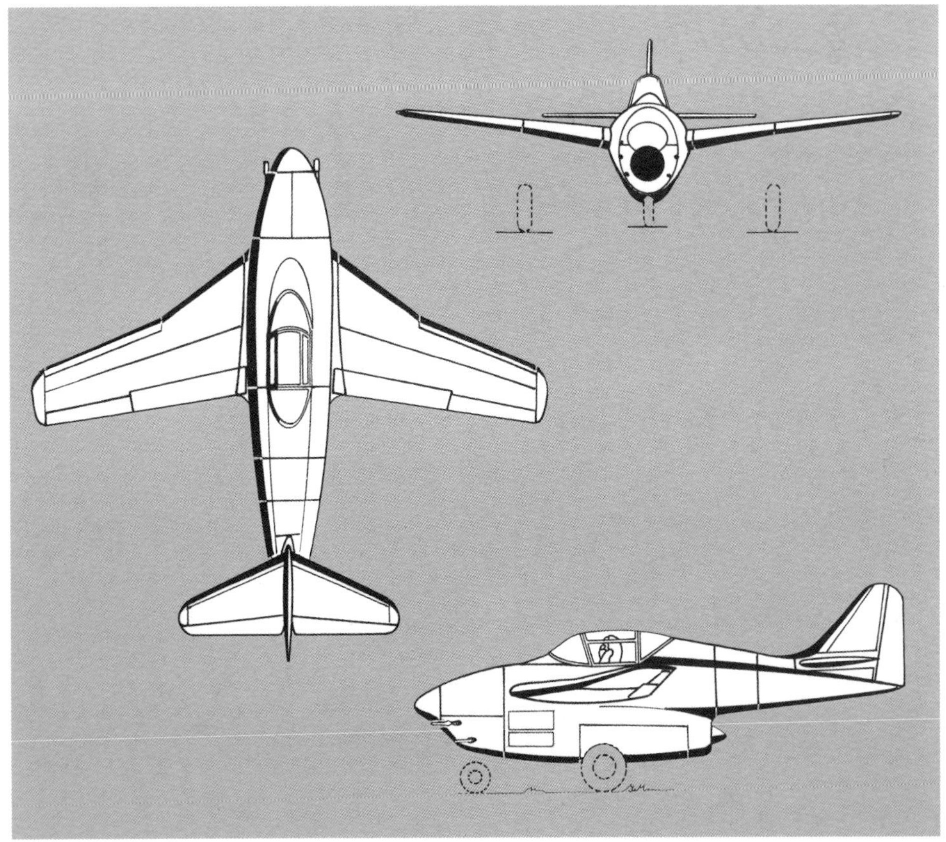

Me P 1092/1a (30.06.1943)

This variant was intended as a fighter-bomber or ground-attack aircraft with inverted gull wings to provide greater stability in dives. The empennage surfaces were similar to those of the Me 262 which, together with the date, leads to the assumption that it was a derivative that led to the P 1092/2. The track of the mainwheels retracting forwards into the wing roots is significantly less than in the other sub-types.

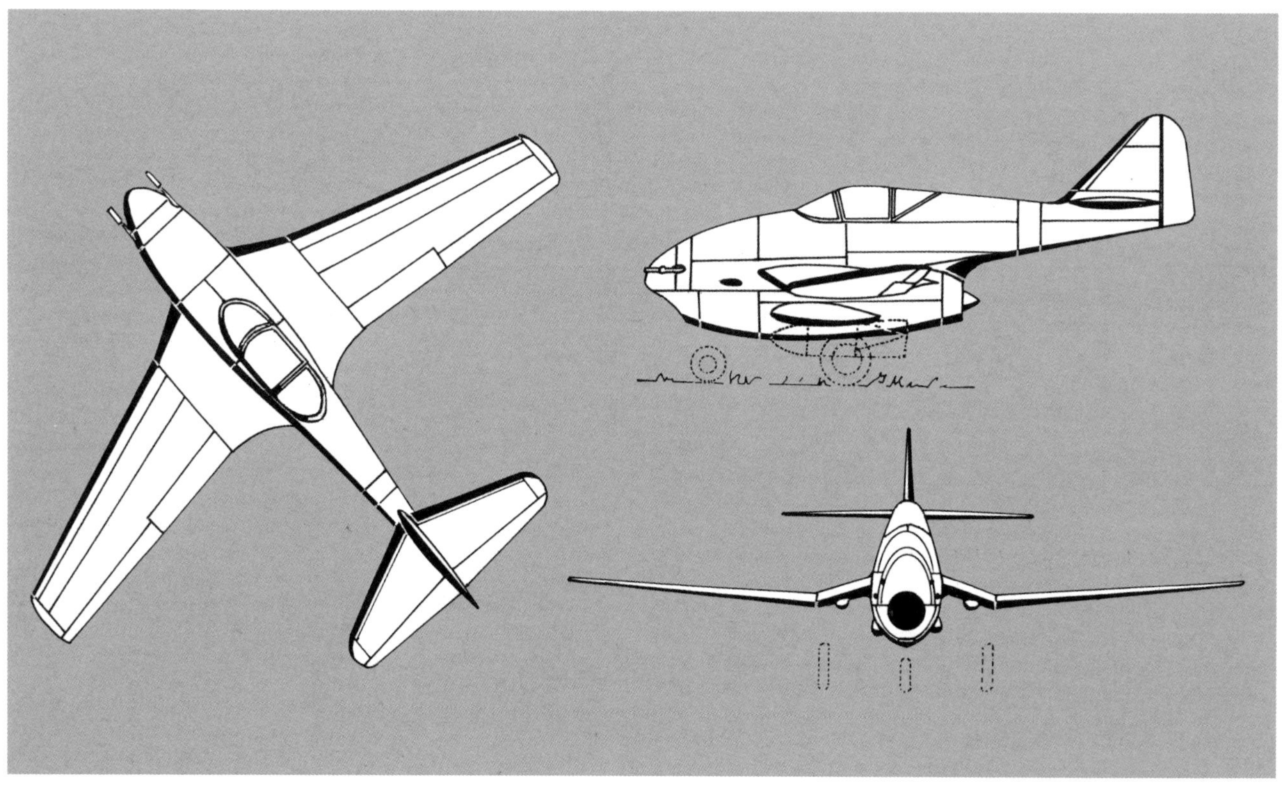

Me P 1092/2 (03.07.1943)

A performance comparison between the P 20 and Me 262 was made with a lighter design which served as a preliminary study for a high-altitude fighter that would have had an increased wingspan. A status was initially reached where its characteristics lay between the P 20 and the Me 262 and in due course, the fuselage volume was increased in order to accommodate a larger quantity of fuel – up to 1,260 litres.

Dimensions

Span	8.85m / 10.00m
Length	8.10m
Height	3.65m
Wing area	12.70m^2 / 14.45m^2

Weights

Equipped	2,626kg / 2,692kg
Flying	3,664kg / 3,730kg

Performance

Max speed	930km/h
Ceiling	11,200m / 12,000m
Range at 11,000m	870km / 970km

Powerplant

1 x 1,015kp thrust Jumo 004C

Armament

2 x MK 103 + 2 x MG 151/15

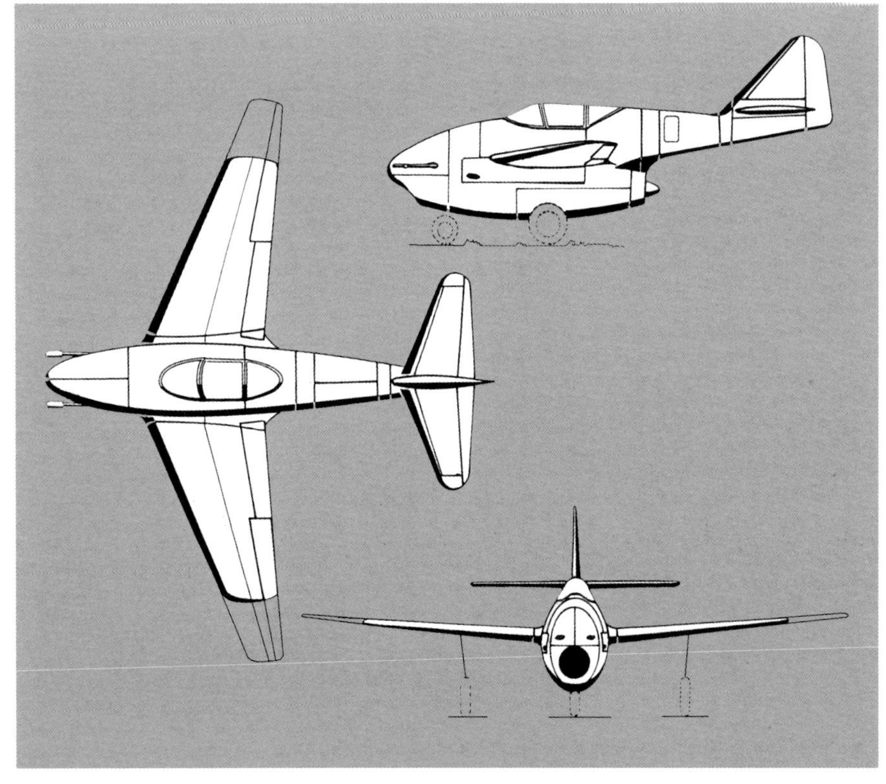

Me P 1092/3 (16.07.1943)

In this next variant the cockpit was located on the rear fuselage, and with more fuel would have had a greater range. Powerplant was still a Jumo 004C; span was 9.40m, length 8.10m, height 3.60m, wing area 12.70m^2 and armament 4 x MK 108; overall weight was somewhat lighter than the preceding proposal.

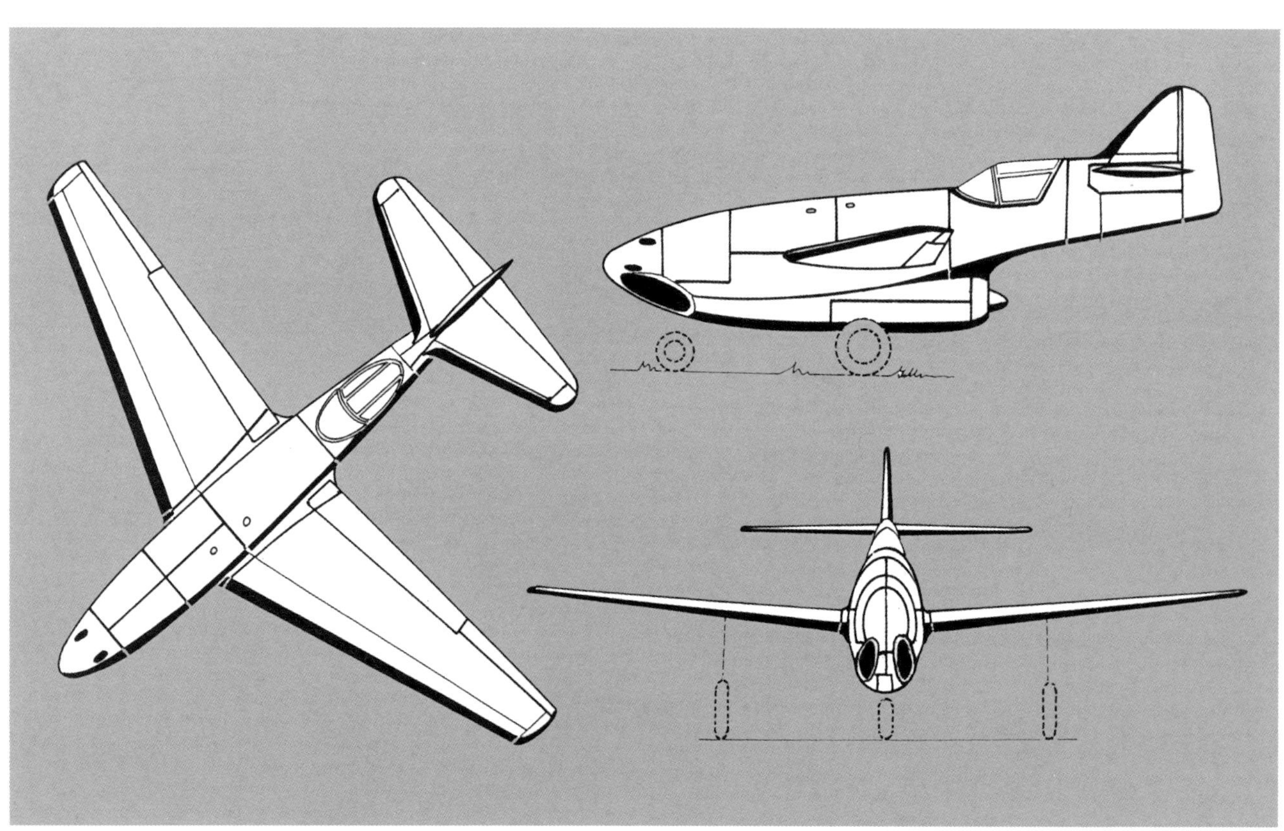

Me P 1092/4 (19.07.1943)

In this variant, the cockpit was again relocated to the forward fuselage and provided the pilot with improved vision, but necessitated a rearward shift of the armament of 4 x MK 103 to the cockpit sides. Overall dimensions were identical to those of the P 1092/3.

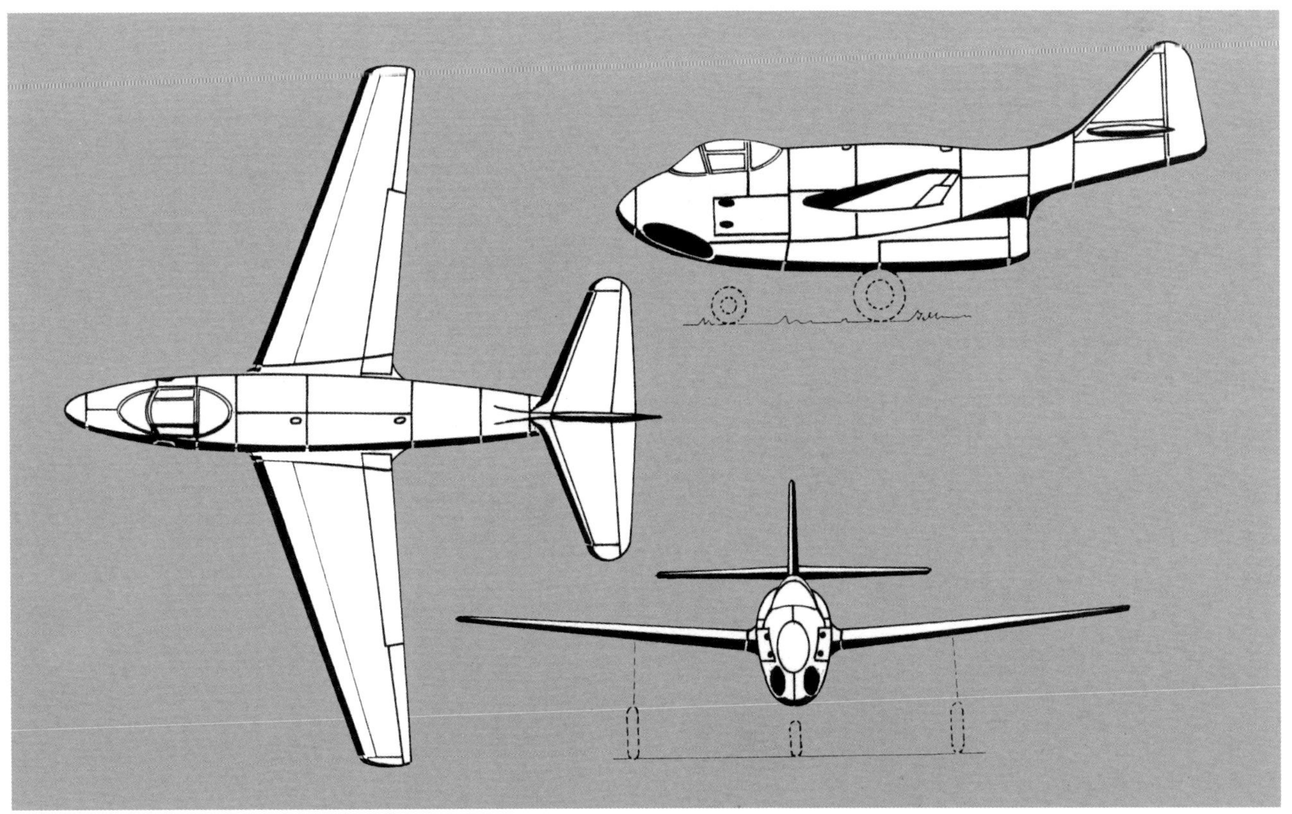

Me P 1092/5 (20.07.1943)

In this last variant of the P 1092 series, with the same overall dimensions as its predecessor, the cockpit was relocated to the centre of the fuselage, the wing and tail surfaces of the previous scheme being retained throughout, the large wing and flaps taken over largely from the Me 262. The larger frontal area of the widened fuselage cross-section did not improve performance, so that work on the P 1092 series was terminated.

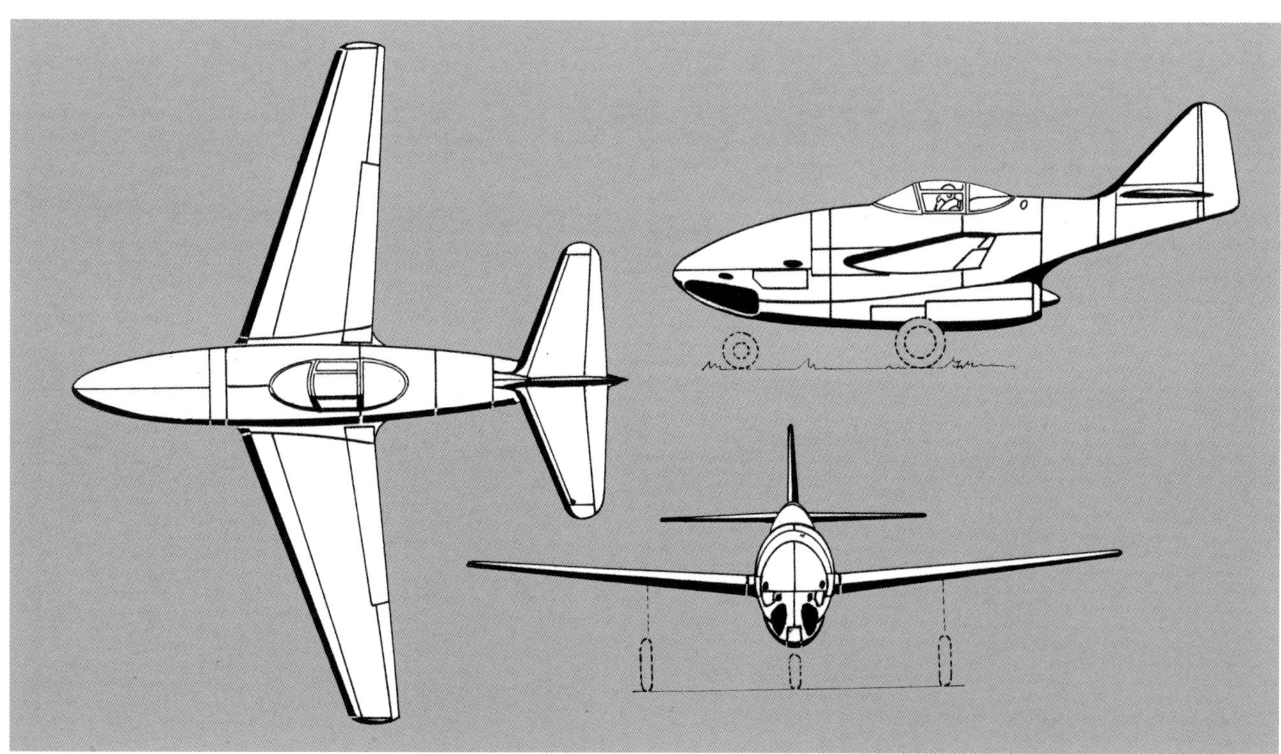

Me P 1095/1 (19.10.1943)

When work on the Me 328 was stopped, an attempt was made to partially rescue the aircraft and led to the Me 328 C powered by a Jumo 004 turbojet, but all else was a failure: too high a wing loading, insufficient range, and a fixed undercarriage. A new design therefore became necessary, consisting of construction components of existing aircraft whereby the fuselage of the Me 328 was largely retained. One P 1095 variant was to have had a wooden wing and incorporated the Me 262 empennage, whilst another featured a somewhat smaller metal wing and Me 328 empennage. [The suffix numerals here are merely to distinguish the variants – *Translator*]

Careful improvements to the final design led to a fighter model that could also be used in the ground-attack, fast bomber and reconnaissance roles. A disadvantage of all three design variants, however, was that the nosewheel lay ahead of the turbojet air intake, with its attendant risk of foreign object ingestion. The wings stemmed from the Me 262 as did the cockpit and controls, the tail surfaces and main undercarriage being taken from the Me 309.

Dimensions and Weight

Span	9.74m
Length	9.71m
Height	3.38m
Wing area	15.30m^2
Flying weight	3,620kg

Performance

Max speed at 6,000m	860km/h

Armament

2 x MK 103 in fuselage nose

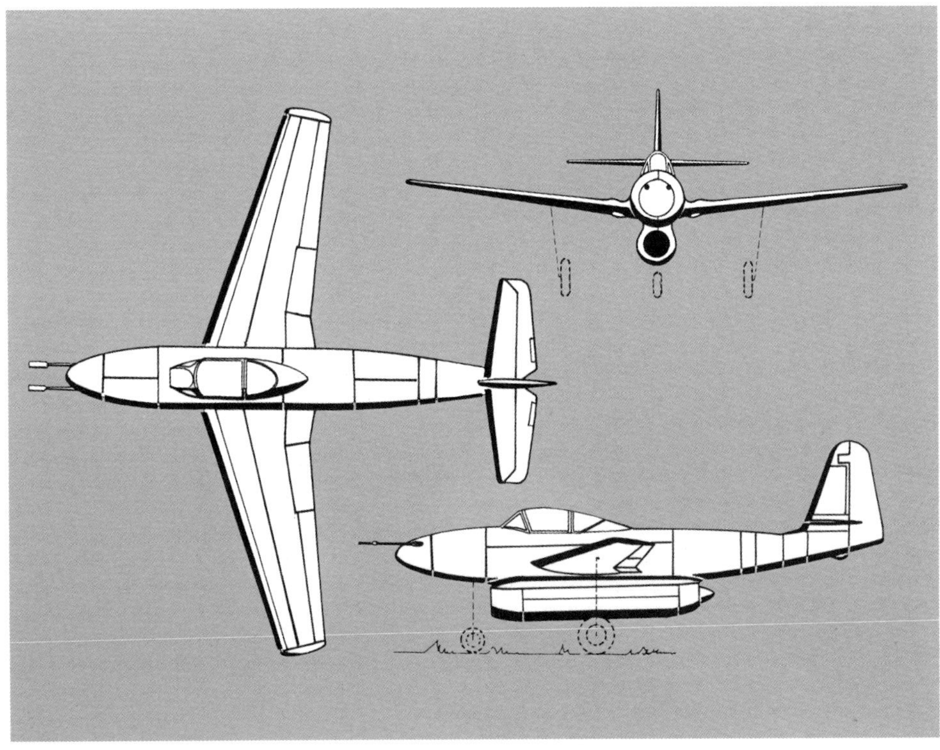

Me P 1095/2 (October 1943)

The Me P 1095 of October 1943 with smaller metal wing and Me 328 tail surfaces.

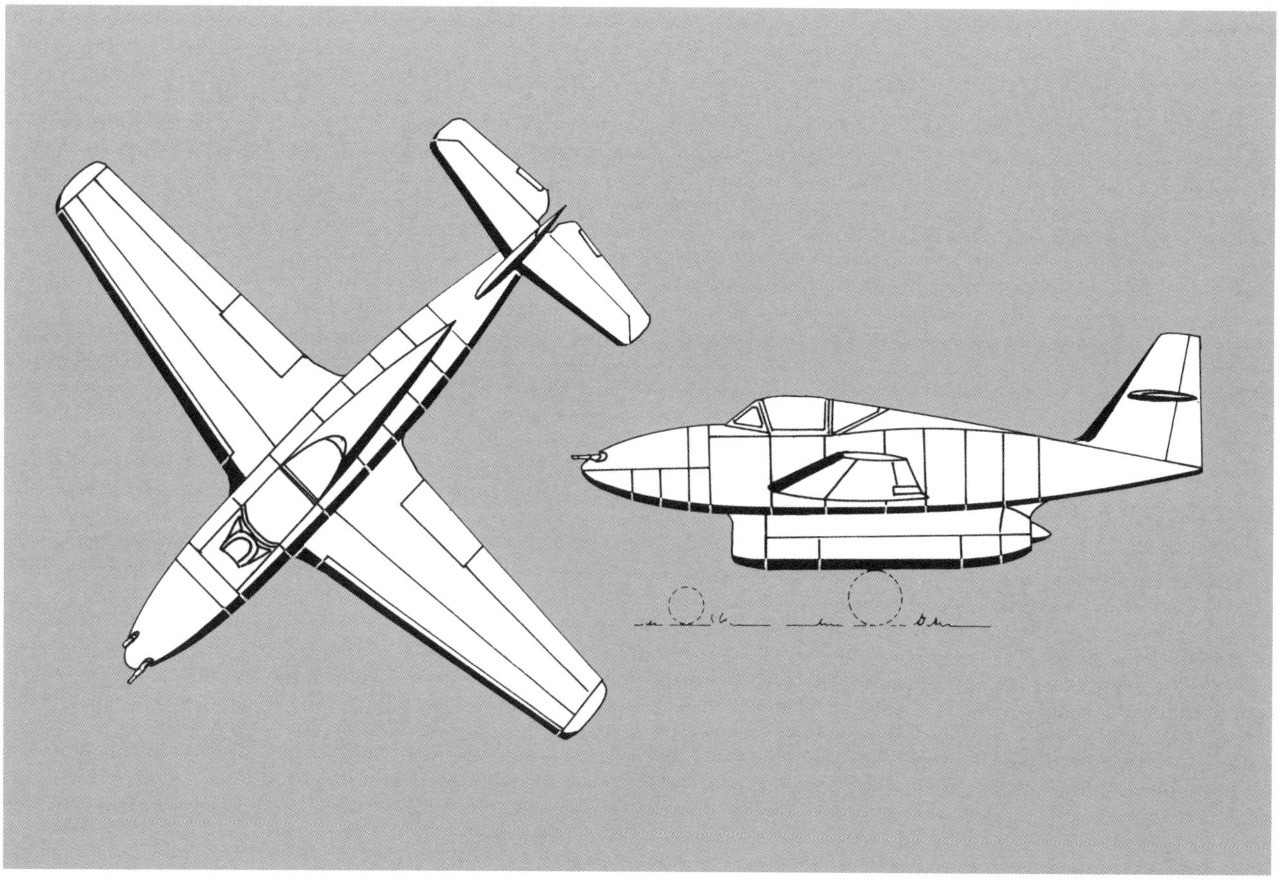

Me P 1095/3 (November 1943)

The Me P 1095 of November 1943 with larger wooden wing and Me 262 tail surfaces.

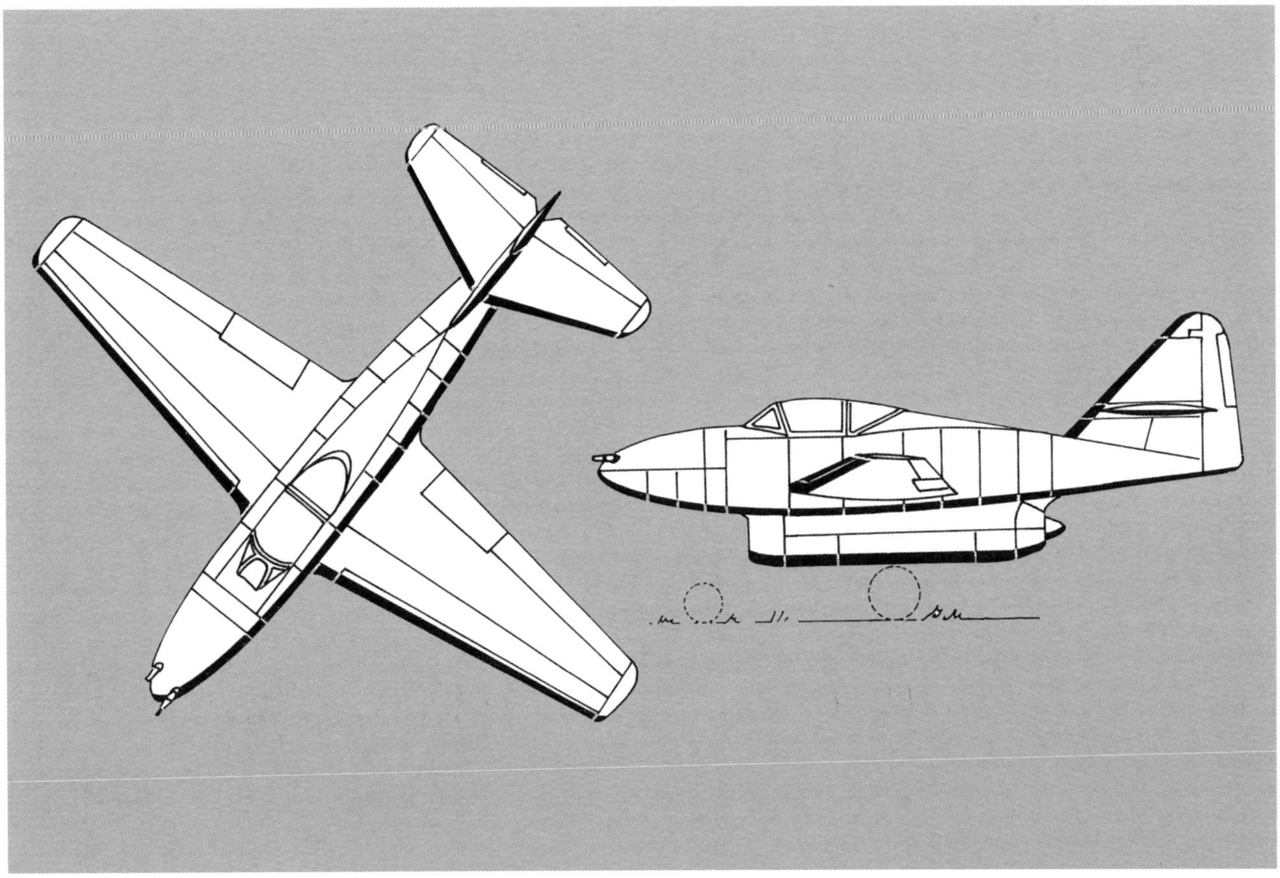

Me P 1099 Jäger / Zerstörer

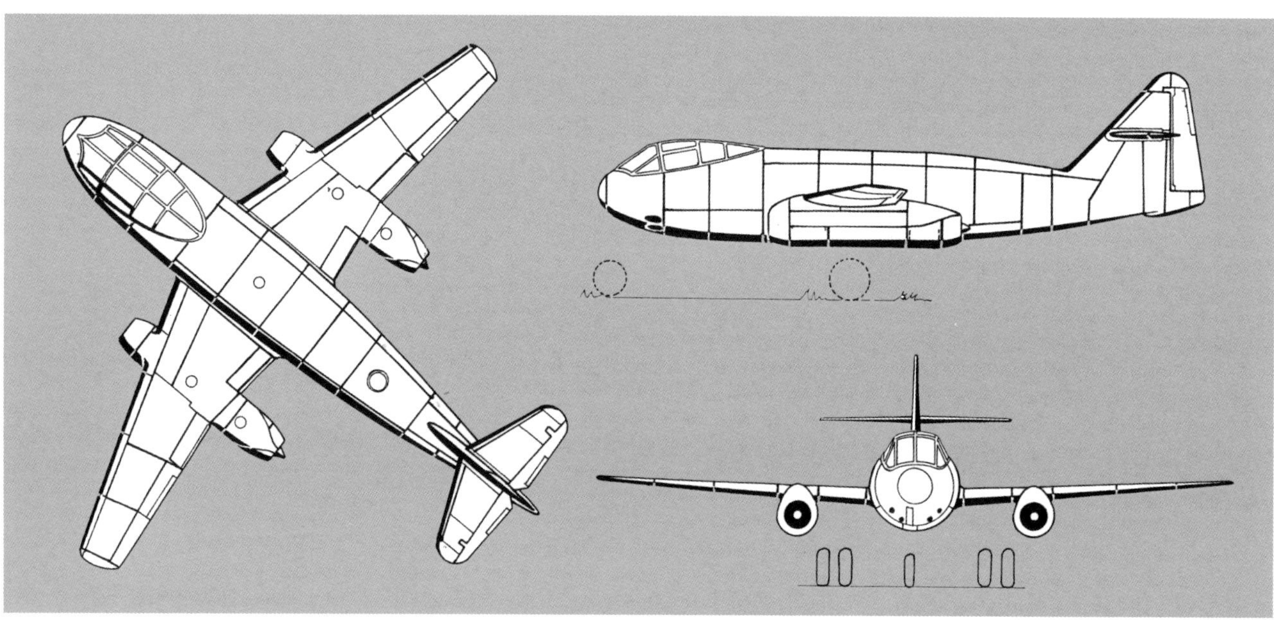

Me P 1099 (Jäger I / Jäger II)

The basic concept of the Me P 1099 proposals stemmed from the Me 262, but with a redesigned fuselage. In the P 1099 (Jäger I), for centre of gravitiy reasons the turbojets were moved significantly to the rear of the wing. Various armament arrangements were proposed which caused the centre of gravitiy position to move, so that with another type of armament, the turbojets could revert to their former position. Initially, 2 x Jumo 004 C were to have been used, to be replaced later by the more powerful HeS 011. The types of armament proposed were:

Jäger I

Version A: 4 x MK 108

Version B: 2 x MK 103

Version C: 2 x MK 108 + 2 x MK 103

Jäger II

Version A: 1 x MK 108 +
1 x MK 112 (55mm)

Version B: 1 x MK 214 (50mm)

Me P 1099 Zerstörer / Heavy Fighter / Night Fighter

Me P 1099 Zerstörer

These Me P 1099 variants envisaged a Zerstörer with 2 x MK 103 + 1 x MK 214 firing forward and 2 x FPL 151 fuselage barbettes; a Heavy Fighter with 4 x MK 108 firing forward + 2 x FPL 151 fuselage barbettes, and a Night Fighter with 4 x MK 108 firing forward and 2 x MK 108 as *Schräge Musik*.

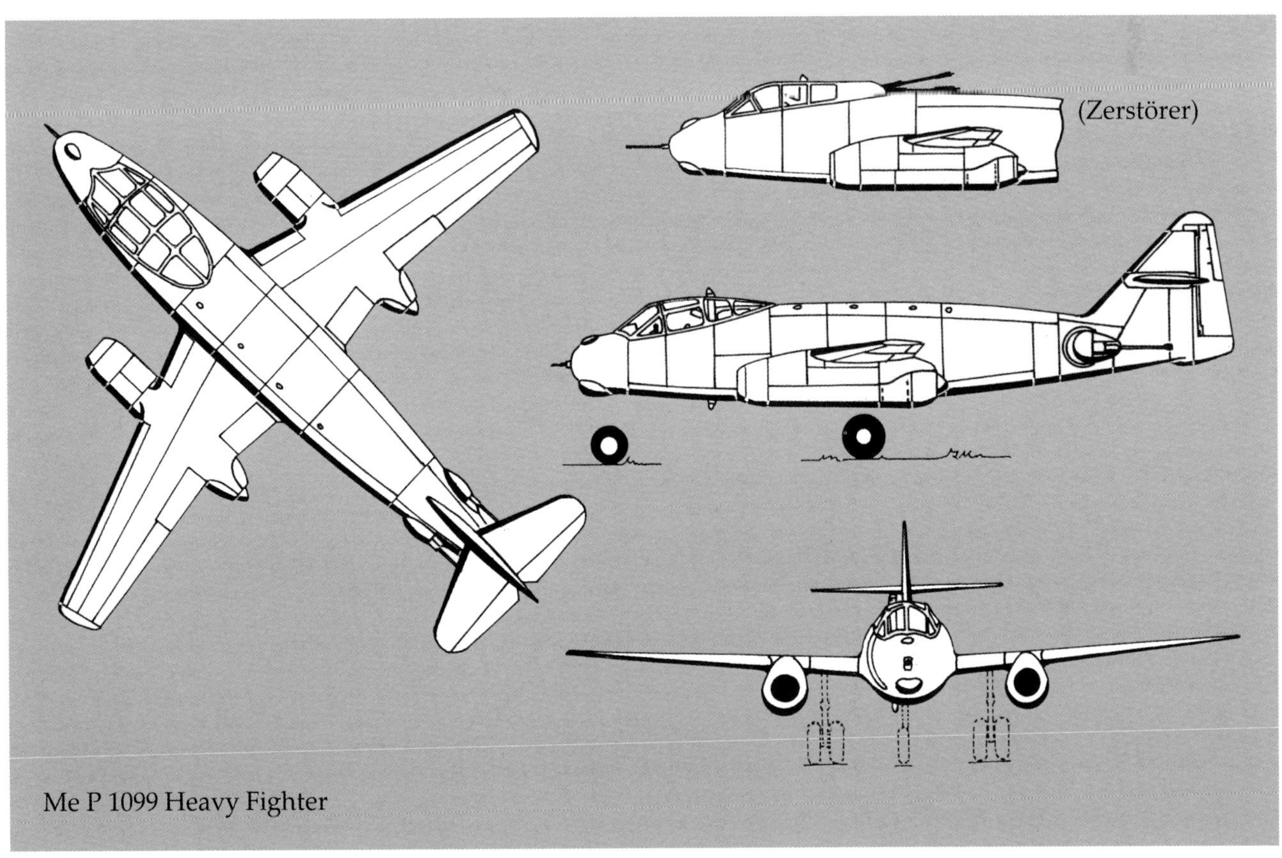

Me P 1099 Heavy Fighter

Me P 1100 Schnellbomber

The Me P 1100 Schnellbomber variants, powered by 2 x Jumo 004C turbojets, were to have carried an internal bombload up to 2,800kg, with provision made for varying forward-firing armament and reduced bombloads. One variant housed a crew of two, whilst a single-seater housed the pilot in a cockpit offset to port. A further variant with swept wings was to have been powered by 2 x HeS 011 turbojets. For more details on the Me P 1099 and P 1100 see *Luftwaffe Secret Projects Volumes 1 & 3* (pages 90-91 and 167-170 respectively).

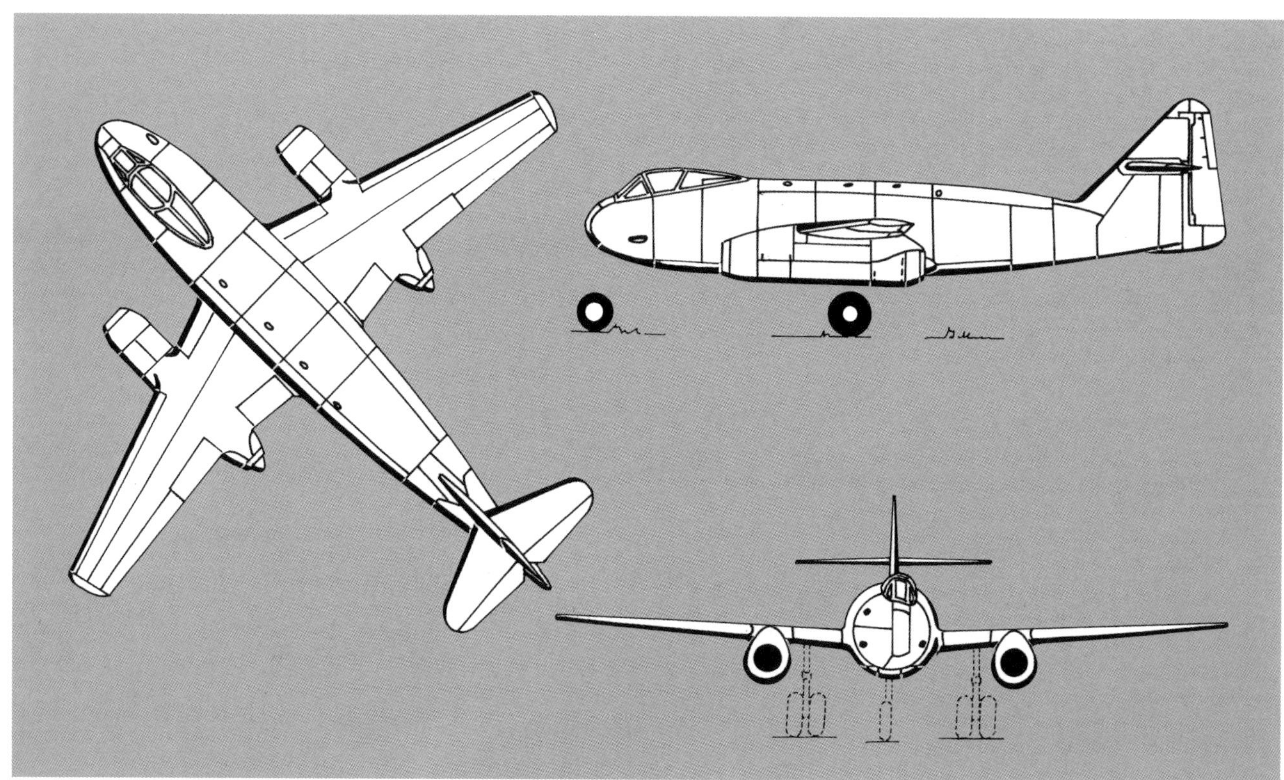

The Me P 1101 Family

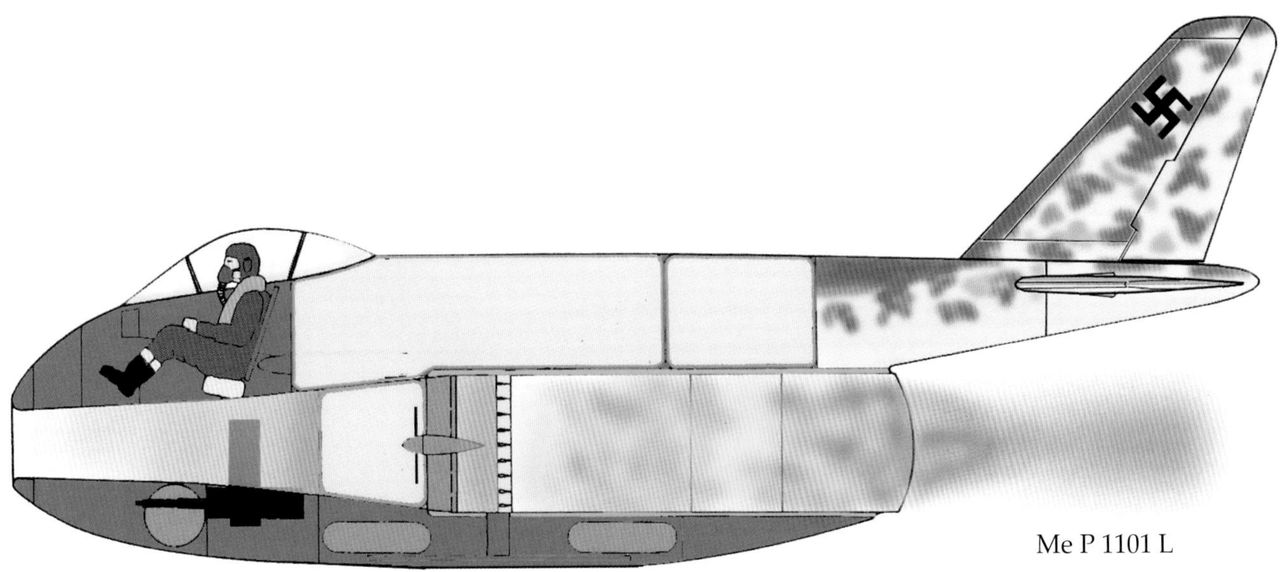

Me P 1101 L

The common designation Me P 1101 actually incorporated several proposals intended for various roles, the list below providing a chronological genealogy of developments.

Date	Designation	Role
25.05.1944	P 1101/97	(not confirmed)
06.06.1944	P 1101/99	4-jet Zerstörer / bomber
29.06.1944	P 1101/XVIII/103	4-jet bomber, trapezoidal wing
01.07.1944	P 1101/XVIII/104	4-jet bomber, crescent wing
11.07.1944	P 1101/XVIII/108	Rotatable biplane wings, alias P 1109
24.07.1944	P 1101/XVIII/?	Single-seat fighter with V-tail
22.08.1944	P 1101/XVIII/?	Further development of preceding project
30.08.1944	P 1101/XVIII/113	Further development of above as Jabo (fighter-bomber)
??.08.1944	P 1101/?	Twin-jet Zerstörer
??.08.1944	P 1101/?	Twin-jet night fighter with compound-sweep M-wings
no date	P 1101/?	Twin-jet swept-wing bomber-formation destroyer
no date	P 1101/?	Tailless, pusher airscrew, bomber-formation destroyer
03.10.1944	P 1101/?	Initial design for a single-jet fighter
08.11.1944	P 1101 V1	Experimental prototype (under construction in May 1945)
13.11.1944	P 1101/?	Series model of the fighter (Entwurf 1)
14.12.1944	P 1101/?	Series model of the fighter (Entwurf 2)
22.02.1945	P 1101/?	Series model of the fighter (Entwurf 3) to series-readiness
no date	P 1101 L	Ramjet-powered variant (illustrated above)

To be sure, one or other P 1101 design study is absent from the above list. To some extent, this may well be established in due course when all authors have more comprehensive details available for publication. Whether the above list is correct in its composition cannot be guaranteed at this point.

The sphere of light-fighter designs by the Messerschmitt firm can only be concentrated upon by omitting the other P 1101 design studies.

Me P 1101/28 Zerstörer

Although this project was worked upon under the P 1101 designation, it somewhat falls out of the orderly lineage as it consisted of a further development of the P 1099 and P 1100. Here again, the possible operational spectrum ranged from the Zerstörer to the bomber role.

Its 40° swept mid-wing is set well forward on the fuselage. Questions not cleared up are the type of armament it was to have carried as a Zerstörer and the mainwheel undercarriage bays (since the turbojets were positioned in-between) as also the configuration of the fuselage nose compartment. For this reason the 3-view shows no armament, and those visible in the flying view are purely fictional.

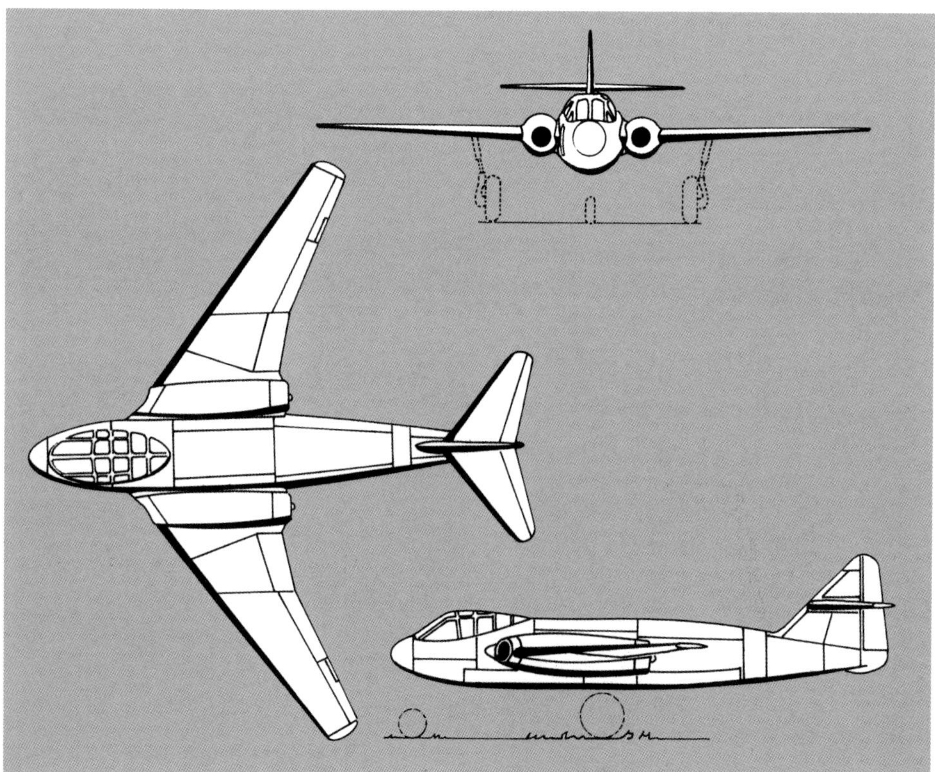

Dimensions

Span	14.30m
Length	12.35m
Height	4.40m

Performance

Max speed	910km/h

Me P 1101/XVIII (24.07.1944)

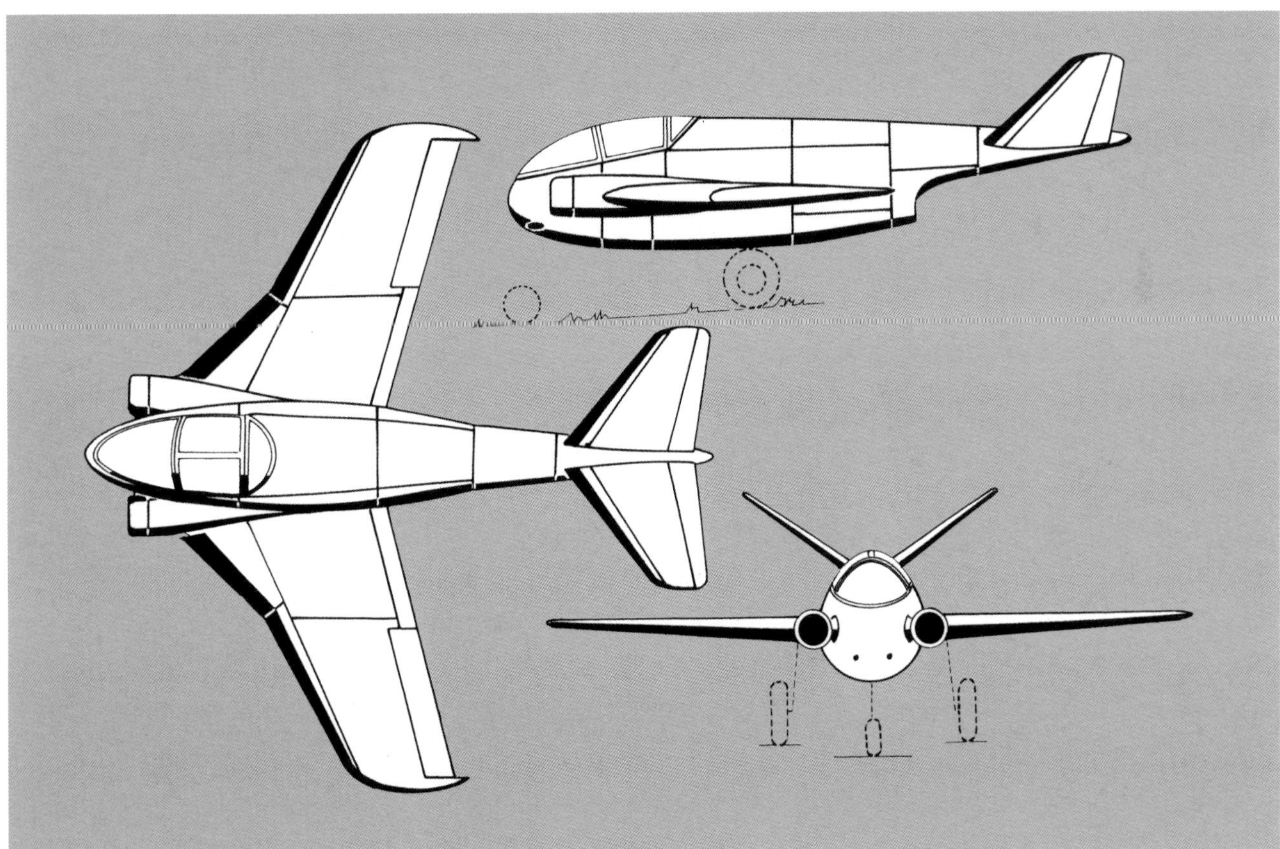

The initial single-seat fighter proposal was a rather plump-looking jet fighter with swept wings, a V-tail and lateral wingroot intakes on either side of a generously glazed cockpit. Although it roughly fulfilled the weight versus performance ratio aimed for, it was still quite far from the latest aerodynamic knowledge.

Span was 7.15m, length 6.85m, fuel load was 710 litres in the fuselage and 2 x 170 litres in wing tanks. The nosewheel retracted rearwards, the mainwheels retracting forwards into the extended wingroots. Armament was 2 x MK(?) in the lower fuselage and provision was made to carry a single external bomb.

Me P 1101 (22.08.1944)

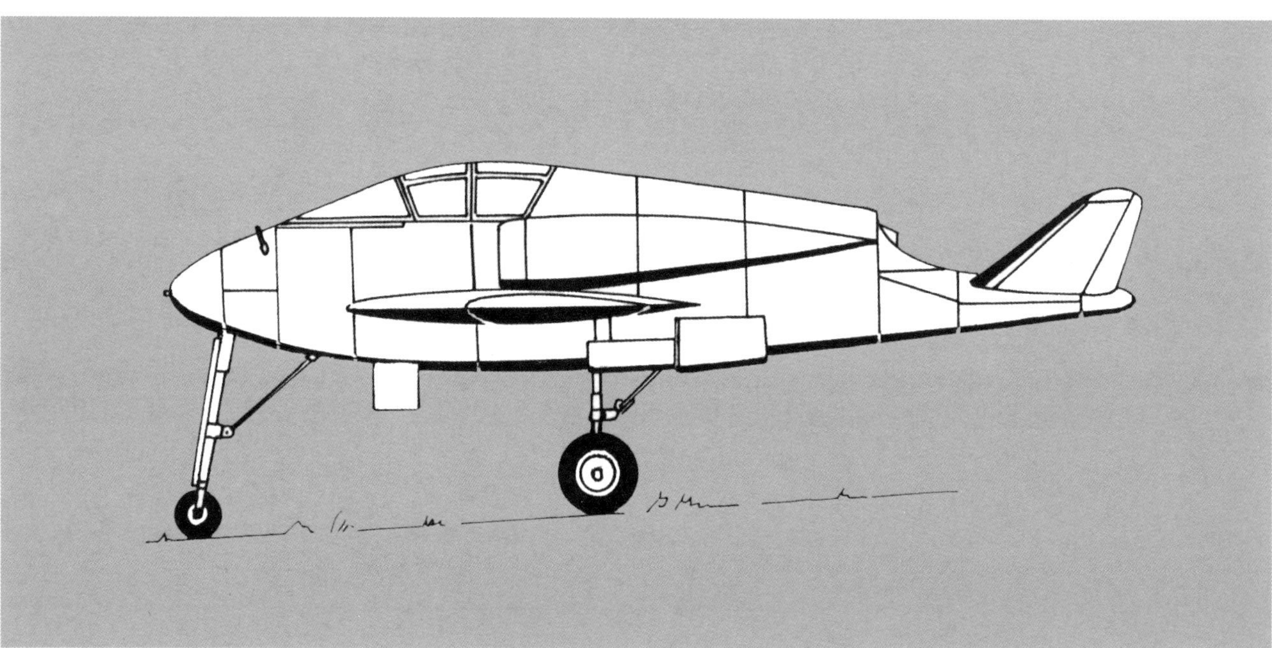

The second proposal shows a more slender fuselage with similarly compound-sweep wings and V-tail, revised lateral air intakes and repositioned turbojet. As it also did not appear to be satisfactory, another solution was proposed a good week later. As often happens, two different drawings have appeared for this aircraft. According to one, published by author Manfried Griehl, the aircraft has a rather stretched appearance, the cockpit leading to the conclusion that it was a single-seater. The final 'crowded' machine was to have been a 2-seater, probably crescent winged, and was to carry an armament of a forward-firing MK 112 and 2 x MK 108 obliquely-firing cannon, with the SG 500 *Jägerfaust* weapon as an alternative.

Me P 1101/XIII-113 (30.08.1944)

This design featured the wing of the Me 262 but with 40° of sweepback, the V-tail being retained. As in the first proposal, the turbojet lay in the lower fuselage, the air lateral intakes being again positioned at the wingroots. Calculations at first indicated the astounding maximum speed of 1,080km/h, but after revised calculations had to be corrected downwards to 1,000km/h. Initial prototypes were planned to be powered by an HeS 011A, the series aircraft having the Jumo 004C, and provision was made in a variant with an auxiliary built-in rocket motor – like that in the Me 262 Heimatschützer (Home Protector).

Dimensions

Span	8.16m
Length	9.37m
Height	3.08m
Wing area	13.50m²

Weights

Equipped	2,624kg
TOW	3,554kg
TOW (max)	4,050kg

Performance

Max speed	c.1,000km/h
Ceiling	14,800m
Range at 7,000m	700km

Armament

2 x MK 108 + 1 x MK 108
or 1 x MK 103 + 1 x MG 151
or 1 x MK 112
or *Schräge Musik* weapons

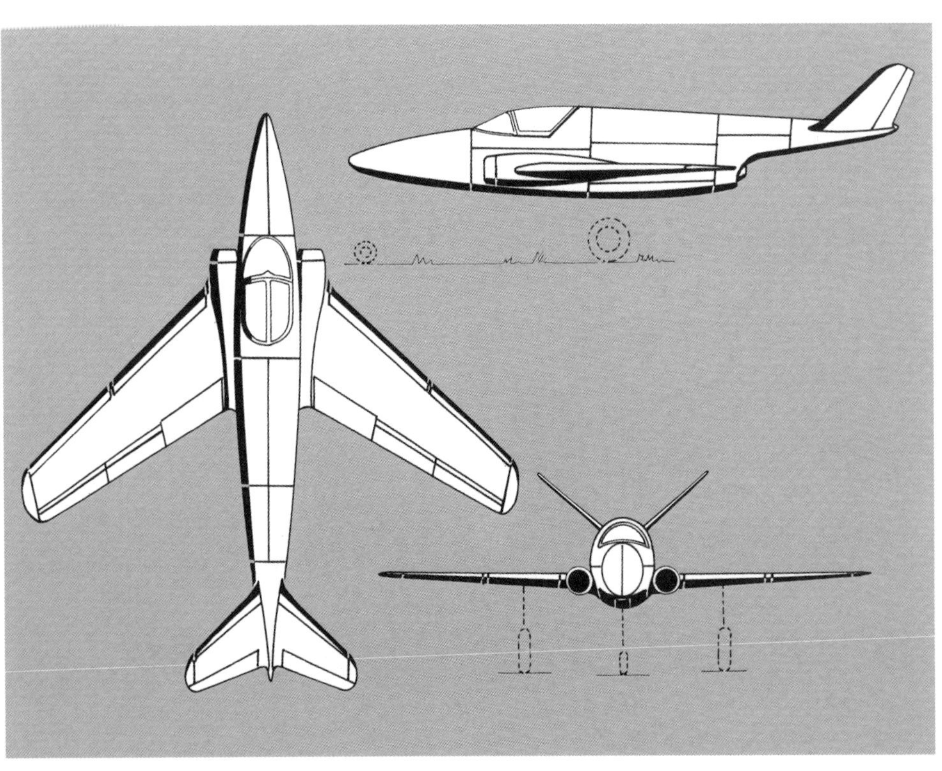

Me P 1101 V1 (14.12.1944)

Dimensions and Weights

Span	8.08m
Length	8.92m
Height	3.72m
Wing area	13.60m²
Equipped weight	2,567kg
Take-off weight	3,863kg
Take-off wt (max)	4,453kg

Performance

Max speed at 7,000m	1,050km/h
Ceiling	13,500m
Climb to 10,000m	10 mins

Armament 2 x MK 108

Powerplant 1 x HeS 011
(with Jumo 004B as emergency solution)

Starting on 30.10.1944, the first configuration drawings for this prototype were initiated, and followed the decision to manufacture an experimental Me P 1101 V1 with which the optimal wing sweepback was to be established. Wing sweep could be varied on the ground between 25° and 45°, and the prototype was almost completely built at the end of the war. It should be noted that it was *not* a variable swept-wing machine, as the sweep angle could not be varied in flight. The P 1102 project, however, pointed the path towards this technology, so that after the war the Americans at the Bell Aircraft Company derived the variable-sweep X-5 out of the captured P 1101 V1 and the variable-sweep P 1102 project.

With the design scheme of 13.11.1944 an aircraft was then developed which by the date of 14.12.1944 was refined into a model fit for series production that had reached its most advanced status as at 22.03.1945. The basic layout incorporated a universal weapons platform that in several roles would determine the future of the Luftwaffe. Below left is a further plan view that shows revised structural alterations made to the wing.

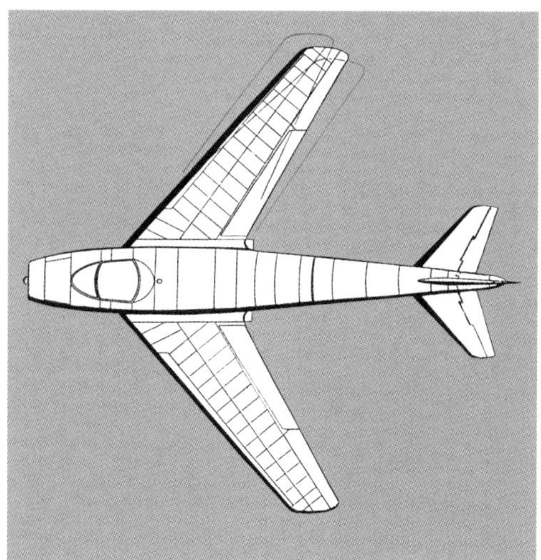

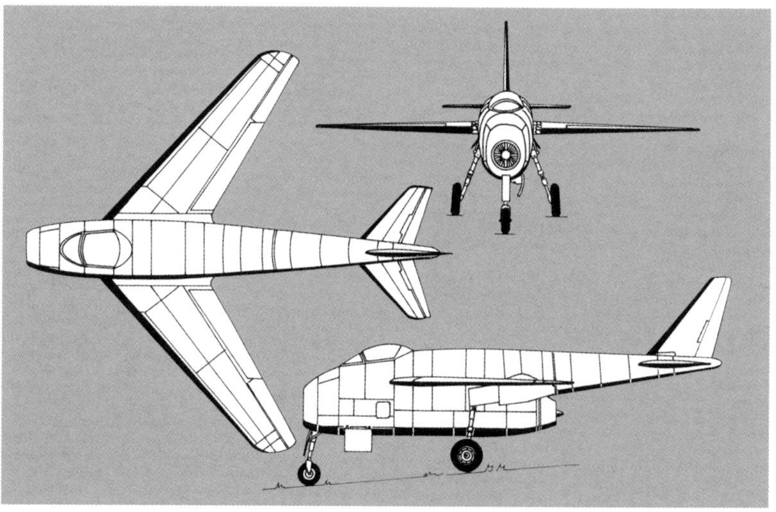

Me P 1101 (22.02.1945)

At the beginning of 1945, design work on the experimental prototype was almost completed. Messerschmitt had interrupted further development of the P 1101 in favour of the P 1106, but had proposed to advance the P 1101 that had a dural fuselage with pressurised cabin and a wooden wing no longer based on that of the Me 262, the tail surfaces likewise constructed of wood. Powerplant was an HeS 011A-0 turbojet.

Dimensions

Span	8.25m
Length	9.18m
Height	3.71m
Wing area	15.25m^2

Performance

Max speed at 7,000m	980km/h
Ceiling	14,000m
Climb to 10,000m	9.5 mins

Armament

4 x MK 108

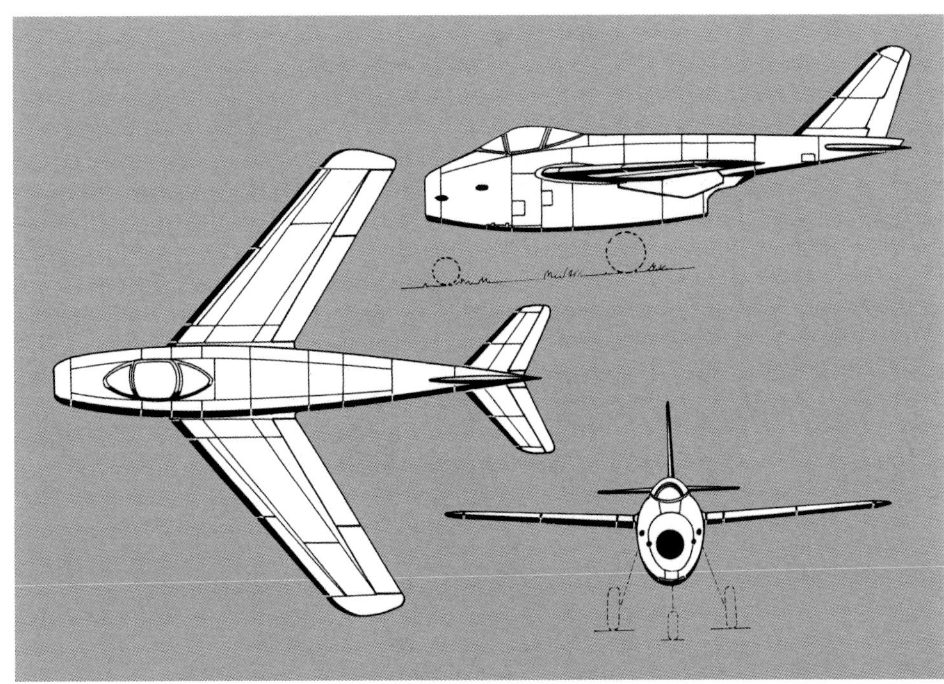

Me P 1101 Night Fighter

The Me P 1101 in its night fighter configuration with T-tail and nose radar housing the parabolic antenna.

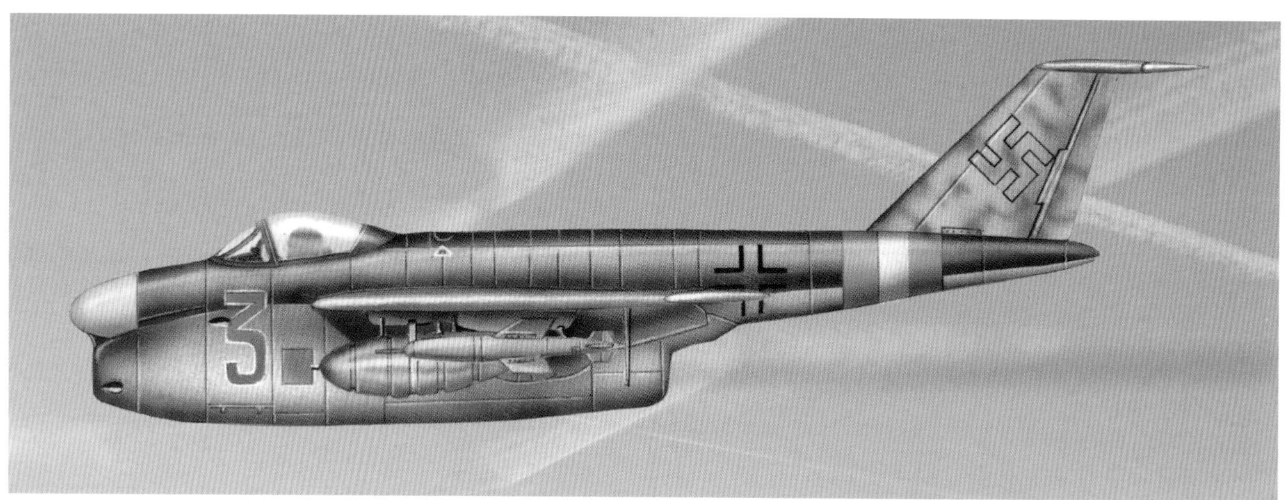

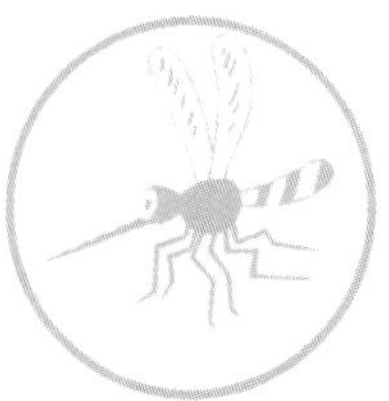

Me P 1101/92 Pulkzerstörer

After heavy-calibre weapons had been tested and successfully put to use in various aircraft ranging from the He 177 to the Ju 87 and Me 262, whether for anti-tank use or for attacks on enemy bombers, projects were also drawn up in which the installation of large-calibre weapons was to have formed the primary armament from the outset.

Although good steerable projectiles against ground targets existed, a self-guided air-to-air rocket was still a weapon of the future. The Boeing B-17 was not called a 'Flying Fortress' for nothing, as it was able to withstand a considerable amount of impacts. But only *one* hit from a large-calibre weapon was enough to destroy it – more than hundreds of smaller projectiles could achieve. The aim was therefore made to consider ever larger cannon as armament, which naturally required aircraft capable of housing such over-dimensioned weapons and of being able to withstand the recoil forces when the projectiles were fired. One of these so-called Pulkzerstörer (bomber-formation destroyers) was the 2-crew aircraft illustrated here.

Dimensions

Span	13.28m
Length	13.10m
Height	4.10m
Wing area	35.00m^2

Powerplant

2 x HeS 011 A turbojets

Armament

1 x 7.5cm Bordkanone or an underslung SD 1700B bomb. A version was also proposed with an external fairing enclosing the bomb but was rejected as unsuitable, especially in the event that two bombs were to be carried.

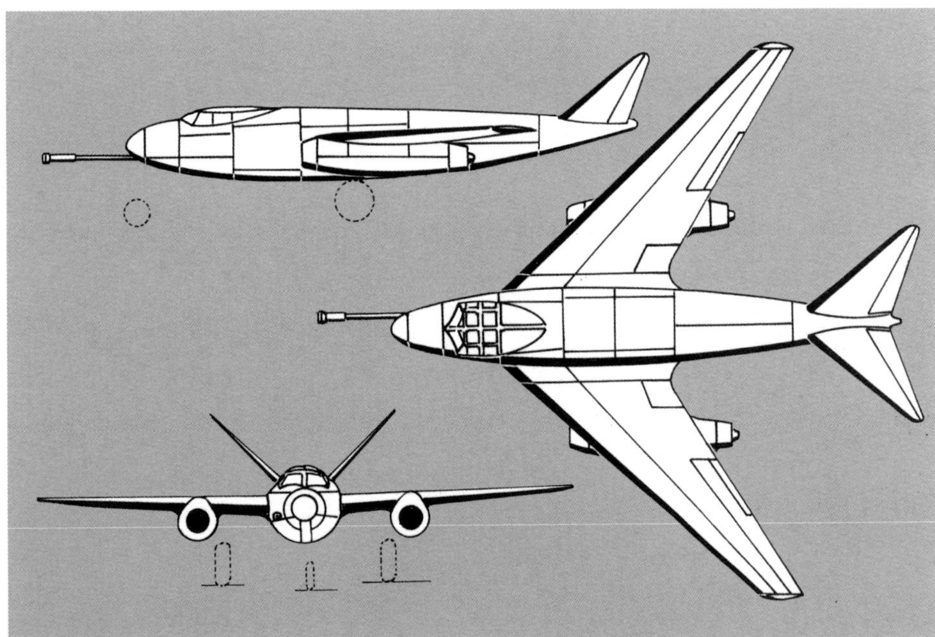

P 1101/92 Zerstörer / Night Fighter

As an alternative to the preceding project, a tailless Pulkzerstörer was drawn up that featured twin fins and rudders at the tips of the swept wings. It retained the forward fuselage, cockpit, and armament of the P 1101/92. Not known is what piston engine(s) driving pusher propellers would be installed, the radiator being in the form of a large hood on the rear dorsal fuselage.

Another proposal, strongly resembling the Arado II, was a 2-seat swept-wing aircraft powered by two turbojets mounted in underwing nacelles. The Me P 1101 drawings of August 1944 lead to the conclusion that its basic configuration was laid out as a Zerstörer and night-fighter. Yet a third (below) featured a compound swept wing: sharp forward sweep on the inner third of the wing, and rearward sweep outboard of the engine nacelles.

Messerschmitt Me P 1101/99 (06.06.1944)

It can be argued as to whether large aircraft in the project stage, all of which were capable of being equipped with large-calibre weapons, belong under the heading Zerstörer or Pulkzerstörer merely because the possibility existed for such weapons to be installed. The Luftwaffe equally needed fast bombers and hence aircraft of this size are the last that will be mentioned in this volume in the Zerstörer category, all others being included in the next volume devoted to bombers.

The 2-seat Me P 1101/99 was to have been powered by 4 x HeS 011 turbojets. Armament was a 7.5cm Pak 40 cannon; its large dimensions also allowed room for 5 x MK 112s. With a wing sweep of 45° and with the above turbojets, it was expected to attain a maximum speed of 960km/h.

Dimensions and Weights

Span	15.40m
Length	15.20m
Height	4.90m
Wing area	47.00m^2
Take-off weight	18,360kg
Fuel load	7,650 litres

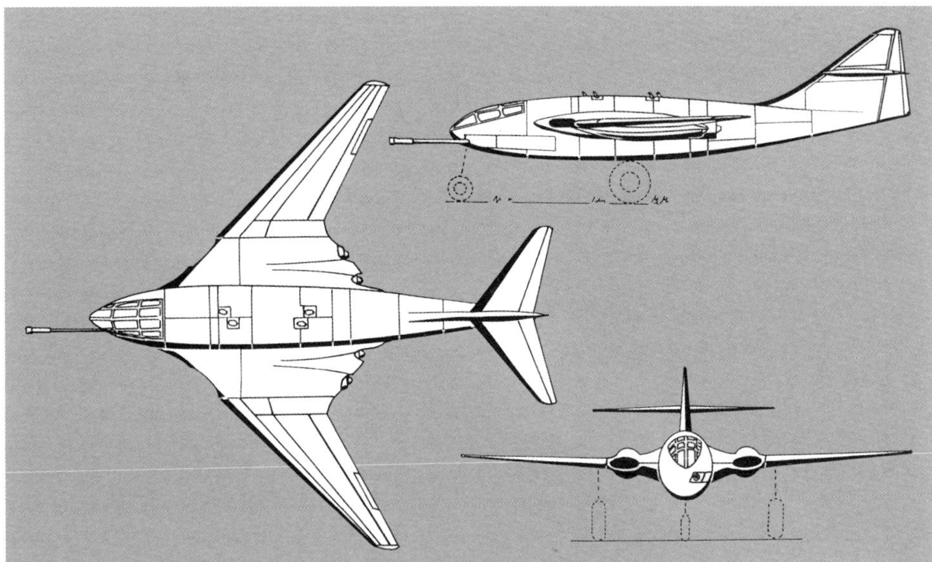

Me P 1102/105 (1944)

Whereas the two underslung turbojets on either side of the fuselage nose are more than conspicuous, it can hardly be believed that yet a third engine was mounted at the fuselage rear, fed from a dorsal air intake ahead of the empennage. Not only that, the $27m^2$ wing geometry of this Schnellbomber and Zerstörer was capable of being altered in flight, making it a true swing-wing aircraft. Variable in sweep between 15° and 50°, it had a calculated maximum speed of 1,010km/h and, with a 3,000kg bombload, had a range of 1,900km. A single-seater, it was powered by 3 x HeS 011 turbojets.

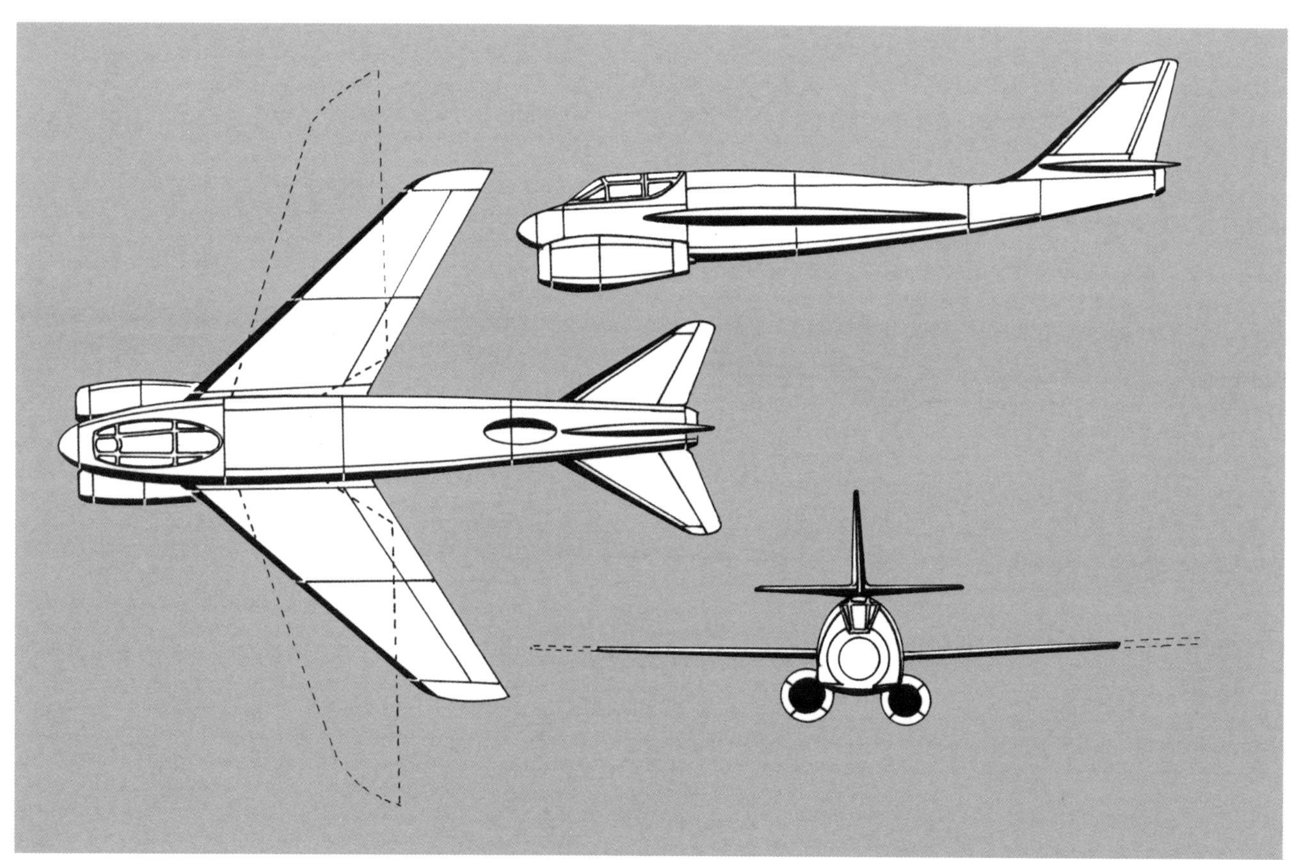

Me P 1103 (06.07.1944)

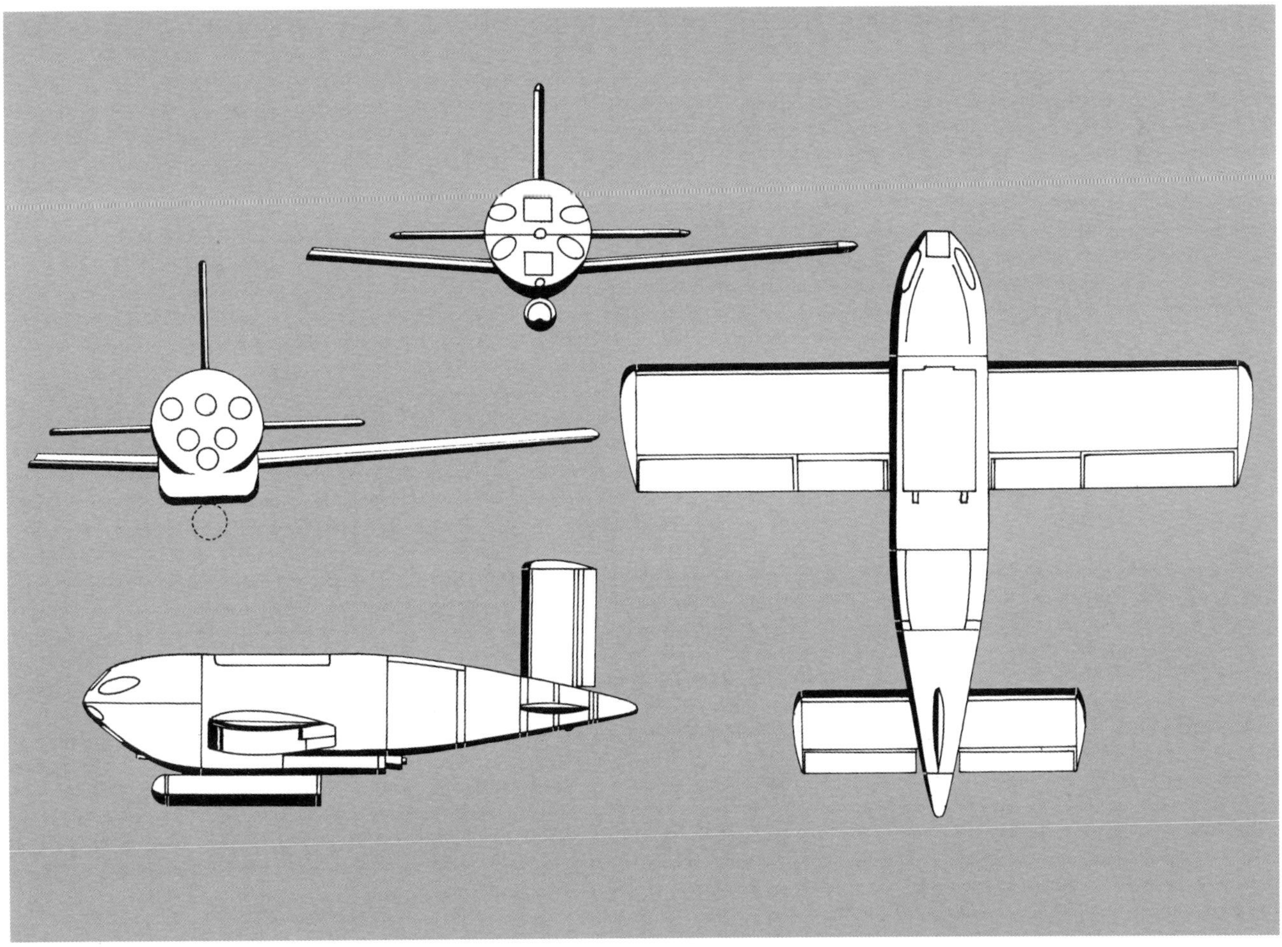

Me P 1103 (12.09.1944)

The designations P 1103 and P 1104 encompassed a number of Bordjäger that were carried aloft and air-launched. The P 1103 of 06.07.1944 with prone pilot and a length of less than 5m was the smallest proposal. Four external solid-propellant RATO units were to have brought it to attack or, alternatively, escape speed. Armament was a single MK 108 beneath the pilot, and auxiliary weapons (Würfkörper 28/32cm) were possible. The project of 12.09.1944 depicts a slightly longer aircraft powered by a liquid-propellant rocket motor, a long-barrelled weapon and seated pilot, with landing on a skid. The earlier project was also to have been used as a Rammer. Precise details of both were not available.

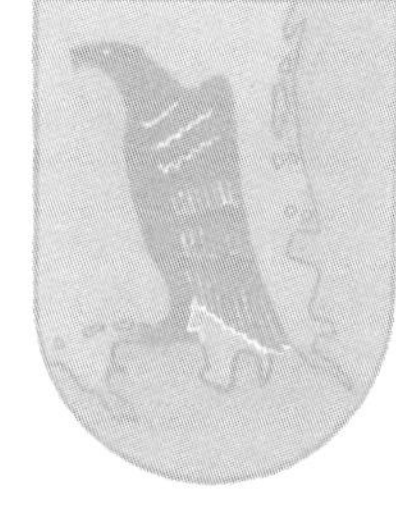

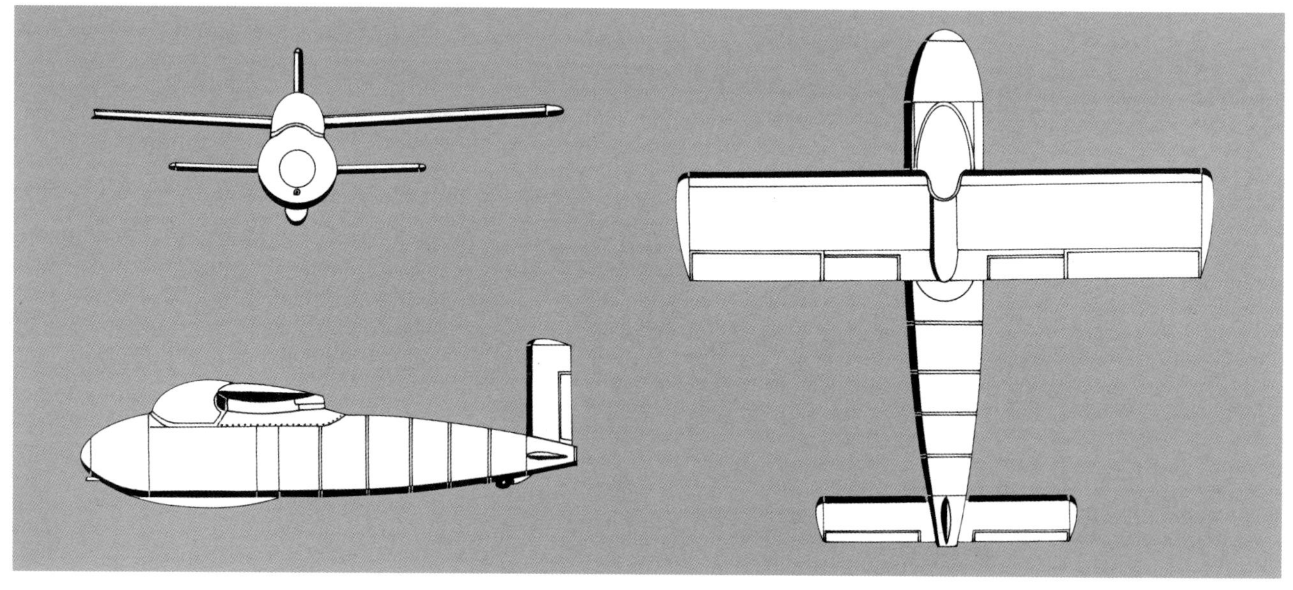

Me P 1103 B (06.07.1944)

With the same overall configuration, simplest type of construction (wood) and rectangular Fi 103 *Reichenberg* wings and tailplane, the P 1103 B had the refinement of retractable narrow-track mainwheels and a nose skid. Accuracy of the data provided cannot be guaranteed.

	Me P 1103/1 ?	**Me P 1103/2 ?**	**Me P 1103/B ?**
Powerplant	4 x Schmidding 109-513	1 x 500kpst HWK RI-202	1 x HWK 109-509A-2
Span	6.20m	5.38m	5.30m
Length	4.70m	5.00m	5.30m
Height	2.08m	1.75m	1.80m
Weight	1,200kg	1,110kg	

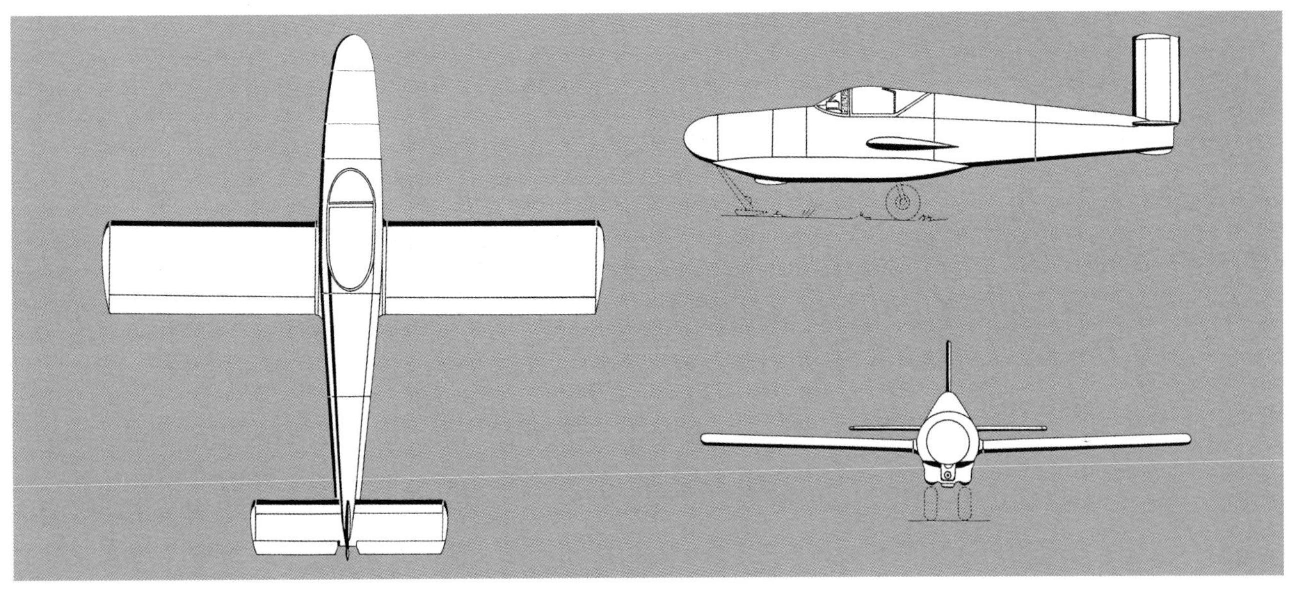

Me P 1104

Me P 1104 (10.08.1944 and 22.09.1944)

Although the Bordjäger – seven in all – were very similar in overall concept, the Messerschmitt AG tendered these in the competition for an Objektschützjäger (target-defence interceptor). By again employing the simplest construction, the P 1104 proposals were equipped with the more powerful HWK 509A-2 rocket motor, which had an auxiliary 300kp thrust cruising chamber.

Work on the project was terminated when the decision had been made to proceed with the Bachem Ba 349 Natter (Viper).

Dimensions and Weight

Span	5.30m
Length	5.00m
Height	1.56m
Max weight	2,540kg

Performance

Max speed	840-930km/h
Range	c.90km

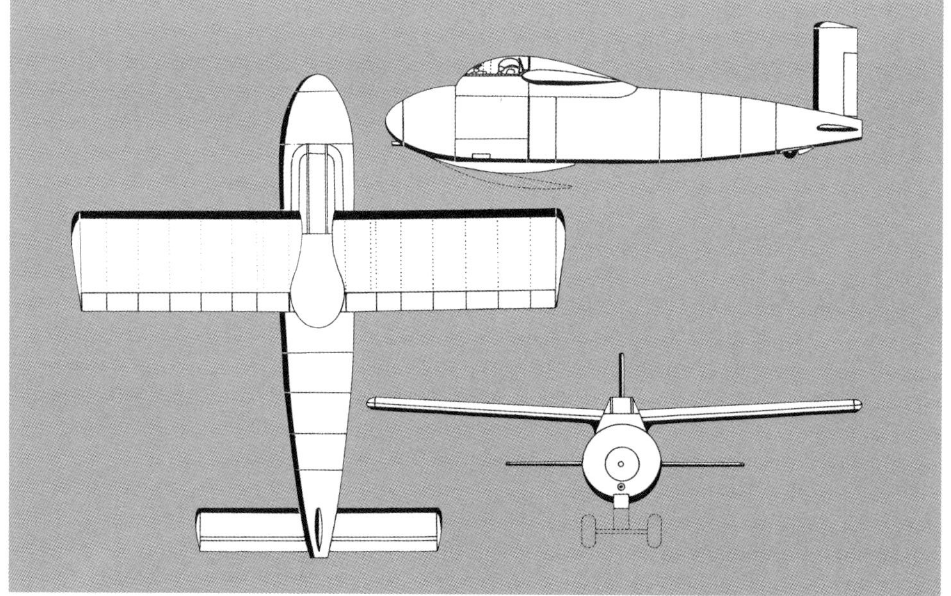

Me P 1104 (10.08.1944)

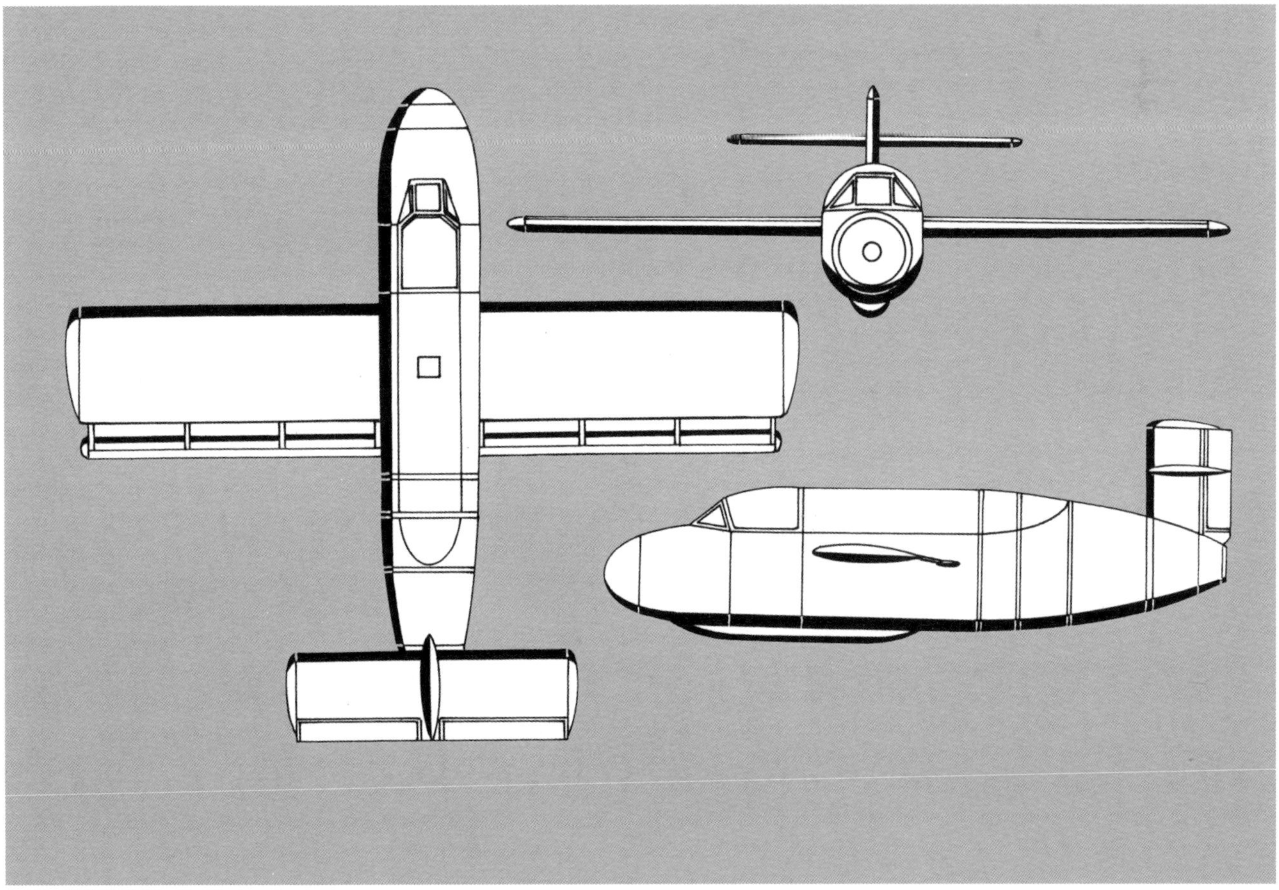

Me P 1104 (22.09.1944)

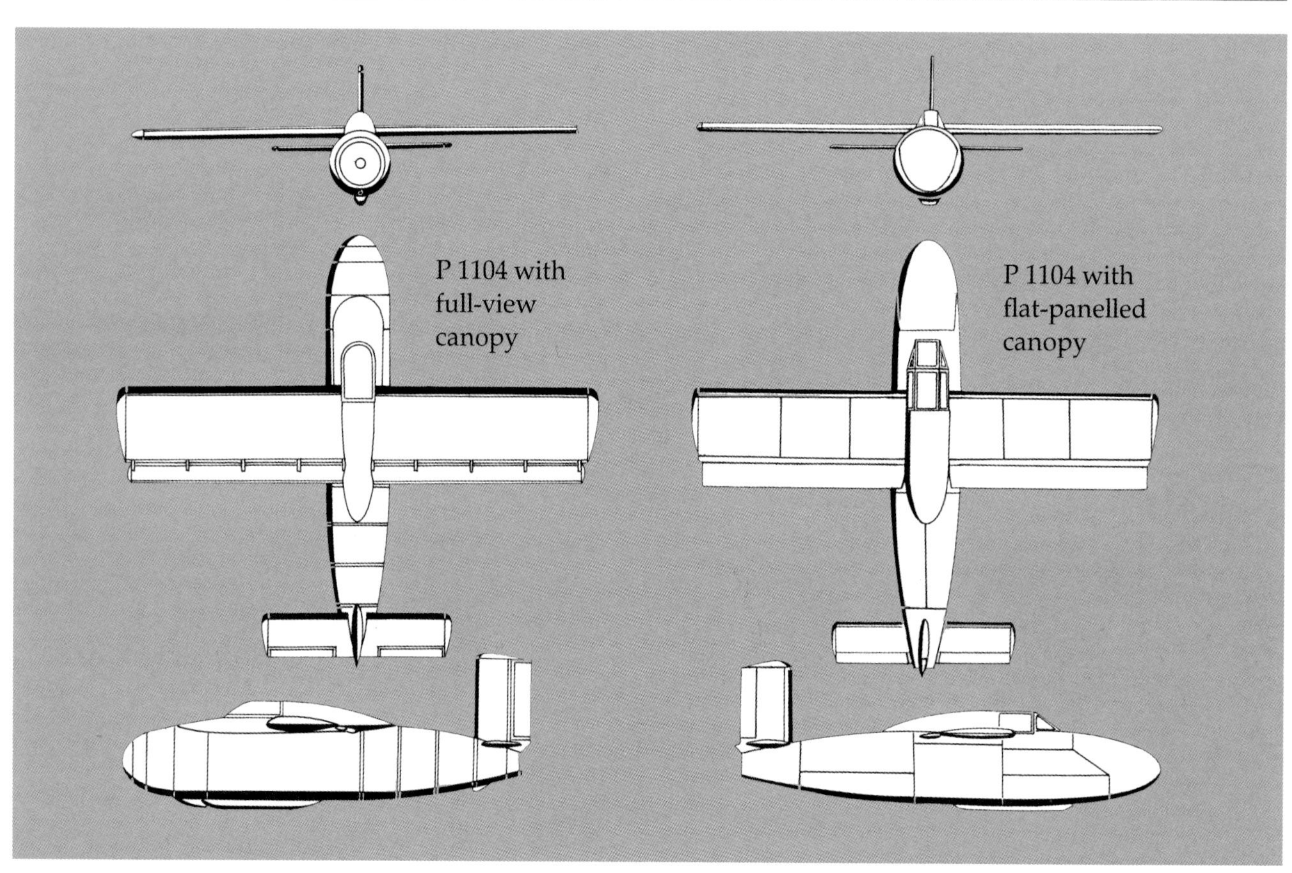

Me P 1106 (12.12.1944)

All in all, the P 1106 projects represented alternative solutions to the P 1101 series. Only the P 1106 R differed in that it was powered by a rocket motor. The basic outlines of the two variants overleaf are shown. Span was 6.74m, length 8.00m, height 3.12m and powerplant an HeS 011.

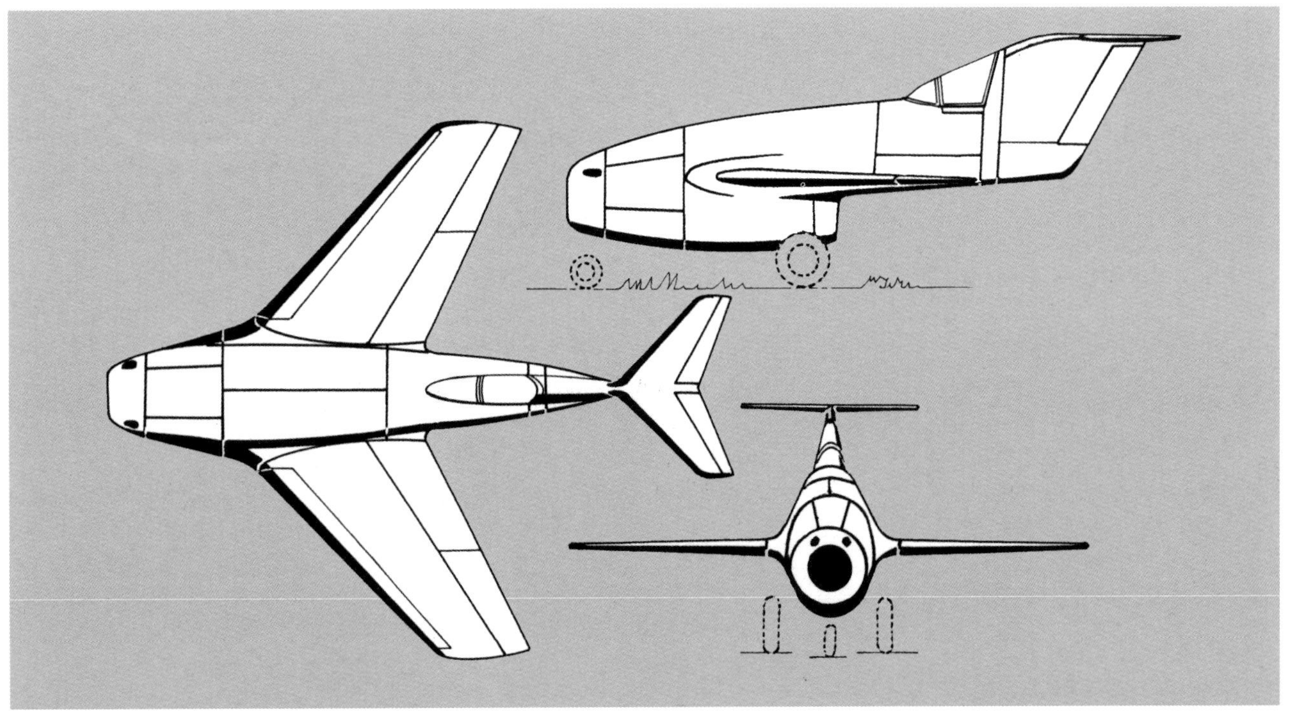

Me P 1106 (End of 1944)

From the design aspect, this appears as an interim scheme between the P 1106 of 12.12.1944 and that of 11.01.1945. Span was 6.00m, fuselage length 6.50m and height 2.85m.

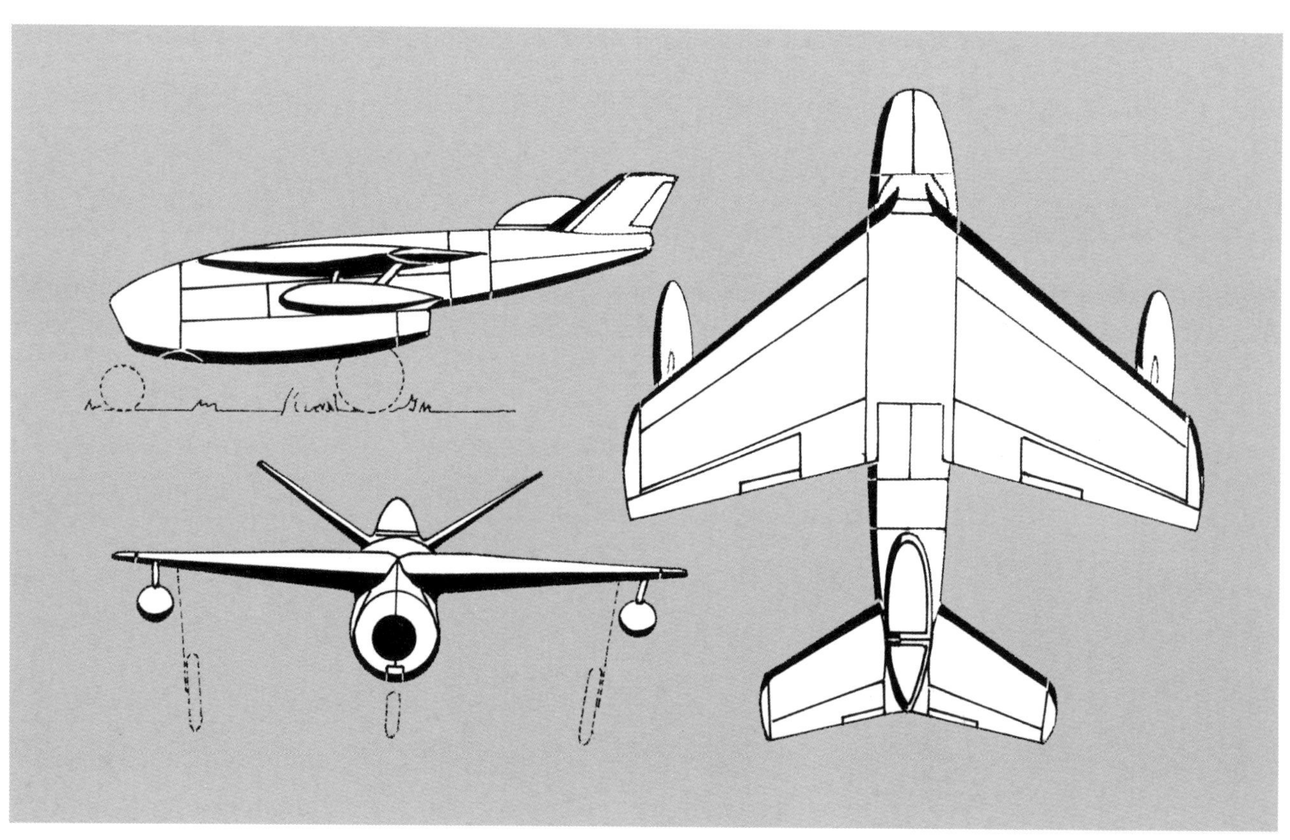

Me P 1106 (11.01.1945)

Dimensions and Weights

Span	6.65m
Length	9.19m
Height	3.37m
Wing area	13.17m^2
Equipped weight	2,300kg
Take-off weight	4,000kg

Performance (1 x HeS 011)

Max speed at 7,000m	993km/h
Ceiling	13,300m

Armament

2 x MK 108 in fuselage nose

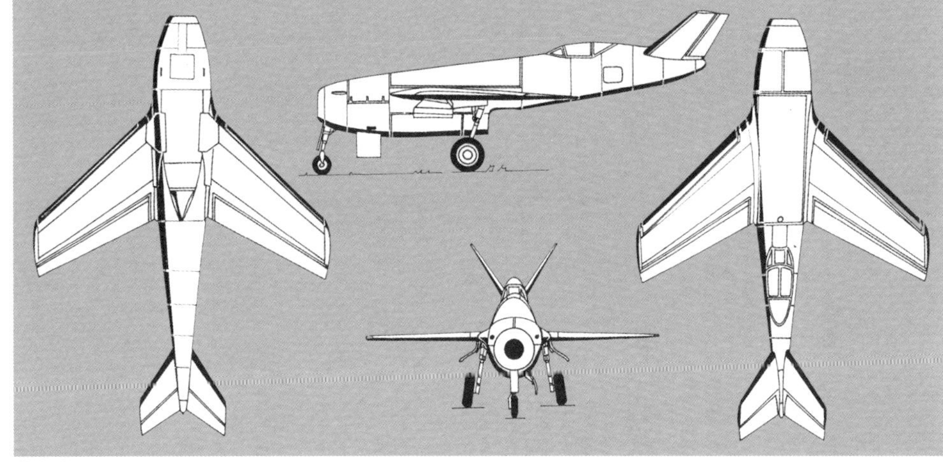

The improved performance and field of vision for the pilot in the parallel P 1101, P 1110 and P 1111 projects led to termination of further work on the P 1106.

Me P 1106 R (14.12.1944)

It would appear that a parallel development of the last P 1106 variant was drawn up under the above date for a rocket-powered version instead of a turbojet. Because of the aggressive nature of the C- and T-Stoff propellants, the use of wood (for the wings) was not possible so that the aircraft had to be of all-metal construction. With the more powerful 2,000kp thrust HWK 109-509 S2 rocket motor, a maximum speed in the supersonic region would have been possible. The quantity of fuel carried was expected to provide this target-defence interceptor with an endurance of 12 minutes and enable a high rate of climb and ceiling as well as an acceptable range to be attained.

Dimensions

Span	6.74m
Length	8.42m
Height	3.05m
Wing area	13.00m^2

Weights

Empty weight	1,700kg
Take-off weight	4,000kg

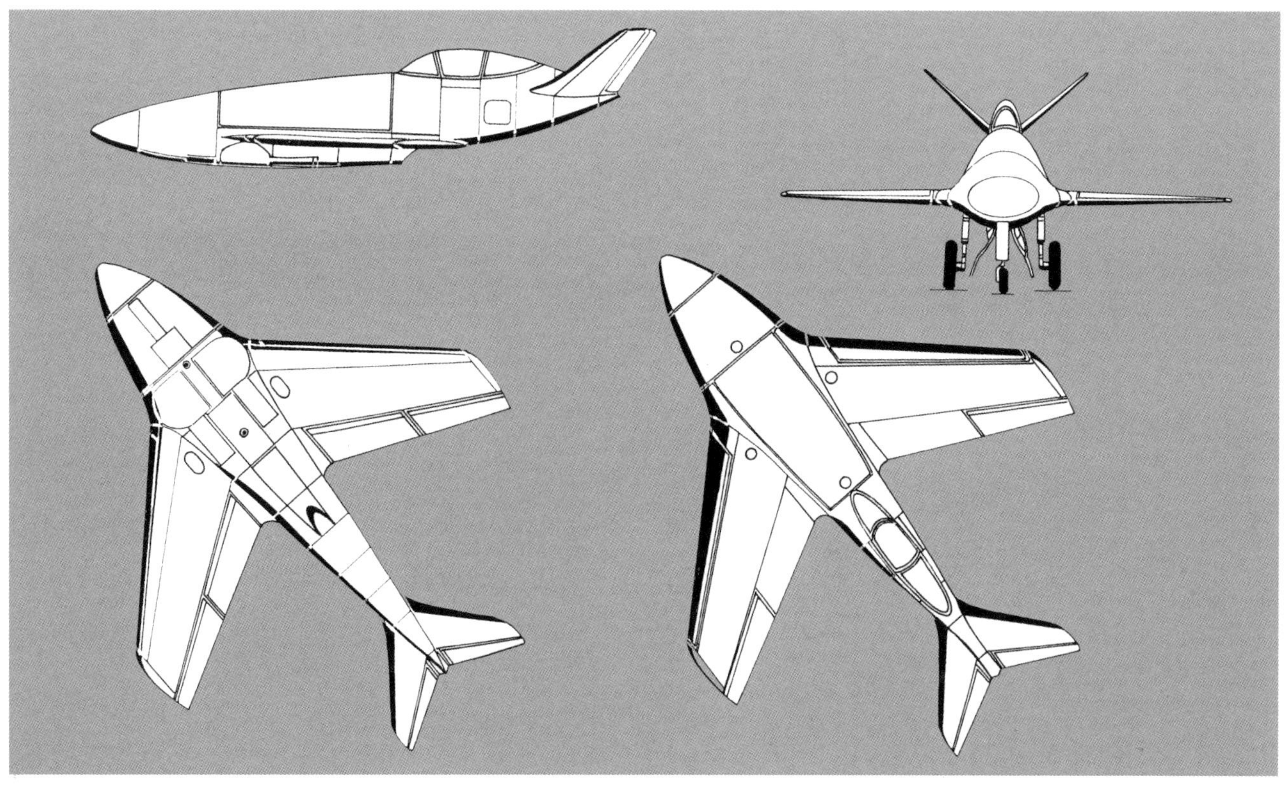

Me P 1109-01 (11.02.1944)

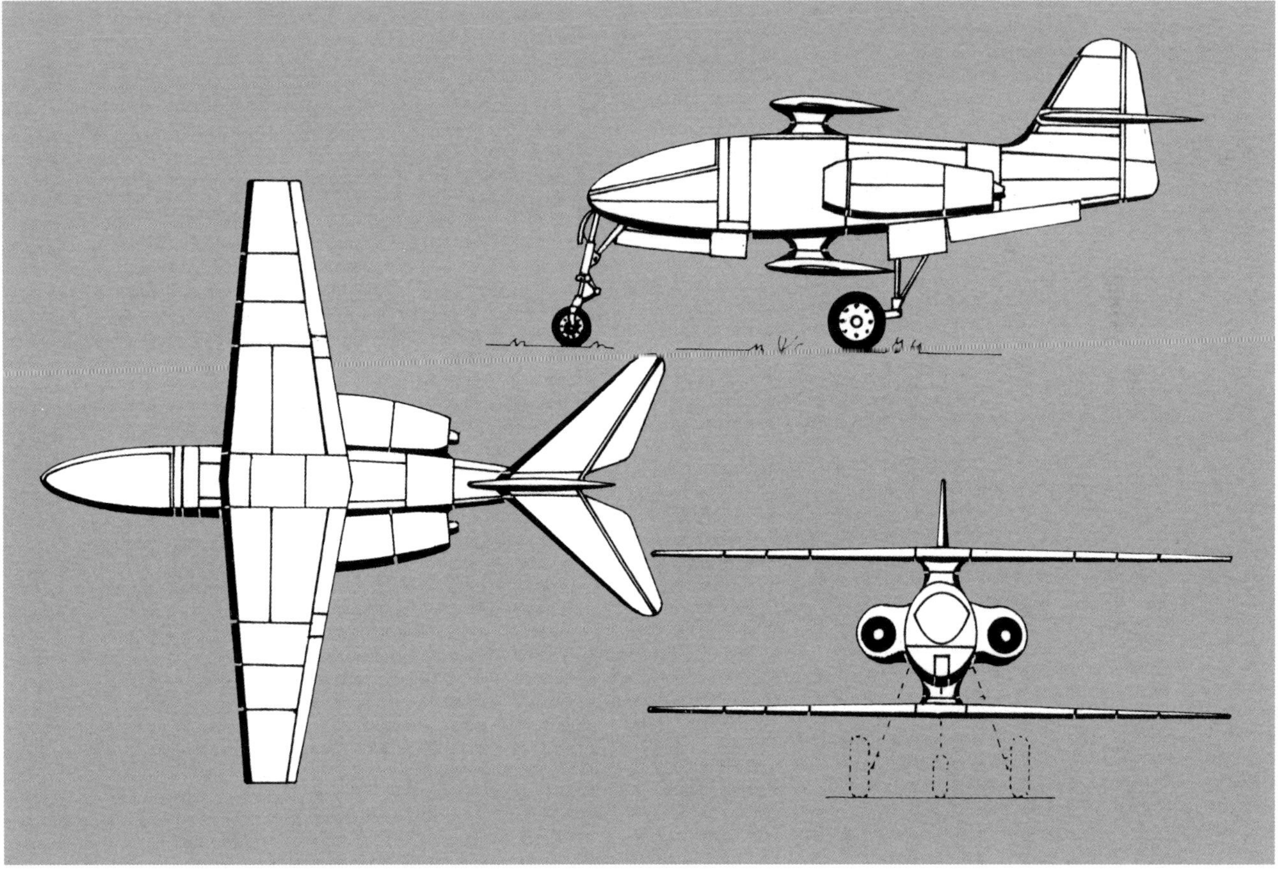

This project number has not been definitely established since design drawings were also made under the P 1101/XVIII-100 series. The idea behind this project corresponds to that of the BV P 202 with the difference that a pair of wings above and below the fuselage, in their normal unswept position for take-off and landing, could be swivelled in opposite directions for high-speed flight. After the war, a sketch was published in France that indicated that the project there was pursued further. Powerplants were 2 x HeS 011 turbojets and dimensions were similar to the Me P 1109-02.

Me P 1109-02 (17.07.1944)

A 3-view drawing of this proposal under the above date was noted as the P 1101/XVIII-108 and insets noted that a single swivel-wing was also considered where only the upper wing was pivoted above the fuselage, all other design details remaining unchanged. Powerplants were 2 x HeS 011 turbojets; span (unswept) was 9.40m, length 12.05m and height (without undercarriage) 3.34m. Performance and armament data are not available.

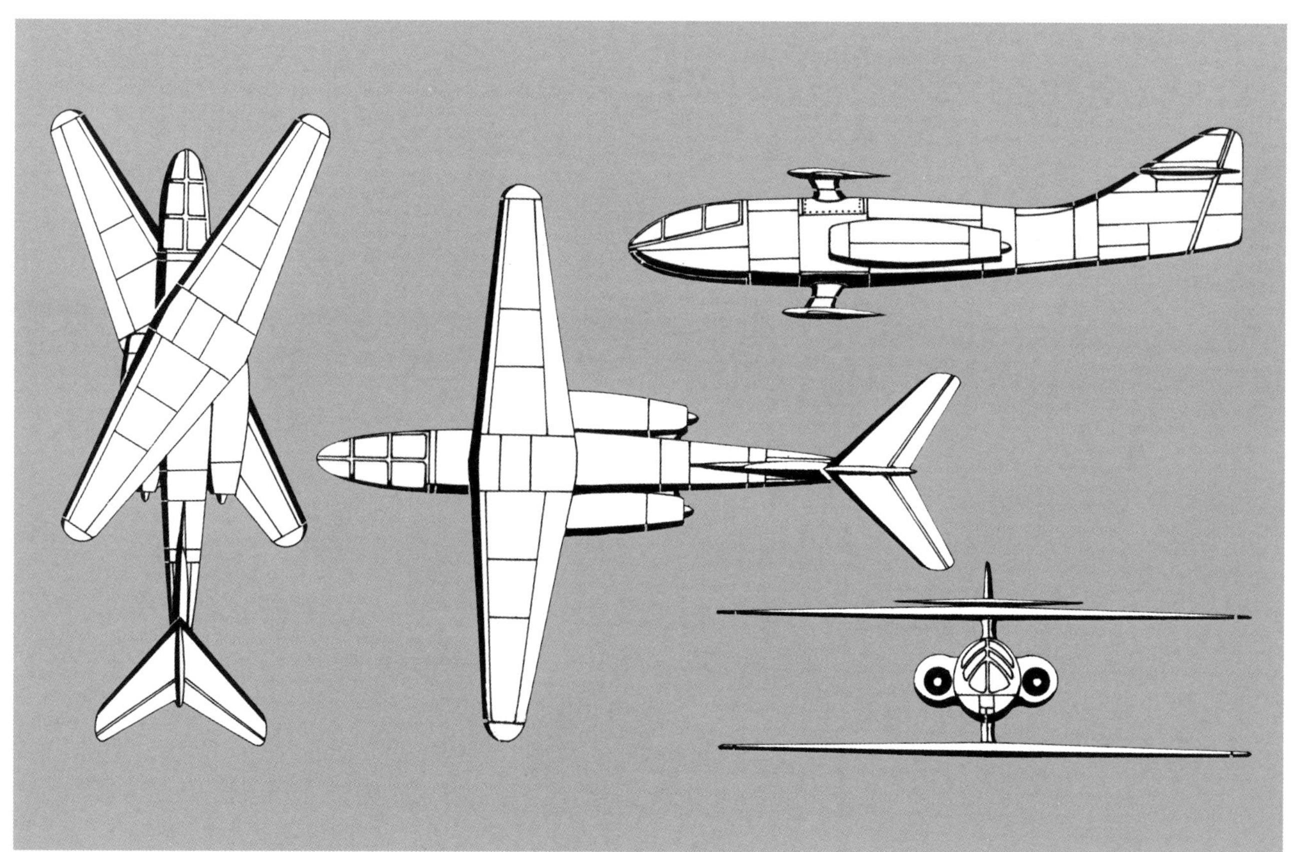

Me P 1110/155 (22.02.1945)

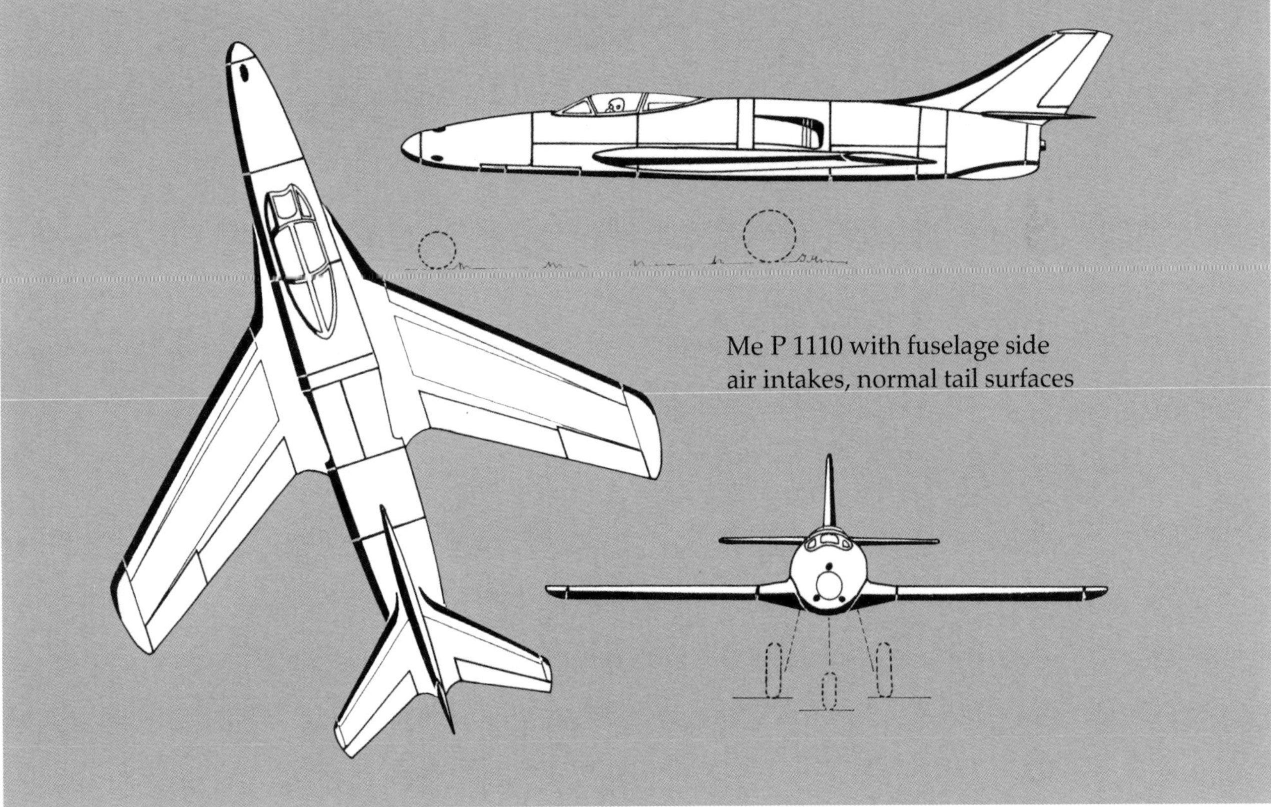

Me P 1110 with fuselage side air intakes, normal tail surfaces

In the P 1110 series of projects, attempts were made (after the P 1106) to again achieve an optimal fuselage shape with a smaller cross-section. The most important question to be resolved was the location and shape of the air intakes for the HeS 011 turbojet housed in the rear fuselage. Three variations were therefore considered that had two features in common: wing strakes that extended forward at the roots to enable higher angles of attack, and a boundary-layer suction blower that would be driven by the turbojet itself. The variant shown here has lateral air intake scoops aft of the wingroot trailing edges.

Me P 1110 (12.01.1945)

The date of this variant indicates that it was an alternative solution in which the HeS 011 air intakes were positioned in extended wingroots that called for rather long ducting. At that time, insufficient information was available on the flow characteristics of the various types of ducts selected and it therefore presented a certain development risk in terms of time.

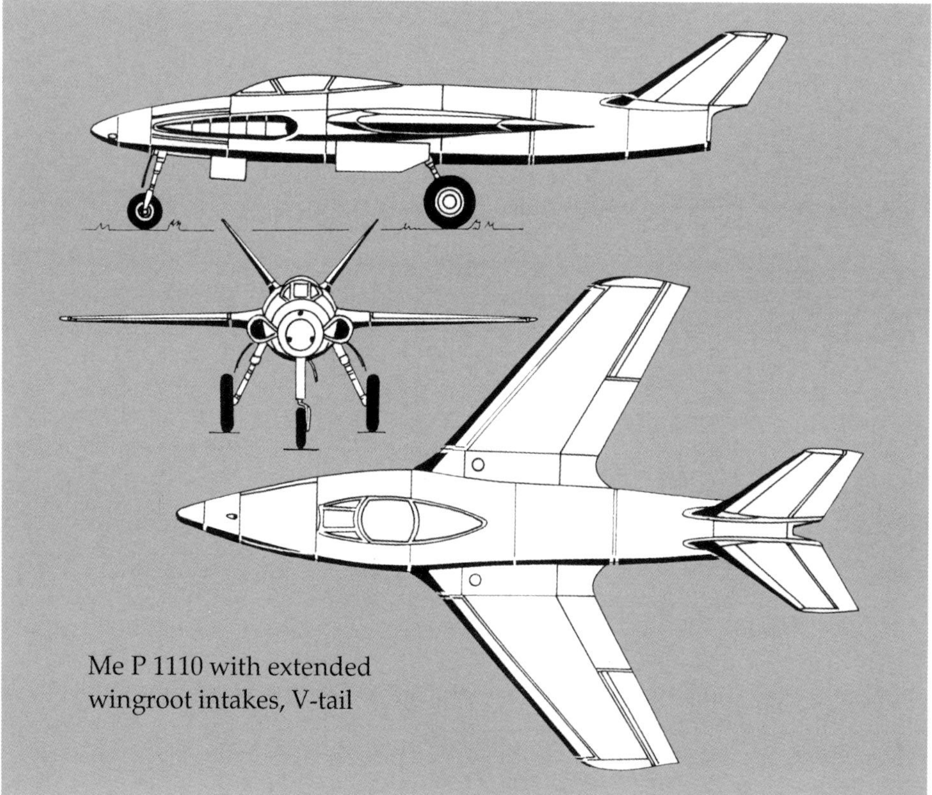

Me P 1110 with extended wingroot intakes, V-tail

Dimensions and Weights

Span	6.69m
Length	9.76m
Height	2.77m
Wing area	13.17m^2
Equipped weight	2,580kg
Take-off weight	4,000kg

Performance

Max speed at 7,000m	1,006km/h
Ceiling	13,100m
Range	1,500km

Armament

3 x MK 108 in fuselage nose

Me P 1110/170 (12.01.1945)

The principal alteration here lay in the annular air intake duct where the fuselage boundary layer was sucked away by a blower driven from the HeS 011 turbojet, the V-tail of the previous scheme having been retained.

Dimensions and Weights

Span	9.66m
Length	9.66m
Height	2.70m
Wing area	13.17m²
Equipped weight	2,580kg
Take-off weight	4,000kg

Performance

Max speed at 7,000m	1,006km/h
Ceiling	13,100m
Range	1,500km

Armament

3 x MK 108 in fuselage nose

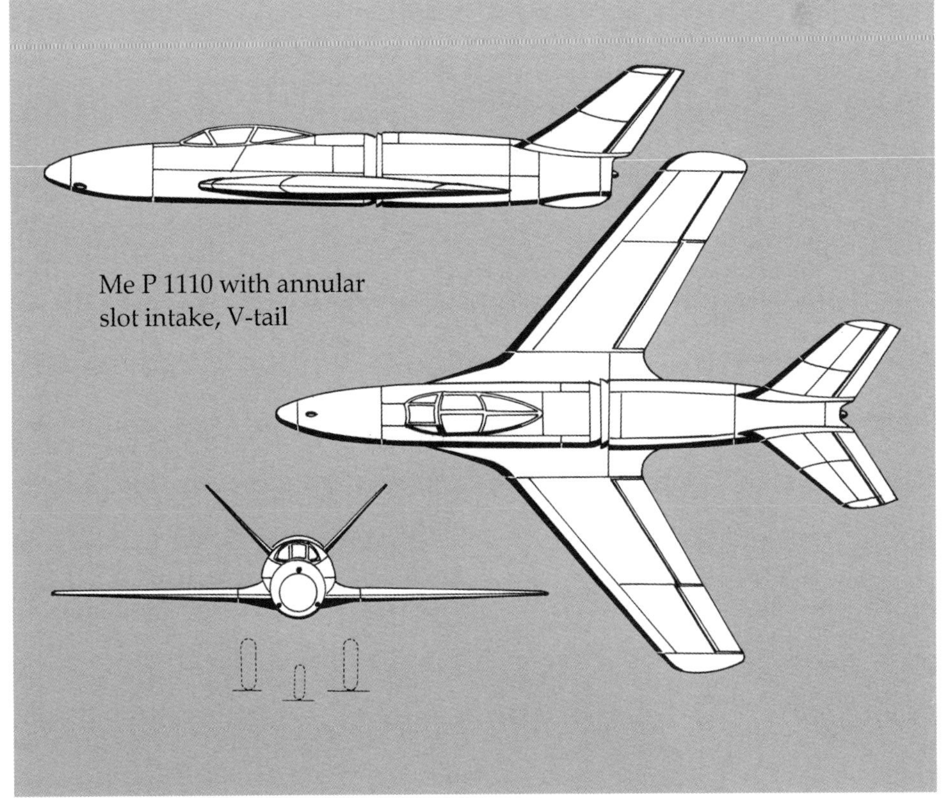

Me P 1110 with annular slot intake, V-tail

Me P 1110 'Ente' (canard)

In mid-February 1945 an unusual concept was drawn up which, although it promised advantages in the low-speed flight regime, raised doubts on the subject of directional stability, for which reason it was soon discarded. Nevertheless, it had a wing sweep of no less than 52° and thus indicated a high maximum speed in excess of 1,000km/h. Span was 5.00m, length 9.60m and height 3.08m.

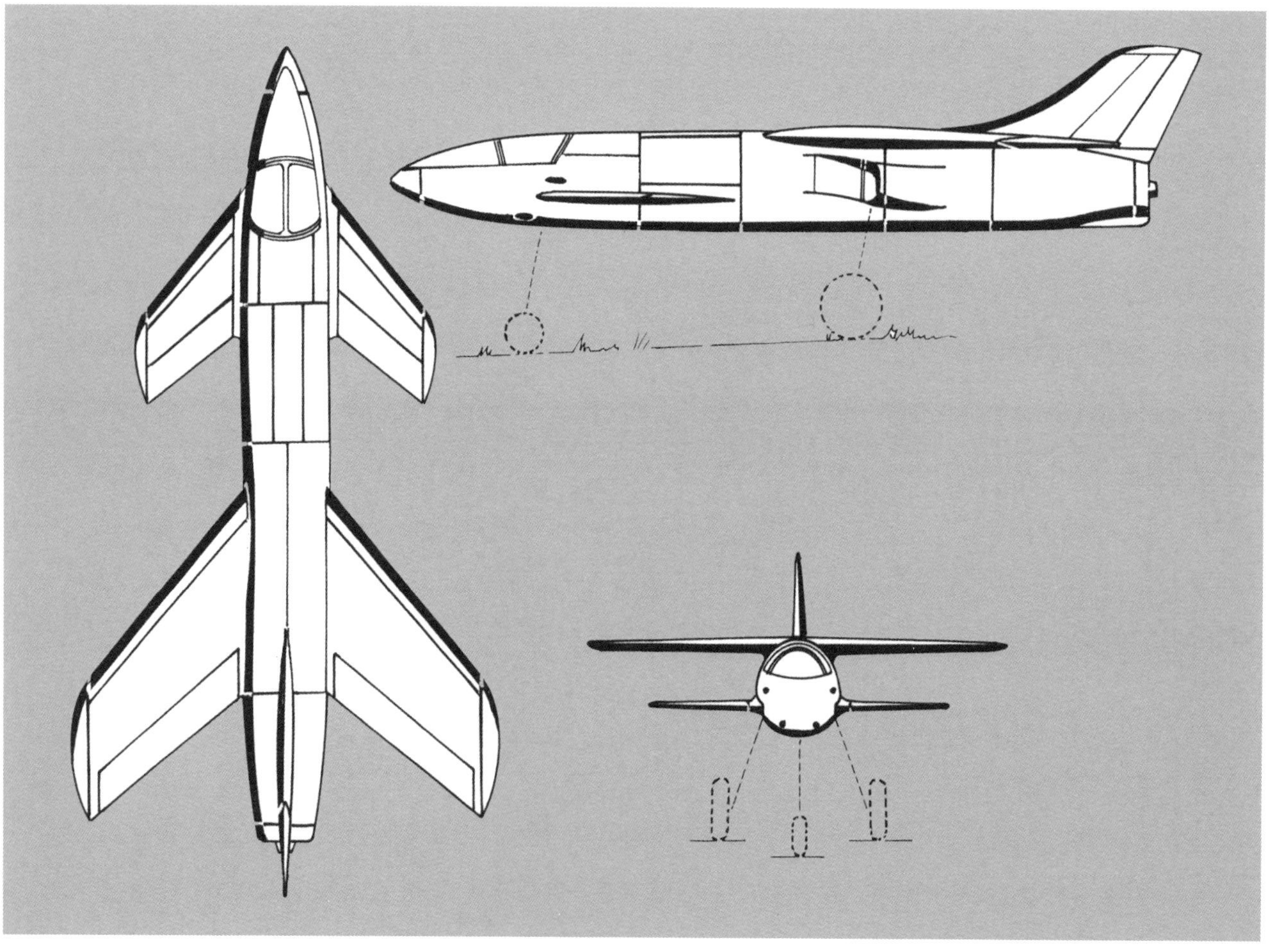

Me P 1111 (22.02.1945)

The drawing of the above date represents the most aerodynamically refined concept combined with wide-track mainwheels and uncomplicated air intakes for the HeS 011 turbojet, so much so that its flying qualities were judged to be extremely favourable. Housing the bulk of the fuel in the wings, however, was a subject of criticism because the generous wing area meant greater susceptibility to enemy fire. As with the P 1110 designs, the P 1111 sought to obtain an optimal solution, and eventually led to the P 1112 variants.

Dimensions and Weights

Span	9.26m
Length	8.92m
Height	3.06m
Wing area	28.00m^2
Equipped weight	2,740kg
Take-off weight	4,282kg

Performance

Max speed	1,000km/h
Ceiling	14,000m

Armament

2 x MK 108 in fuselage nose with provision for two more.

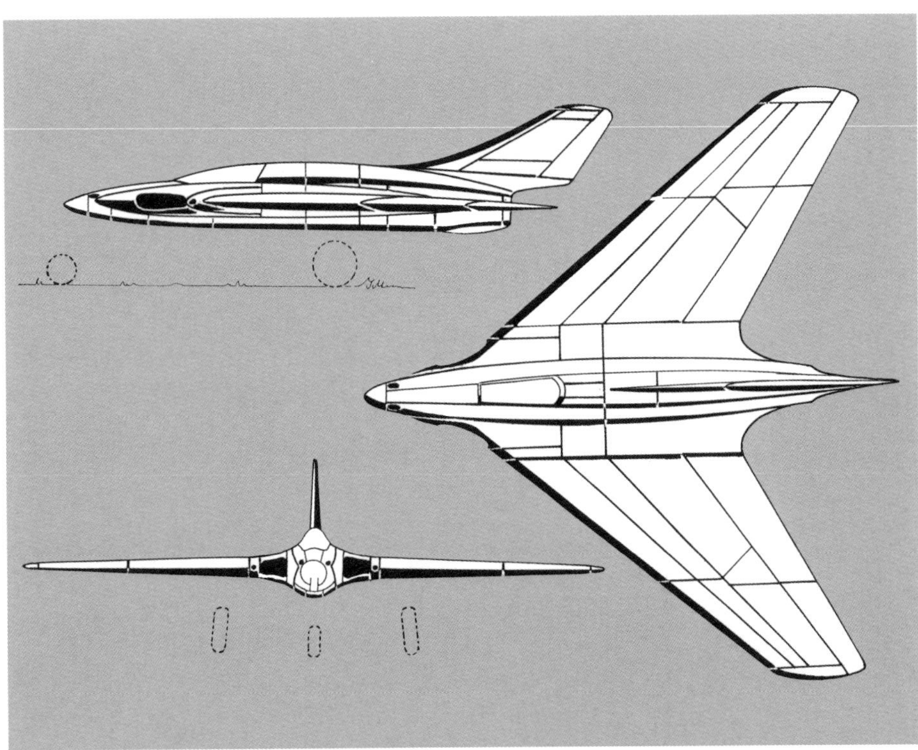

Me P 1112 Night Fighter

The drawing number IV/155 dated 24.02.1945 shows an aircraft closely resembling the previous P 1111. Although the drawing is clearly marked (P 1112 Night Fighter), it appears elsewhere as the P 1111 and it is possible that it was redesignated at some stage. It nonetheless has the basic configuration of the P 1111 with its generous wing area, but is powered by two HeS 011s housed at the wingroots that required a revised form and necessitated a second crew member for the night fighter role. For this reason, the centre of gravitiy position was altered and the fuselage lengthened whereby the swept fin and rudder was set further back. Span was 12.70m and length 10.40m, but no other data is known.

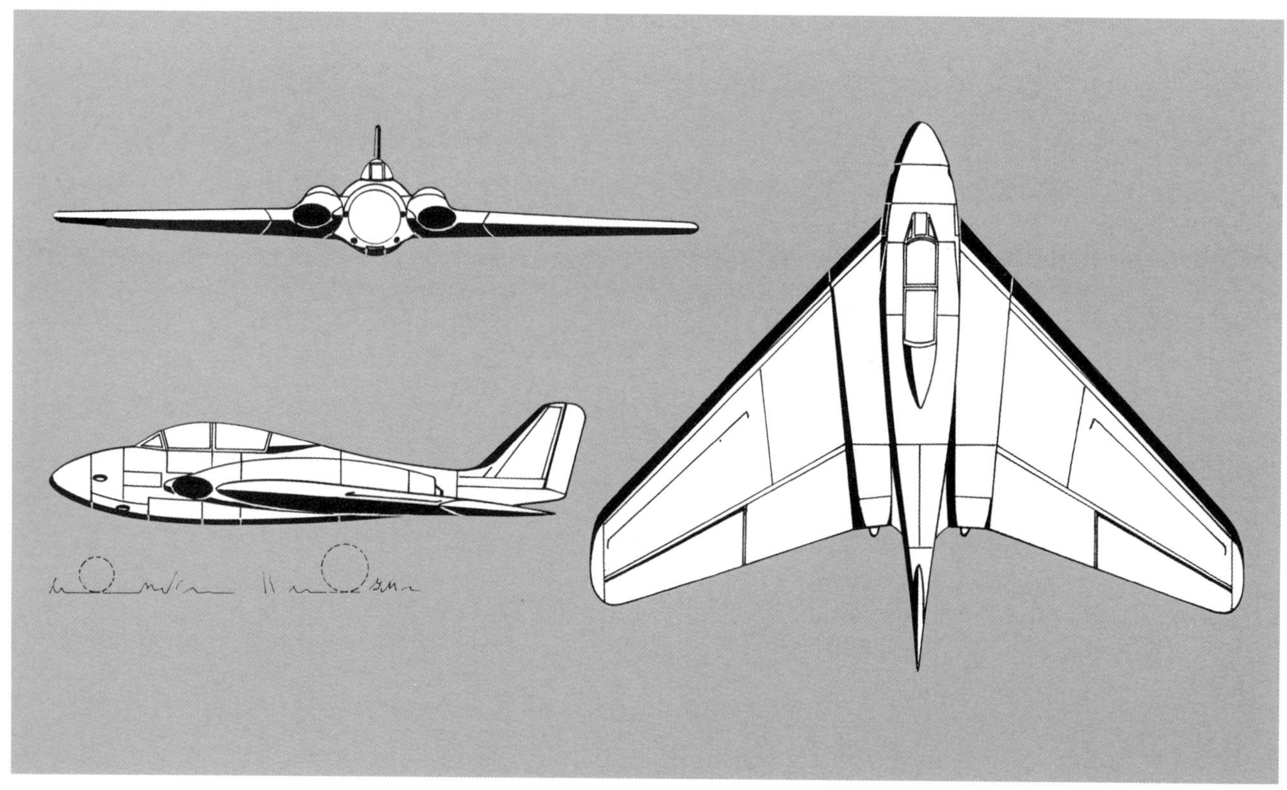

Me P 1112 S-1 (27.03.1945)

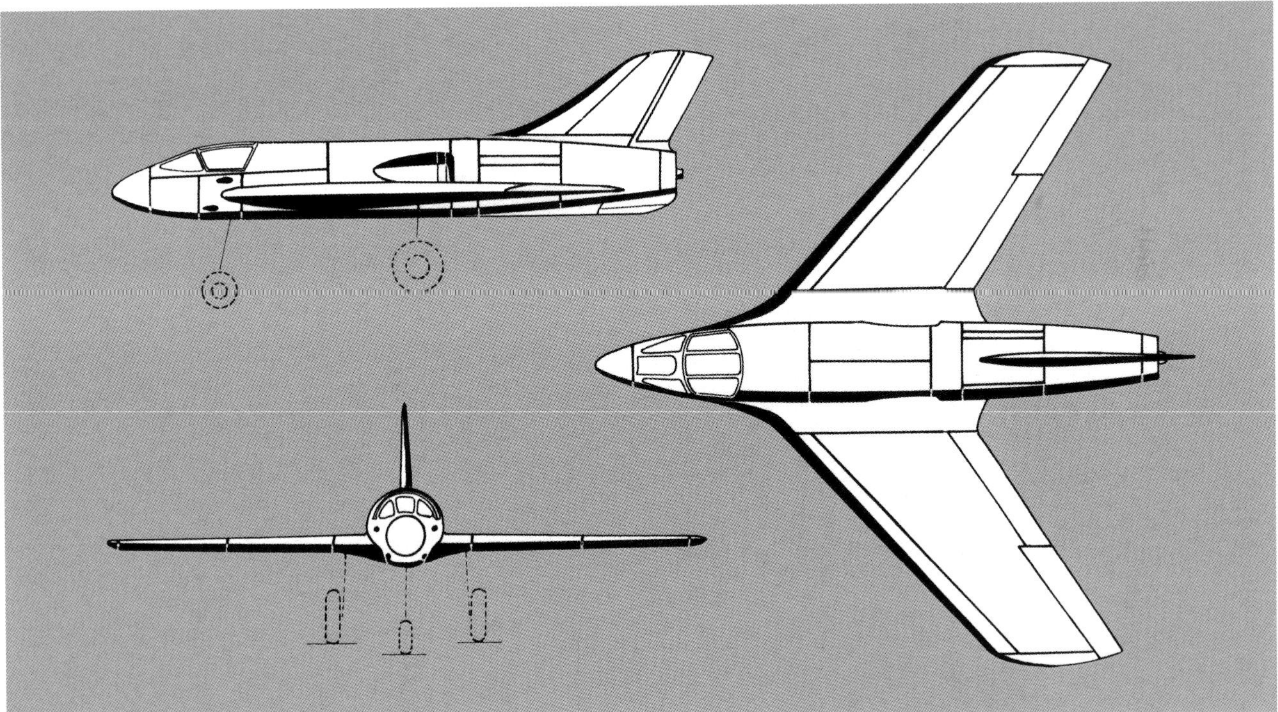

The experience gained with preceding projects was incorporated into the P 1112, of which three variants were drawn up. The wingroot forward extensions were retained and whilst the S-2 had the wing planform of the P 1111 with its extended wingroot air intakes, the S-1 and V1 both had fuselage side air intakes for the HeS 011. Whereas the S-1 and S-2 had a single swept fin and rudder, the V1 featured a V-tail and in this form was intended for the production version. The pressurised cockpit's front windscreen, faired into the fuselage nose profile, was to have consisted of 10cm thick armoured glass, the pilot seated in a semi-reclined position so as to make room for nosewheel retraction and the lateral armament bays. When it is considered that these projects had an overall length between 8 and 9m and hence not greater than the Me 109, the distribution of fuselage space is nothing short of astounding.

Me P 1112 S-2 (March 1945)

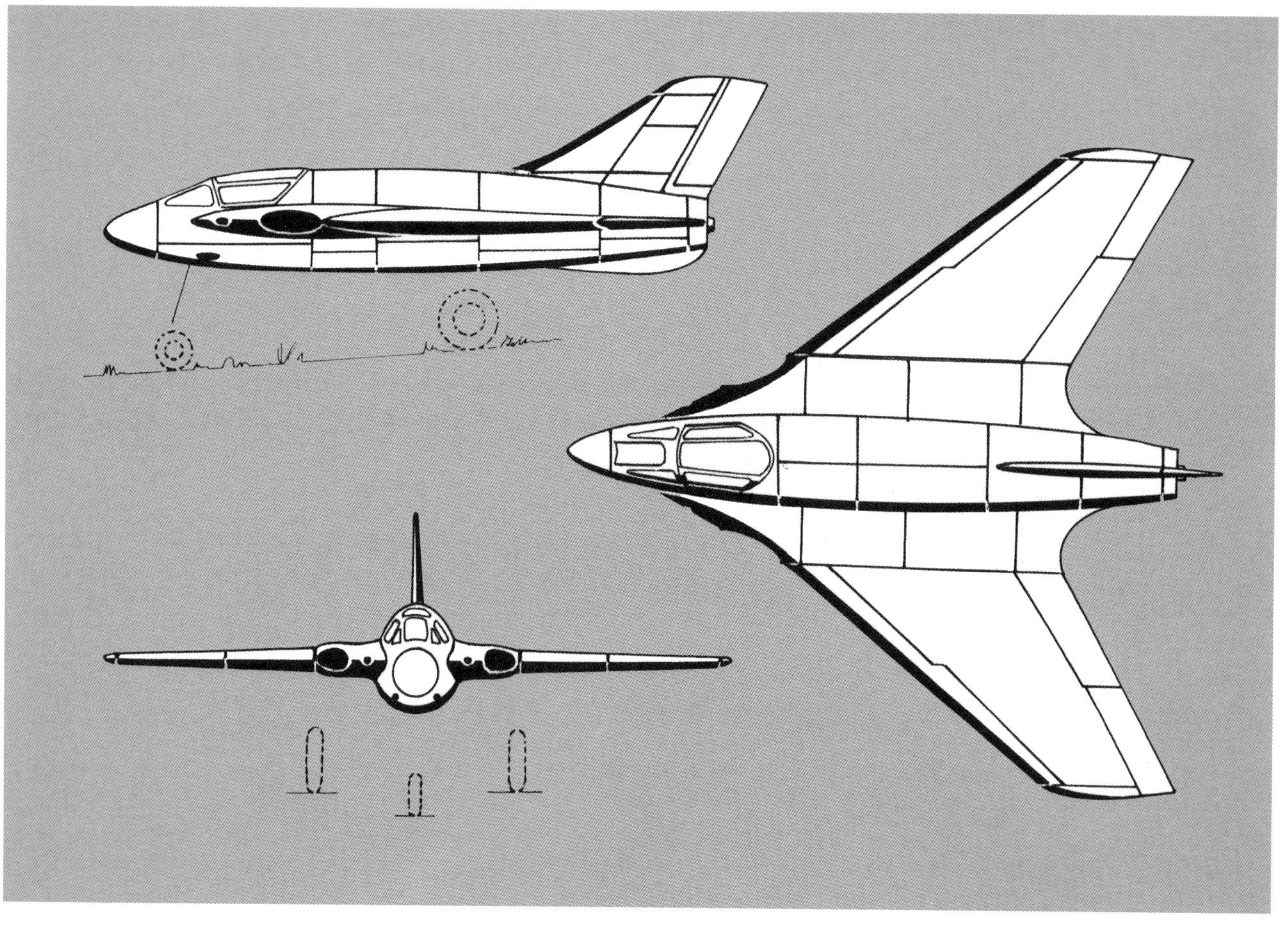

Me P 1112 V1 (30.03.1945)

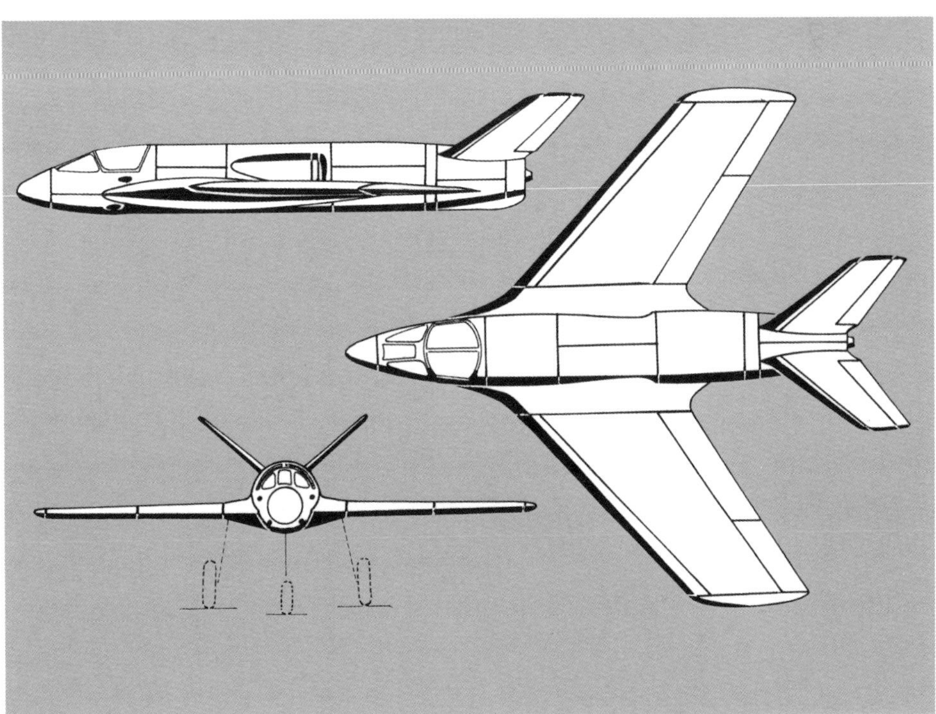

Dimensions

Span	8.16m
Length	9.24m
Height	2.84m

Weights

Equipped weight	2,290kg
Take-off weight	4,673kg

Performance

Max speed over 1,000km/h

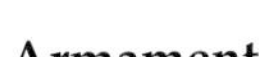

Armament

4 x MK 108 or 1 x MK 214 in dorsal fuselage, or 1 x MK 112 offset beneath the forward fuselage, the latter weapons being intended for the Pulkzerstörer role.

Me P 1112 Variant

A Me P 1112 variant as depicted in postwar literature.

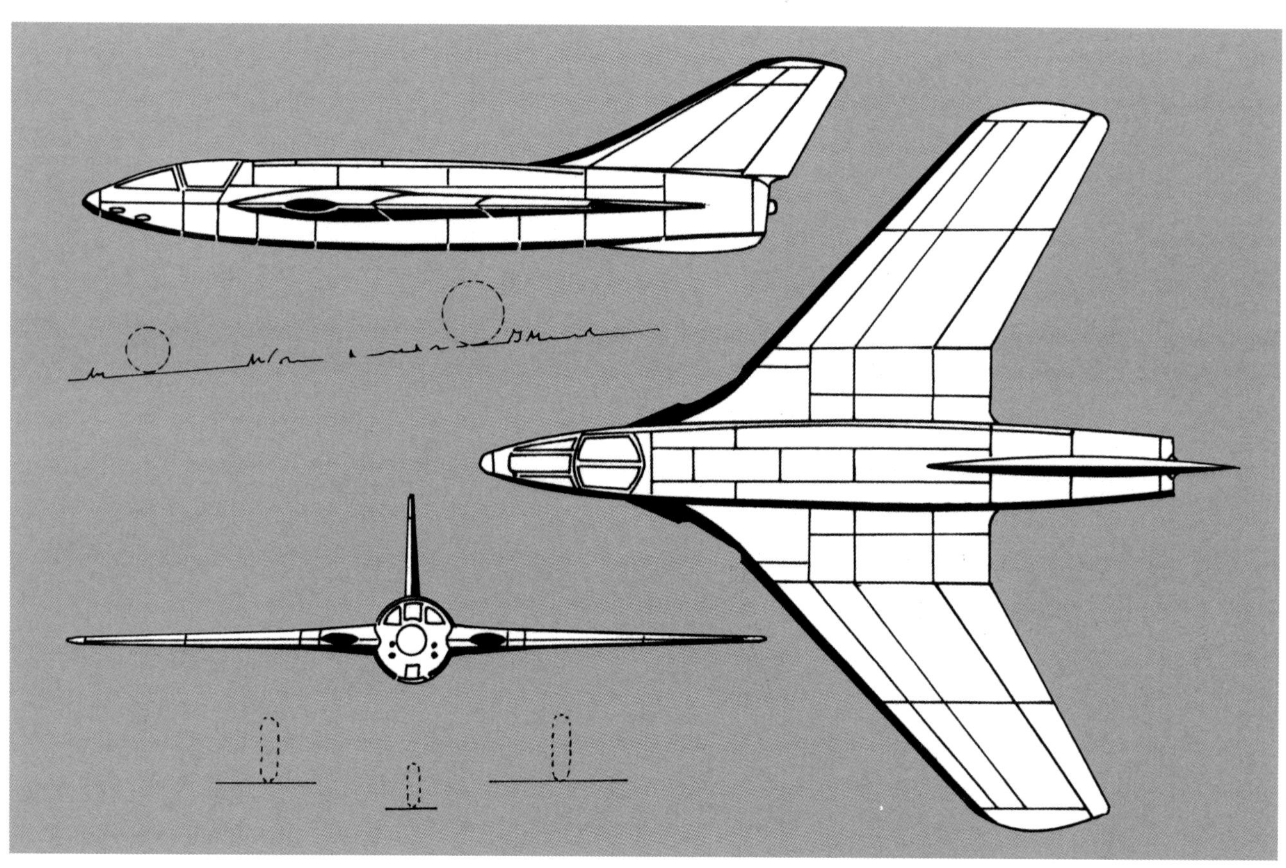

Me 'Schwalbe'

A project number for the 'Schwalbe' (Swallow) Zerstörer is not known, but Me P 1115 has been conjectured by some writers. Evident is that the project is the most radical of all the unusual configurations and resembles no other Messerschmitt design study. Forming the bulk of the fuselage are two superimposed turbojets, their air intakes bifurcated to allow for the cockpit enclosure and nosewheel bay, the short rear fuselage cone with lateral air brakes, the flattened nose compartment and armament projecting fore and aft of the engine nacelles. The wide-track mainwheels retracted forwards and inwards aft of the main spar into the roots of the thin wing having trailing edge ailerons and inboard elevators that were the sole flight controls. The wing, with its fixed outboard fixed slots, resembled that of the Me 163 B and presumably had hardpoints for bomb suspension mechanisms. Of the total of six fuel tanks, four were housed in the wings and two in the fuselage between the engine nacelles.

With a span of 9.05m, length 8.90m, height 2.75m, wing area 20.00m² and take-off weight 4,030kg, the 2 x 1,195kp thrust turbojets were reportedly expected to accelerate the aircraft to around 950km/h.

Me 'Libelle'

In the 'Libelle' (Dragonfly), the fuselage has the form of an elongated egg with generous cockpit glazing, the compound-sweep 10% thick mid-wing having wingroot intakes for the unknown 450kp thrust turbojet, with a V-tail mounted at the extremity of the slender rear fuselage boom, all three wheels of the tricycle undercarriage retracting into the fuselage. Conceived as a light-fighter, the project gives the impression more of a lightly-armed close-reconnaissance aircraft and with a span of 7.00m, length 7.30m, height 2.00m, wing area 10.00m^2 and take-off weight 1,000kg, it was thus much smaller than the He 162.

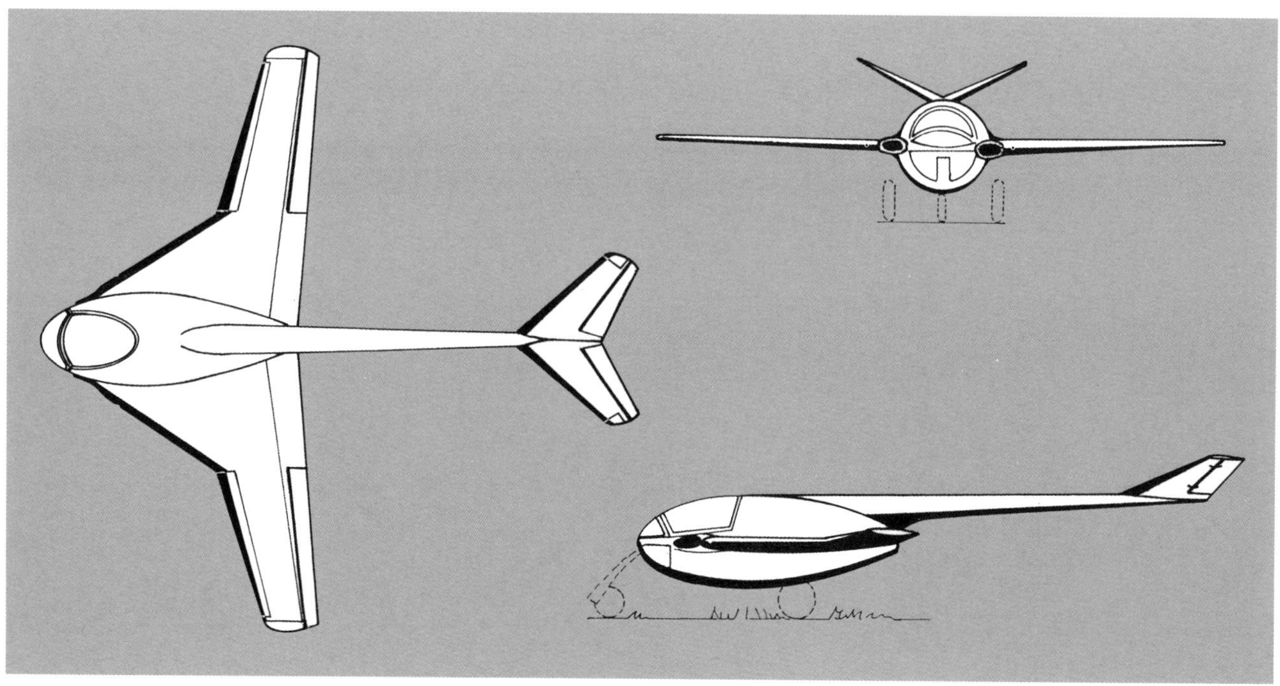

Me 'Wespe'

A fighter drawn up in two variants, one (not illustrated here) had a Me P 1112-type slender fuselage with a low-profile cockpit canopy situated at the centre of its length, the single 1,195kp thrust turbojet at the rear fed by a long intake duct situated at the nose and passing beneath the cockpit floor. The mid-positioned tapered swept wing with its outboard slats housed the inward retracting mainwheels. Unusual was the very sharply-swept fin and rudder, the swept tailplane mounted half way up the fin. The other variant is the one illustrated here.

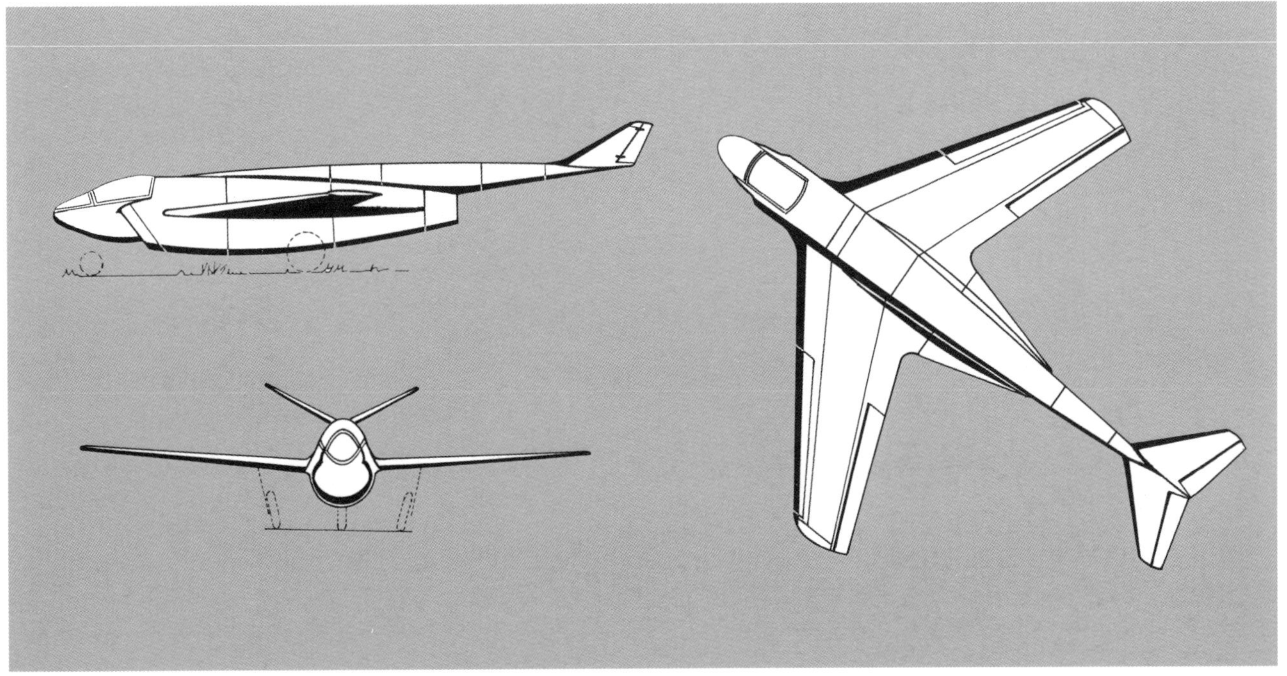

Me 'Wespe'

The variant also shown here differed from the other scheme in having a shortened fuselage featuring a nose cockpit, rearward-retracting nosewheel, crescent-shaped turbojet air intake for the turbojet behind the cockpit and a V-tail mounted on the extremity of the tailboom. As before, the mainwheels retracted forwards and inwards to rest in bays behind the main spar at the wing roots, which extended in long fillets to the turbojet exhaust nozzle. Span was 8.65m, overall length 10.00m, height 2.30m, wing area 15.00m² and take-off weight 3,000kg. Performance data is not known, but presumably lay in the 1,000km/h region.

Unnamed Zerstörer I

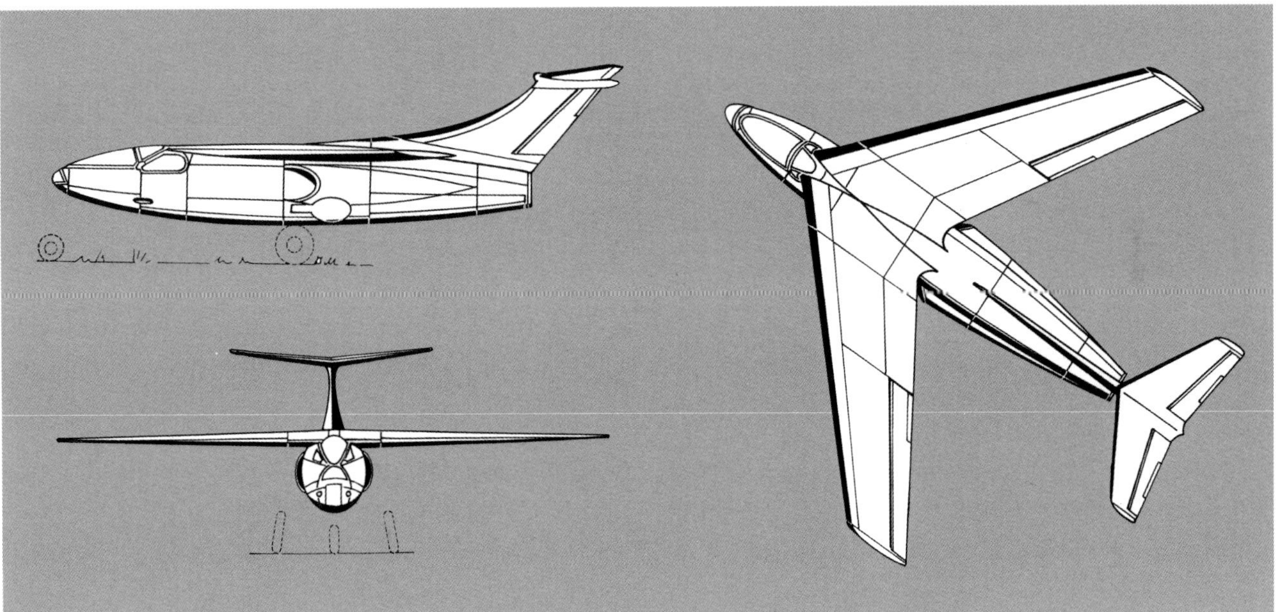

Although principal dimensions of the unnamed 'Zerstörer with T-tail' are known, the cutaway side-view drawing showed an unknown turbojet with what appears to be a multi-can combustion chamber, the unit closely resembling the basic Jumo 004 but with a shorter compressor section. In this design, the nosewheel retracted rearwards into the cockpit ahead of the pilot's seat, the canopy blending into the fuselage nose contour, with the mainwheels retracting rearwards into the fuselage beneath the lateral turbojet air intakes. Larger than the preceding projects, it had a swept shoulder wing and sharply swept empennage surfaces. Span was 11.80m, fuselage length 10.30m, overall length 12.20m and wing area 28.00m^2. Assuming the take-off wing loading was held to around 200kg/m^2 (as were the 'Schwalbe' and 'Wespe'), the quoted 7,000kg weight is certainly too high, and in such a case, would have been much less.

Another Zerstörer project (on next page) which has been illustrated elsewhere and denoted here as the Zerstörer II, with the exception of the T-tailplane, shows a rather different swept wing aircraft whose chief novelty is the sweptforward fin and rudder. No dimensions, weight or performance data are known.

Unnamed Zerstörer II

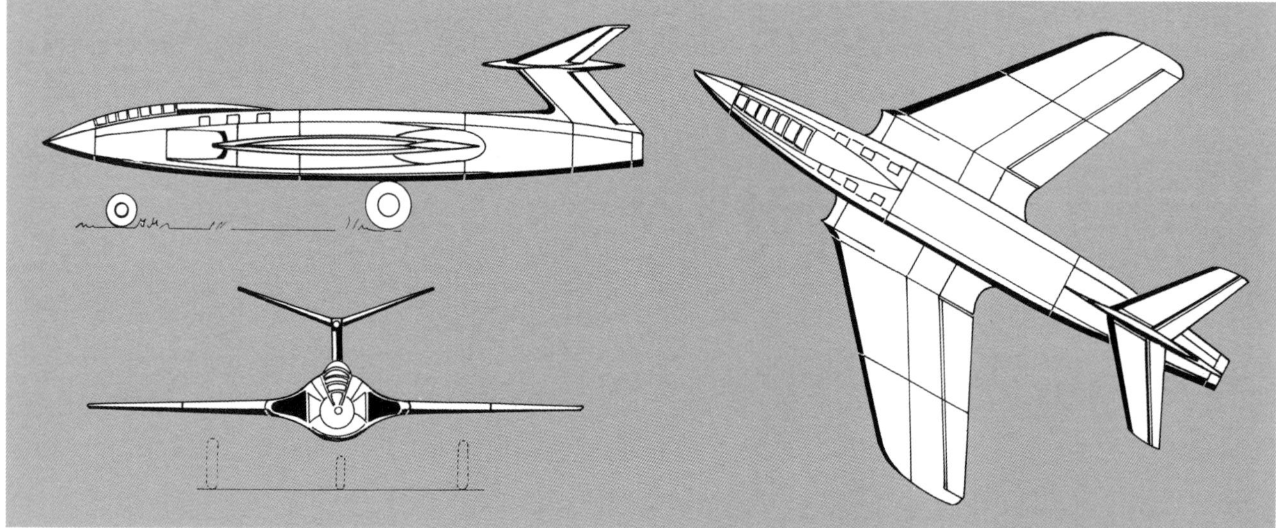

Li-Me 'Bomb-Carrying Glider'

Described in other publications as the DFS Bombensegler (bomb-carrying glider) of mixed wood and metal construction, but whose design origin remains uncertain, this Lippisch-type delta-winged aircraft supporting a cruciform empennage was to have carried an underslung 1,000kg bomb in 'Deichselschlepp' (towed attachment) behind another aircraft to altitude and released to approach its target in a steep dive. After bomb release, the pilot was to distance himself in a fast glide from the danger area and initiate the compressed-air installation behind the cockpit to eject a balloon that would be inflated in stages, slowing down the glider to the point where he could exit by parachute. Span was 4.28m and length 7.25m.

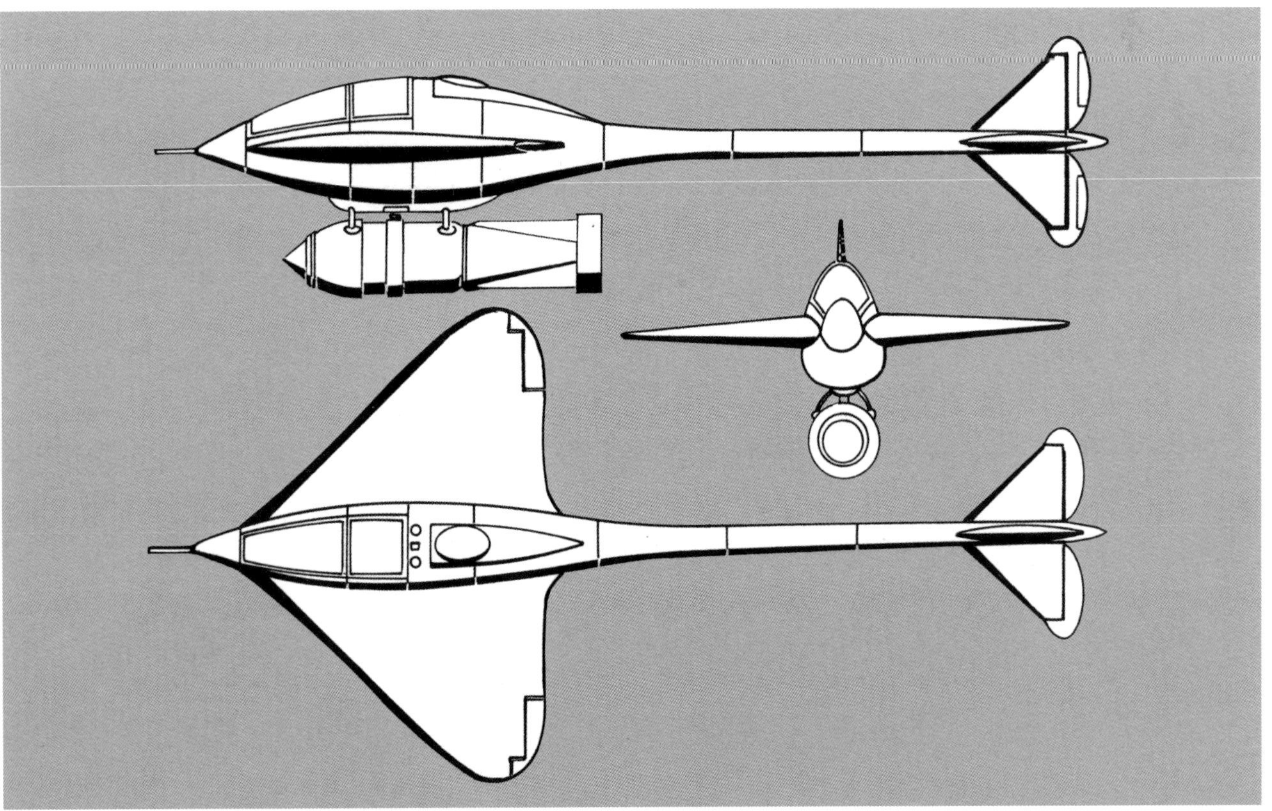

Skoda-Kauba Flugzeugbau

Sk P 14-01 (21.03.1945)

This lesser-known firm was established under RLM initiative in 1942, headed by the Austrian designer Otto Kauba and integrated into a part of the Skoda Works, but in fact was the Avia Aircraft Works in Cakovice near Prague, Czechoslovakia.

Powerplant of this single-seat fighter, one of the latest to be proposed in early 1945, was a high-temperature 1.50m-diameter ramjet of Dr.-Ing. Eugen Sänger of the DFS, who had flight-tested ramjets of different diameters on a Do 17Z and a Do 217E. In one P 14 variant, span was 7.00m, length 9.85m, height (on trolley) 4.20m and wing area 12.50m^2, whilst in another, span was 7.90m and length 9.50m. In one scheme, fuel carried was J2, but provision had been made to carry a mixture of J2 plus coal dust, with which experiments were under way before the war's end. With J2 alone, take-off weight was 2,850kg, and with J2 + coal, was 3,100kg. Armament was 1 x MK 103 firing through the canopy above the pilot, take-off being with the aid of two powerful RATO units. Estimated maximum speed was 1,010km/h at sea-level and 925km/h at 15,000m, with an absolute ceiling well over 18,000m.

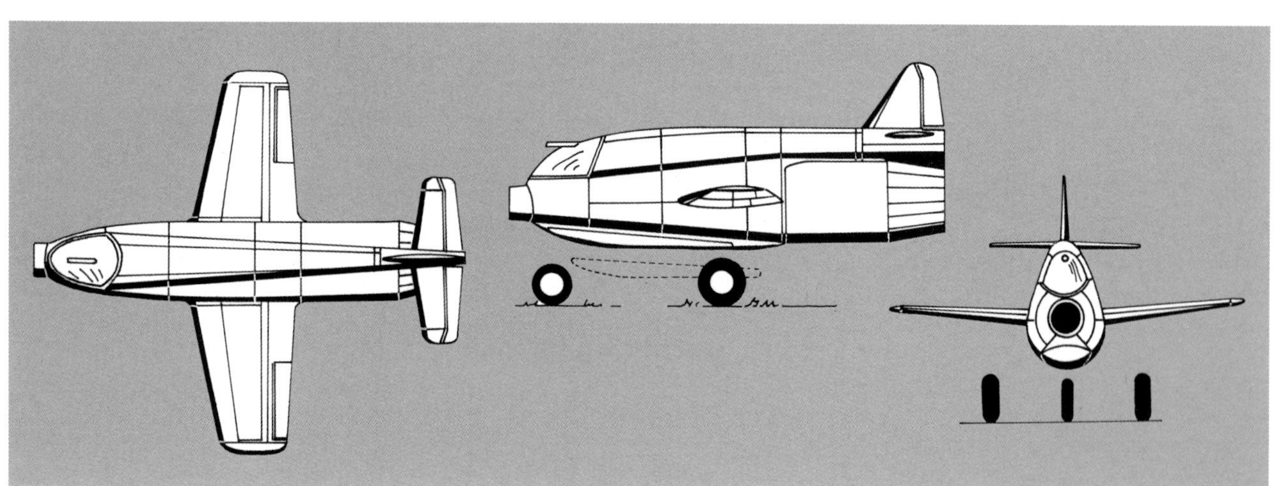

Sk P 14-02 (March/April 1945)

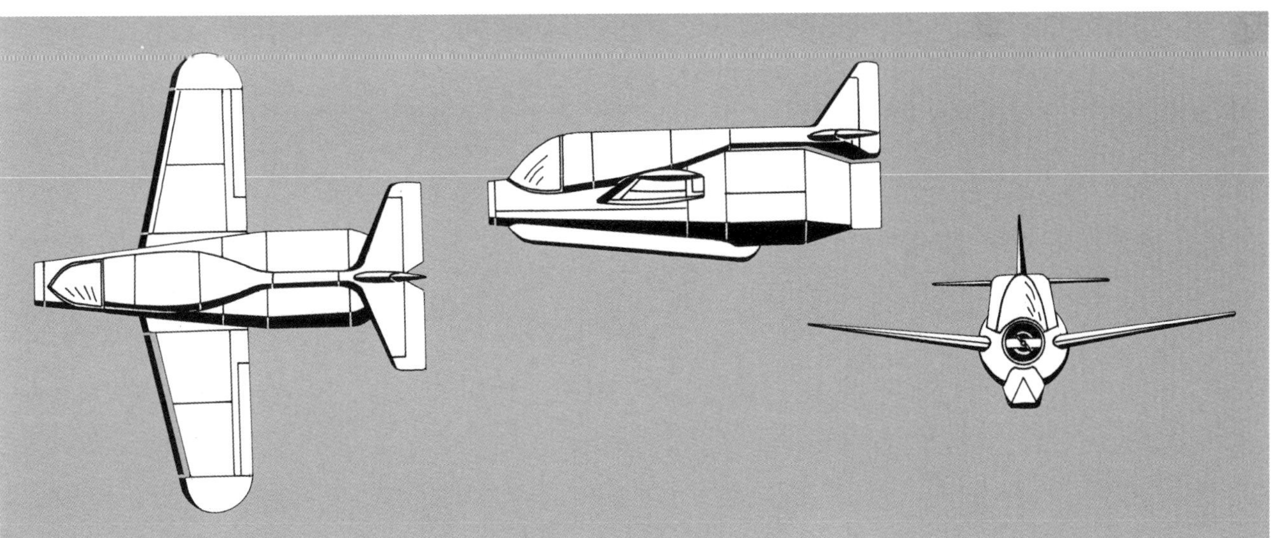

Translator's Note: The aircraft depicted here, described in recent years by some well-known authors in their books as the 'Sk P 14-01' or 'Sk P 14-02 of March-April 1945' was in fact a predecessor of the Sk P 14. This particular 2-seater aircraft, capable of carrying bombs in the ventral fuselage pannier, with span 12.00m, length 10.90m, wing area 30m^2 and ramjet maximum diameter 2.50m, at 7,000kg had well over twice the take-off weight of the Sk P 14 and had been proposed by Dr.-Ing. Eugen Sänger in 1942 – a fact that should be apparent from the rounded wingtips of this older design. At 12,000m altitude, estimated maximum speed was 750km/h and endurance 50 minutes.

So 344 (22.01.1944)

Engineer Heinz Sombold of the Ingenieurbüro Bley in Naumburg designed this mixture of a rocket-powered aircraft and anti-aircraft projectile. Its principal weapon load consisted of a 400kg weight high-explosive warhead which was expected to destroy a number of US bombers flying in mass-formation boxes. Just how right this expectation was, was displayed at the beginning of 1945, when the pressure wave of an unmanned explosive warhead test at 3,000m altitude carried out for this purpose in Ötztal in Tyrol, caused losses among the civil population, so that further trials had to be relocated to the EdL Peenemünde-Karlshagen. The So 344 was to have been carried aloft by a specially-converted bomber and, after release, fly in a parabolic arc towards its bomber-stream target. To avoid defending enemy fighters, a Walter rocket motor with sufficient fuel to make good an escape was to provide the power to achieve a high approach speed. The warhead, a type of air-mine, detonated automatically. Span was 5.70m, length 7.00m, wing area 6.00m^2, loaded weight 1,350kg and powered endurance 25-30 mins, an armament of 2 x MGs being provided for defensive purposes, the aircraft landing on a skid following a glide after its fuel was expended.

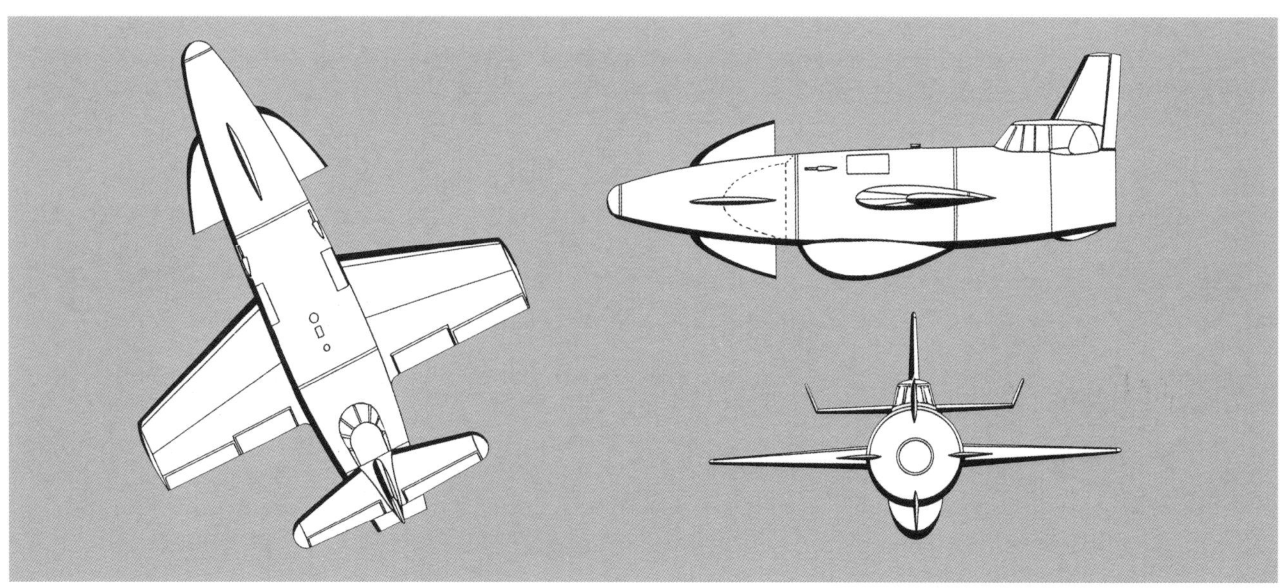

Ram-Fighter (25.08.1944)

Dipl.-Ing. J Stöckel at the Blohm und Voss firm drew up a number of such Ramschussjäger (ram-fighter) projects, that illustrated dating from 25.08.1944. The mixed-propulsion system consisted of a ramjet whose annular intake diffuser enclosed a series of rocket chambers within the duct that brought the aircraft to initial ramjet operating speed. The sole weapons load in this suicide-mission aircraft was 200kg of high-explosive housed in the steel fuselage nosecap but, as Hitler had forbidden such operations, thought was given to a second variation in which the pilot would be able to eject prior to ramming. Span was 7.00m, fuselage diameter 1.00m and length 7.20m.

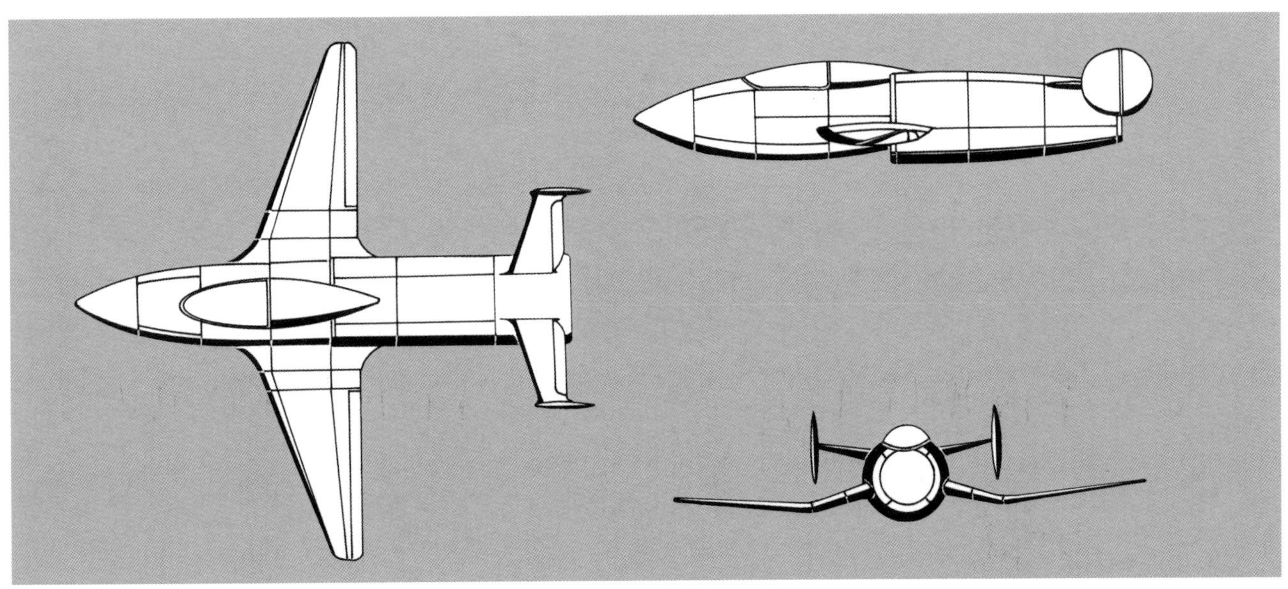

Ram-Fighter (20.8.1944)

Another proposal of his depicted an aircraft of similar overall layout with a likewise mixed-propulsion system, but with a central liquid-propellant rocket motor within the ramjet duct. Here, the nose warhead was replaced by a fuselage nose suitably strengthened for a ram attack that would follow a first attack where two small bombs would be released from underwing mountings. Span was 4.00m, fuselage diameter 0.80m and length 5.20m, the pilot in this project being accommodated in a seated position. In both projects, the small aircraft was carried aloft to altitude by a mothercraft and released in a similar manner to the Bv P 214 'manually-guided rocket projectile' mentioned in Volume 1 of this series.

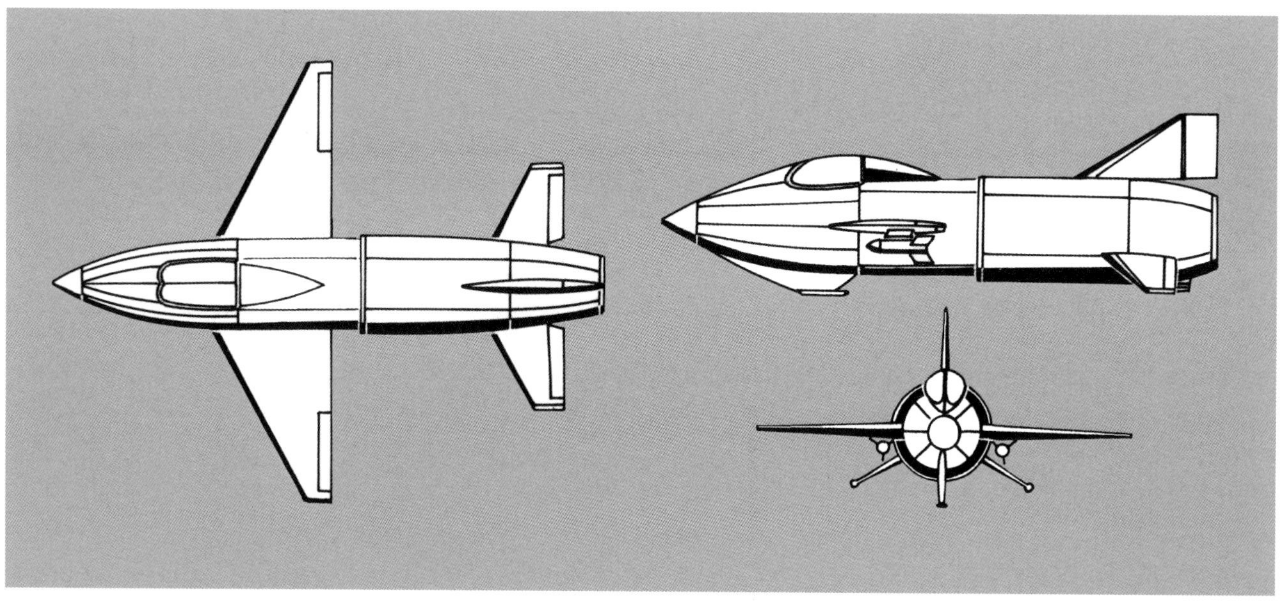

Publisher's Note: For further details of the Sombold and Stöckel Ramschussjäger see *Luftwaffe Secret Projects: Ground-Attack and Special-Purpose Aircraft, Vol. 3,* Midland (2004) pp. 236-237.

Interceptor I (06.07.1939)

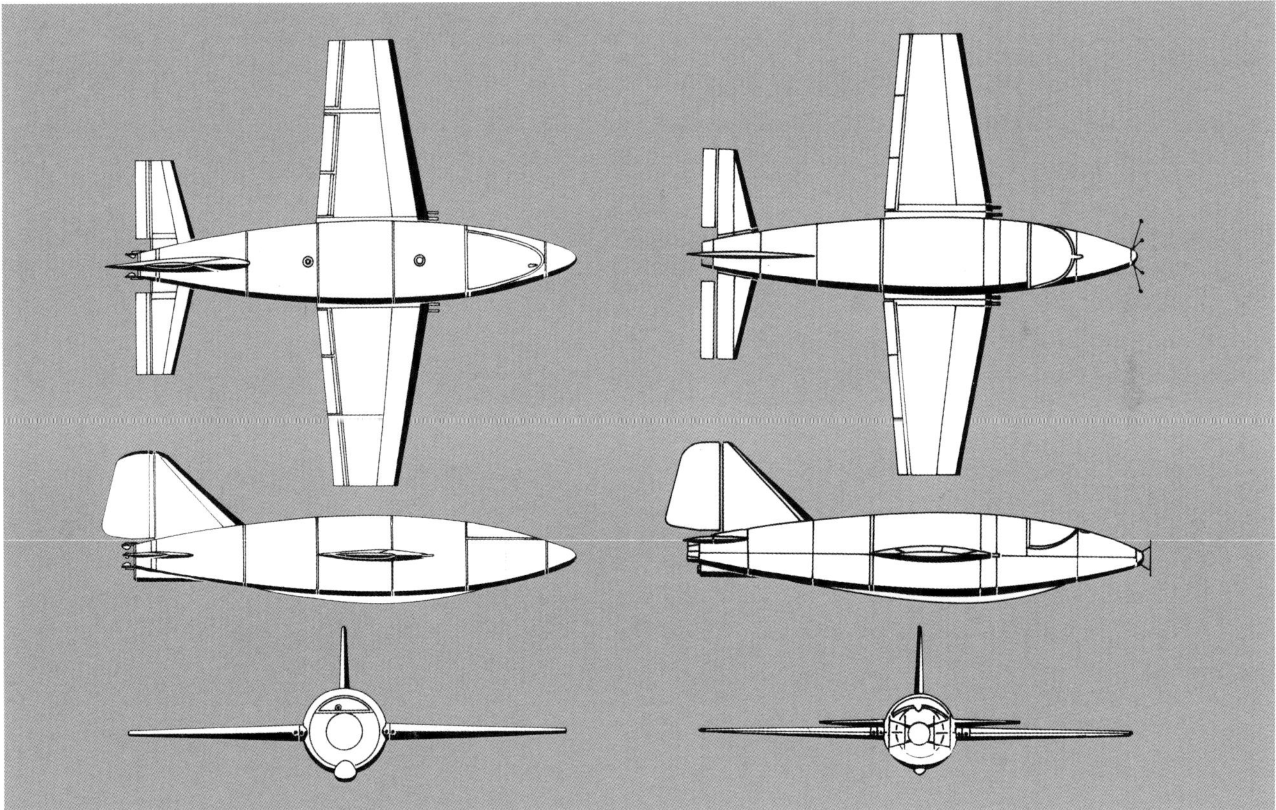

This proposal by Dr. Wernher von Braun at the HWA Peenemünde envisaged a vertical-take-off rocket-powered interceptor that would be rolled out from storage in a large assembly hall and launched in pairs from vertical guide rails. Upon identification of a target by radar, a control centre would calculate the optimal flightpath and steer the fighter automatically like an anti-aircraft rocket to an altitude of 8,000m, at which point the pilot would take over control and start a low-thrust rocket motor to conserve on fuel. Following his attack and fuel expenditure, the aircraft would continue as a glider before making a skid landing at its home airfield. Both the main and cruising-chamber rocket motors consisted of an A3 missile powerplant burning A-Stoff (liquid oxygen) and M-Stoff (methyl alcohol), pressure being provided by a nitrogen supply. Storage and handling of the low-temperature propellants, however, was regarded as problematic. Span was 8.50m, length 9.30m, height 3.02m and payload 5,000kg. Attack speed was 700km/h, ceiling 8,000m and armament 4 x MGs in the wingroots.

Interceptor II

The next rocket-powered interceptor design was based on the technology of the A6 rocket and had a 10,160kp thrust main chamber and a 770kp thrust cruising chamber, the T-Stoff/Z-Stoff and Visol/SV-Stoff propellants, which could be stored at average temperatures, were viewed as being less problematic than liquid oxygen. Although the projects were handed over to the Fieseler firm, which in 1941 drew up similar proposals – the Fi 166/I and Fi 166/II described in Volume 1 – they did not find favour with the Luftwaffe. Projects such as these were revived again by Wernher von Braun in 1944, when the Heinkel P 1077 'Julia' and the Bachem Ba 349 Natter also appeared. Span was 8.60m, length 9.30m, height 3.20m and armament 4 x MGs in the wing roots. Attack speed was 690km/h and ceiling 8,000m.

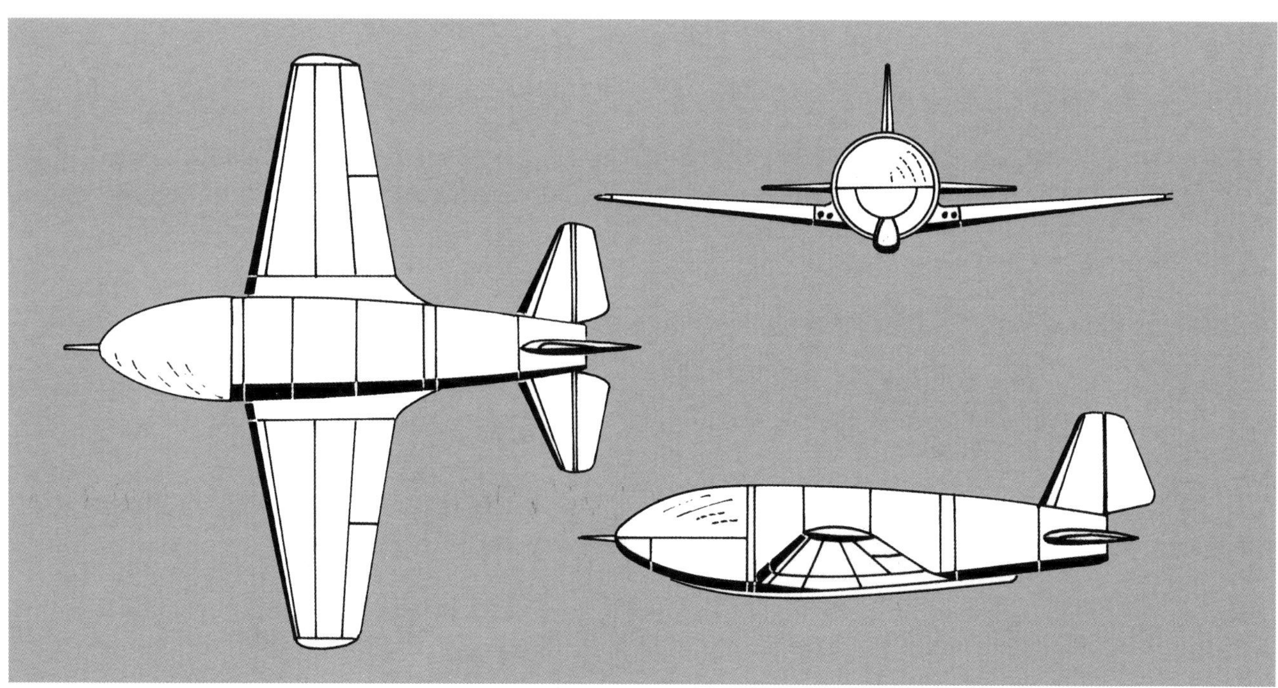

Luftschiffbau Zeppelin

'Fliegende Panzerfaust'

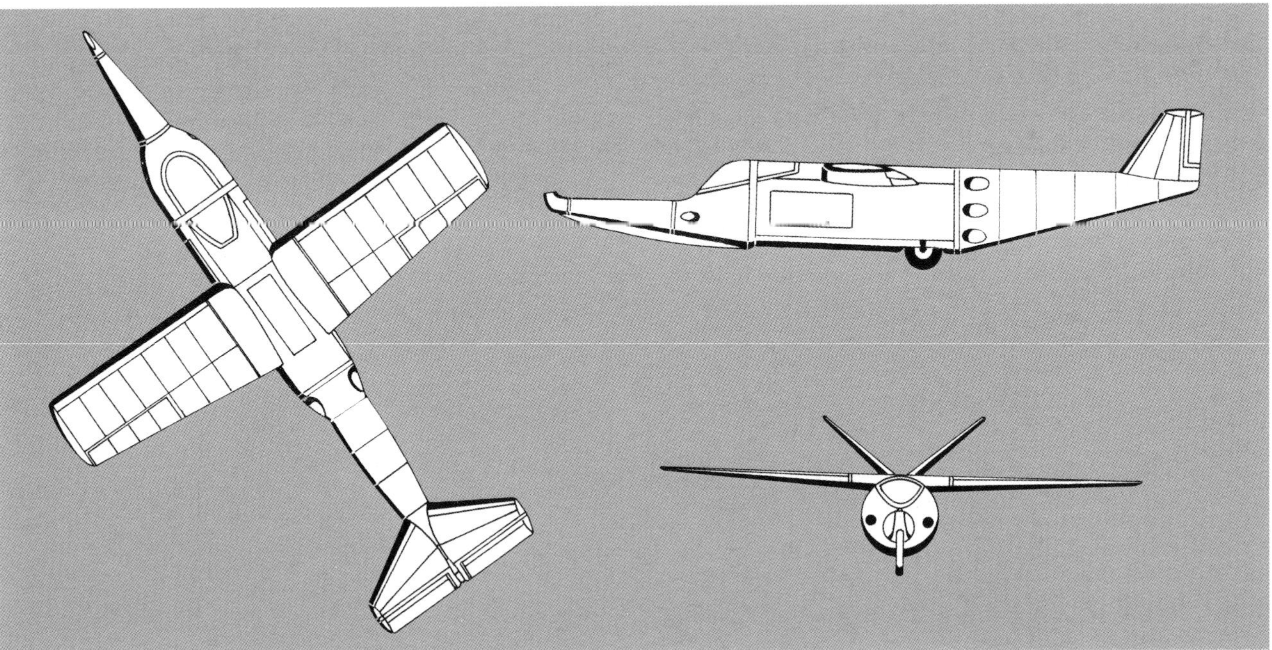

During the war the Luftschiffbau Zeppelin GmbH of Friedrichshafen undertook manufacture of large-capacity transport aircraft such as the Me 323 Gigant (Giant) and in 1944 participated in the development of towed fighters and Bordjäger. The standard Me 109 fighter was to have towed this small 'Flying Bazooka' aloft using the 'Starrschlepp' (rigid pole-tow) method. Upon release at altitude, it was to be accelerated to its attack speed of 850km/h by its battery of six SG 34 solid-propellant rockets. Following a first attack against the enemy bombers with unguided rockets, the aircraft was to perform a final ram attack with its wings, the prone pilot, ensconced in the blown-off fuselage nose, thereafter saving himself by parachute. The wing was strengthened to withstand a ram attack, the remainder of the aircraft likewise brought to earth by parachute for re-use. A mock-up was built in January 1945. Span was 4.50m, length 6.00m, height 1.50m, wing area 3.80m^2 and flying weight 1,200kg.

'Rammer' (November 1944)

The operational principle here was the same as the 'Flying Bazooka'. The same high-strength materials were to have been used for both projects as were employed for the Fw 190 A-8/R2 ram-fighters of IV./JG 3. An optimistic assessment indicated that the wing, without any negative effect on the rammer's speed and stability, would be able to shear-off the tail of a B-17 bomber. The 'Rammer' was likewise to perform an initial attack releasing its 14 x R4M rockets enclosed in the nose and then perform a ram attack. Span was 4.90m, length 5.00m, height 1.20m, wing area 6.50m^2, flying weight 860kg and attack speed 780km/h.

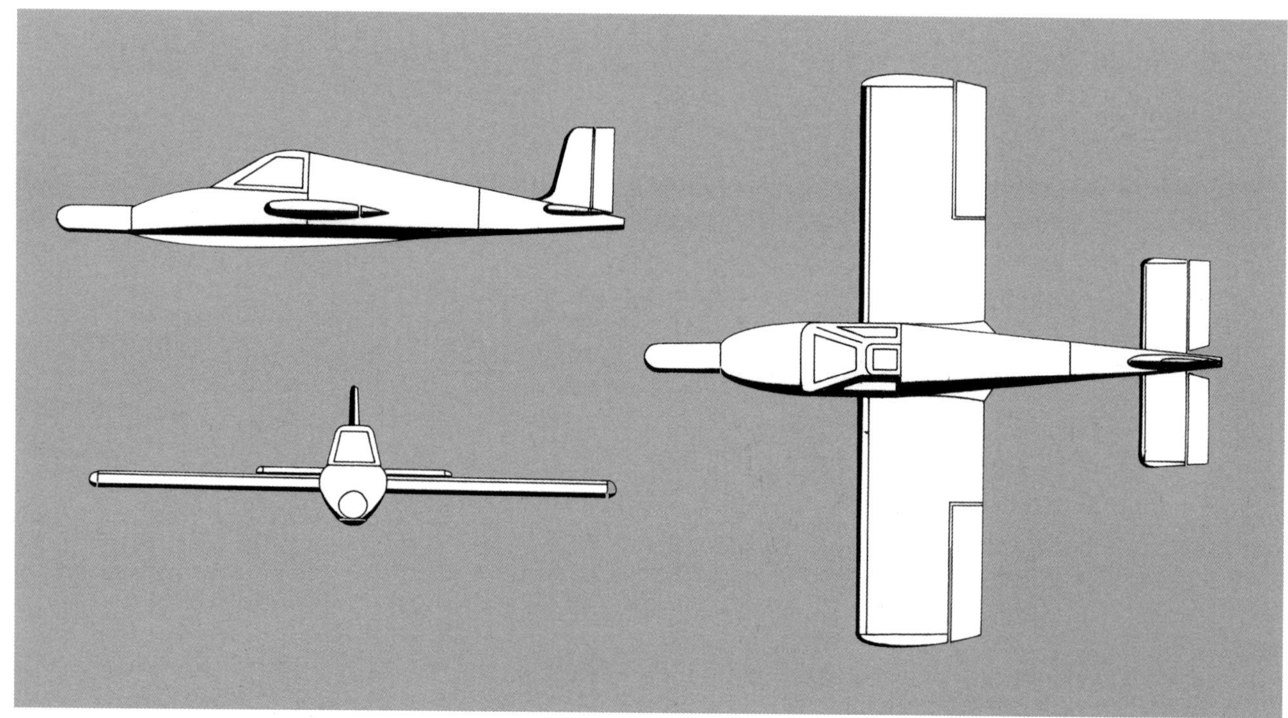

Epilogue

This survey of the large realm of German aircraft projects is planned to be continued in further volumes that will contain details of heavy bombers, high-altitude fighters, vertical take-off and tail-sitters, helicopters and disc-wing aircraft (such as the Schriever, Habermohl and Belluzo types).

Where unproven, questionable, as well as unbelievable projects are scattered in diverse publications, all will be included, even if it should turn out later on that one or other is a complete fantasy, or due to lack of concrete documentation, has been reconstructed. It will not, however, be a complete summary, but instead, merely an overall picture of what has been published or touched upon during the course of several decades.

For the sake of a few 'fakes', the many genuine projects should not be under-evaluated or even become questionable, and it may well turn out that in the course of time, one or other curiosity will become exposed as a falsity. However, such is not looked upon as a self-appointed task by the author, but instead, a matter for the experts. The aim of these volumes is to encourage the aviation historian to conduct ever more and careful research.

For financial reasons, a continual revision is not possible, and should initially be done by the reader. If and when much new material should become available, this task will be tackled. Until then, I trust my readers will have much pleasure on this topic and in my books.

Ingolf Meyer, 2006

LUFTWAFFE ADVANCED AIRCRAFT PROJECTS TO 1945
Volume 1: Arado to Junkers

Ingolf Meyer

Continuing his research into the experimental aircraft produced by the Third Reich, Ingolf Meyer has unearthed a remarkable range of aircraft, many of which did not appear in the earlier and highly successful *Luftwaffe Secret Projects* series. This, the first volume in the series, covers around half of the fighter and ground-attack designs mooted. In alphabetical format, each project is illustrated in colour while b/w drawings show its salient points.

Hardback, 297 x 210 mm, 192 pages, 172 colour illusts, 160 3-view dwgs
1 85780 240 3 **£29.99**

LUFTWAFFE SECRET PROJECTS
Fighters 1939-1945

Walter Schick & Ingolf Meyer

Germany's incredible fighter projects of 1939-45 are revealed in-depth – showing for the first time the technical dominance that their designers could have achieved. With access to much previously unpublished information the authors bring to life futuristic shapes that might have terrorised the Allies had the war gone beyond 1945. Full colour action illustrations in contemporary unit markings and performance tables show what might have been achieved.

Hbk, 282 x 213 mm, 176pp, 95 colour artworks, c160 dwgs and c 30 photos
1 85780 052 4 **£29.95**

LUFTWAFFE SECRET PROJECTS
Strategic Bombers 1935-45

Dieter Herwig and Heinz Rode

In this companion to the enormously popular volume on fighters, Germany's incredible strategic bomber projects 1935-45 are revealed showing the technical dominance that their designers could have achieved if time had allowed. Had the war gone beyond 1945 the aircraft described would have set it on a markedly different course. Comparison with later Allied and Soviet aircraft show the legacy handed on, right up to today's stealth aircraft.

Hbk, 282 x 213 mm, 144pp, 100 colour artworks, 132 b/w photos, 122 dwgs
1 85780 092 3 **£24.95**

LUFTWAFFE SECRET PROJECTS – Ground Attack & Special Purpose Aircraft

Dieter Herwig and Heinz Rode

This third volume in the series takes a close look at a varied range of about 140 ground attack and special purpose aircraft types including Kampfzerstörer (multi-purpose combat aircraft), multi-purpose and fast bombers, explosive-carrying aircraft intended to attack other aircraft, air-to-air ramming vehicles, bomb-carrying gliders and towed fighters, and airborne weapons and special devices (rockets, cannon, flamethrowers etc).

Hbk, 282 x 213 mm, 272pp, 154 colour illustrations, 168 b/w photos, 196 dwgs
1 85780 150 4 **£35.00**

GERMAN AIR-DROPPED WEAPONS TO 1945

Wolfgang Fleischer

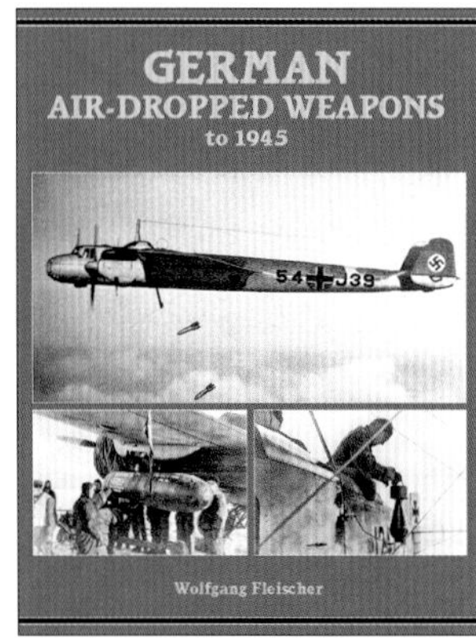

This traces the development of German air-dropped ammunition from the crude, 'aeronautical artillery' of WW1 to the advanced remote-control bombs of WW2. Major topics within the book include demolition bombs, incendiary bombs, special dropped ammunition, sea-dropping ammunition and dropping containers. A comprehensive illustrated listing gives information on 100 different bombs, 22 canisters and 50 of the most important bomb fuses.

Hbk, 282 x 213 mm, 240pp, 200 b/w photographs with over 200 drawings
1 85780 174 1 **£24.99**

GERMAN SECRET FLIGHT TEST CENTRES TO 1945

H Beauvais, K Kössler, M Mayer and C Regel

A group of German authors, some of whom were involved at the time, have brought together a history and overview of the establishment and activities of government flight-test centres in Germany from its resumption in the 1920s until the end of the Second World War. Major locations included are the research facilities at Johannisthal, Lipetsk, Rechlin, Travemünde, Tarnewitz and Peenemünde-West.

Hardback, 282 x 213mm, 248 pages 270 b/w photos, sketches, 8pp of col
1 85780 127 X **£35.00**

WAR PRIZES: THE ALBUM
A Pictorial Compendium of Axis Aircraft Operated by the Allies During & After WW2

Phil Butler

Illustrates in much greater depth the aircraft types featured in the original *War Prizes*. The photos are presented in alphabetical order of manufacture and are accompanied by detailed captions. Each type is illustrated in the markings of the Allied countries which operated them. There is much new information on Axis aircraft which found their way into Russian hands.The majority of photographs in this book were not published in the original *War Prizes*.

Softback, 280 x 215 mm, 128 pages, 297 b/w and 63 colour photos
1 85780 244 6 **£18.99**

Military Aircraft in Detail
HENSCHEL Hs 129

Dénes Bernád

This, the second volume in the series, is a comprehensive guide to the Hs 129 dealing with its development and operational career. It includes many photographs of the type in service and specially commissioned line drawings and colour artworks designed to illustrate all the variants, including those which never progressed beyond the drawing board. The camouflage schemes applied to the aircraft are also examined.

Softback, 280 x 215 mm, 96 pages, c150 colour and b/w photos, artworks
1 85780 238 1 **£16.99**